Japan and Her People

Anna C. Hartshorne

Edited by BRENT MASSEY and
CHRISTOPHER WEST

Foreword by Lian Hearn

Massey, Brent; West, Christopher
    Japan and Her People / Edited by Brent Massey and
    Christopher West

        p. cm.
        1. Japanese Culture. 2. Japanese History. 3. Japan Travel. I.
        Title.
        ISBN 978-0-9790397-2-0

Printed in the USA and UK

http://www.culturetype.com

Contents

FOREWORD TO NEW EDITION BY LIAN HEARN

IN one of my favourite parts of her early 20th century travel book, Japan and Her People, Anna Hartshorne reminds her readers that a stranger is never quite in touch with the country until he has spent a night in a real Japanese yadoya, eaten with chopsticks and slept on the floor. She then escorts us to her pet inn "which shall be called the Sign of the Pine Tree, because that is not its name", situated on the coast somewhere between Volcano Bay and the Inland Sea, and describes the enchanting rituals of staying in such a place. At the end she concludes there is something wanting, "Ume, in her pretty Quakerly dress, and the hibachi between us, and the night wind crying outside." Something about the scene she evokes set me to reminiscing of yadoya and ryokan I've stayed at with close friends, H-san or M-san, and the special pleasures of travelling in rural Japan.

Over one hundred years separate Anna's journeys from mine. So much has changed. When she was writing, the countryside around Yokohama was "exceedingly pretty", it took an hour to get from Ueno to Shimbashi by horse tram, and the gardens of the old Kaga yashiki were home to pheasants which took off in flight seconds before an earthquake struck. Now earthquakes are predicted on sophisticated electronic equipment, Ueno and Shimbashi are stations on one of the most complex and efficient subway systems in the world and the pretty surroundings of Yokohama are buried

Great Gate, Nikko

in the concrete conurbation that covers most of the eastern coast-line of Japan.

Anna Hartshorne who was born in 1860 went to Japan with her father, a Quaker missionary, in the 1880s and, after his death, returned there to teach in several schools, most importantly the Joshi Eigaku Juku (Girls' English School) which was founded by her close friend, Ume: Tsuda Umeko, who was sent to America, at the age of seven, with the Iwakura Mission and became a pioneer of women's higher education in Japan. She met Anna Hartshorne when they were both students at Bryn Mawr: at the end of her life Anna was almost her only remaining friend.

Japan and Her People, first published in 1902, was Anna's only book, but she had an unexpected influence on Western ideas about Japan. She helped Nitobe Inazo write one of the first books that attempted to explain the Japanese to the West: *Bushido: the Soul of Japan* (1900), a book that is still in print today. Nitobe was married to another of Anna's close friends, Mary Elkinton, and when a breakdown in his health prevented him from working, Anna transcribed at his dictation. We can only speculate how much of the finished work on the chivalry and ethics of the samurai, with its comparisons to Western literature, was Anna's contribution. Nitobe, and no doubt Anna too, intended the book to be a bridge between Japanese tradition and the Christian countries of the West. Neither of them could have foreseen how this largely fabricated version of the Way of the Samurai would be seized upon, first with uncritical enthusiasm by Western admirers of Japan and then by the Japanese government itself to exhort loyalty to the Emperor and the nation. The glorification of bushido has been one of the most enduring misconceptions about Japan and its worldwide repercussions are still felt today.

The end of the 19th century, thirty years after the Meiji Restoration saw the fall of the Tokugawa bakufu, was a time both of intense change in Japan and enormous fascination in the West for an extraordinary, strange and exotic country. Japan was the place to visit: everyone who had any interest in travel found their way there and wrote about it, while 40,000 to 50,000 Americans and Europeans felt called to go there to live and work, maybe to preach and convert, certainly to educate and train. One of them was Basil Hall Chamberlain who wrote that "Old Japan was to us a delicate little wonder-world of sylphs and fairies," while "England and America were a wonder-world to the Japanese of irresistible genii and magicians." It was to cater for this increase in the travel industry that Anna wrote her book, part guide, part history: she gravely advises visitors to Japan to do their reading beforehand otherwise they will be baffled by what they see, with no other response than to remark, "How funny!" or "How absurd!" In her own preface she says, half-despairingly, "How shall I make them understand?"

Anna's own reading included Chamberlain, W.E. Griffis, the Marquis de la Mazeliere, Lafcadio Hearn, Pierre Loti, and many others. Some of the events of history that she gives as true cannot be verified: for example that Tokugawa Ieyasu died of a battle wound. We can only guess that this was one of the many legends that in the 19th century were still indistinguishable from fact. Perhaps Nitobe Inazo was her source, influencing her as she influenced him, or perhaps she heard these anecdotes from Ume or her father Tsuda Sen, a curious and eccentric character who among other achievements grew the first asparagus in Japan and of whom Anna wrote "How could he ever have been repressed into the samurai mode!"

The main focus of her story is that tumultous period when Japanese life balanced on the cusp between old and new: the fifty or so years that stretch between the obasan who kept silk worms in her loft and remembers days long before the Black Ships (the arrival of Matthew Perry in 1853) to her grandchildren who work in the water-powered filiature under the hill. I envy Anna being in Japan at this time: I've often wished I could be one of those 19th century travellers who saw old Japan before it was industrialized, before it disappeared for ever. Unlike Isabella Bird, who visited Japan in 1878 and spent several months there, Anna lived in Japan for many years. Isabella delights us with her experiences in wild Japan, the discomfort, the "fishy and vegetable abominations know as Japanese food", the fleas, the bad tempered horses, but the only Japanese person she came to know at all well was her servant, Ito. She was an observer of the country; Anna was an inhabitant and her view is more gentle and affectionate–and generally more informed.

All this makes reading her book feel as if you are travelling through Japan with a delightful and knowledgeable companion, with wide-ranging interests, the keen eye of an artist, and a lively sense of humour. Everything fascinates Anna: in one chapter she goes from house building to Buddhism, to peonies, to the use of kura, to the "energetic divinity" Tenshin, ending up in the garden of the Mito yashiki. "I have strayed too far," she says guiltily. We want to cry, "No, no!" and beg her for more, but luckily she has already taken flight again talking of hot springs, and the proper way to take a Japanese bath which leads her to Rudyard Kipling, then to hermits under waterfalls, which reminds her of the legend of the Cat of Nabeshima and then of fox possession. She has a natural sympathy for the Japanese and their country; she gives gentle advice, on the use of chopsticks for example ("they are not to be held one in each hand like a knife and fork"), but while she is never unkind she can be quite tart about her fellow-countrymen. She compares Commander Perry to the cowboy, Fighting Bill, "who was asked to take up the collection in church", dismisses the activities of missionary women ... "well, they surely have their reward somewhere" and observes perceptively, "The Japanese are always borrowing but always change the loan to suit their own intense individuality–a habit which is often very distressing to those who believe Western civilisation the only reliable brand."

Interested in everything, shocked by nothing–she writes with ease about mekake, or the globe trotters and their "mousmees", or the salons and grog shops of Hokkaido, only rarely pulling back and saying, "but this is quite too large a subject to enter on"–Anna Hartshorne is above all an extraordinarily gifted writer, able to bring to life the bustling streets of Tokyo or the tranquillity of the ancient shrine of Enoshima with astonishing vividness. If she has a fault it is one common to many 19th century writers on Japan: they are so impressed by the achievements of the Meiji government that they are blind to its shortcomings. There is no place in Anna's book for comments on the suppression of the people's rights movement or the backlash in the late 1890s against women's education. Her book is non-political and inoffensive, but it is unfair to expect anything else. The 1891 publication of Alice Bacon's book, *Japanese Girls and Women*, co-written by Tsuda Ume, had already exposed Ume to hostile criticism in Japan. Anna's book posed no threat to her friend nor to any of the other women involved in the struggle for female education.

It's sad that Anna wrote no other books: presumably the various commitments of her life, a life which seems to have been lived in the service of others, prevented it. She devoted her life to Japan and hoped to retire in her adopted country but the deteriorating political situation of the 1930s persuaded her to return to America. After her death a memorial service was held in Tokyo in 1957; everyone who took part had been a student of hers. It is impossible to calculate how many lives this talented and self-effacing woman influenced. The reissue of her book means her influence will continue to be felt and many more readers will take delight in her company.

I would like to acknowledge Barbara Rose's Tsuda Umeko and Women's Education in Japan for information about Tsuda Umeko used in this foreword.

Lian Hearn
May, 2007

PREFACE
TO THE 1ST VOLUME EDITION

EVERY ONE who goes to Japan writes home at first on thin Japanese paper, unfolding yard after yard of the neat rolls, and measuring now and then, perhaps, to see how much one really has written. That is in the early days, when all seems half unreal, when one says "fairy like" and "funny" at every other breath. But just because everything is so different, so utterly unlike all we have ever known, that former life itself seems presently to recede, to grow unreal; we cease to wonder, cease to find anything strange at all. Then the long letters drop to a page or two, and in writing of the simplest experiences of daily life we stop to think half despairingly, "How shall I make them understand?"

Out of that effort to be understood, and from the answers to the questions so frequently asked here in America, these rambling pages have grown. If they have any value, it is due to the patient teaching of friends during three happy years in Japan; most, among many, to Miss Ume Tsuda, of Tokyo, and to Dr. Inazo Nitobe, whose suggestions and supervision of a large portion have made the attempt possible. Of books, Chamberlain's (Murray's) "Handbook" and his "Things Japanese" have been always at hand since I first began to know a little of Japan; in history I have followed especially Mis. de la Mazeliere's "Histoire du Japon," and the "History of the Empire of Japan," published by the (Japanese) Board of Education for the

Chicago Exposition; in art, Fenollosa and La Farge; in literature, Aston, with others who are referred to here and there.

To all my thanks are due; to all, but especially to those–whether of our own race or another–who made for me and mine a place and home, in a land not ours.

Anna C. Hartshorne

PHILADELPHIA, January, 1902.

1

INTRODUCTION

NOWADAYS a journey to Japan is not at all a formidable matter; there are already six steamship lines crossing the Pacific, their voyages ranging from twelve days to three weeks, and once across travel is little more fatiguing than in Germany or Italy, and far less so from all accounts than in Spain. The chief difficulty for Americans seems to be to find out beforehand what to expect in the way of climate and physical conditions; when to go; what to take and what to leave behind; what there is to see and how much time is needed to see it.

The seasons largely control the choice of routes, the northern lines being most desirable for summer and early fall, the San Francisco ones for winter and March or April. The very best months in Japan, so far as weather goes, are October and November, and even most of December; the next best March to early June. Winter is short and sharp, a good deal like Southern Italy, and equally uncertain as to temperature and sunshine; summer hot and wet (except in the northern island, Yezo), especially in August and September, when there are the severest storms and a heavy, muggy atmosphere.

Was it a Londoner or a Philadelphian who said of his birthplace, "We don't have climate here; we have weather?" Thanks to the monsoons, Japan gets both; that is to say, from June to October the wind is mostly south and wet, from October to May northwest and dry, with a lively period of unsettlement between changes. This brings the rain in June, just when it is needed for the rice, and blows it away at harvest time. Between the summer rains come bursts of hot sunlight, and everybody airs their houses and closets, and whatever is not already well dried and put away in air-tight chests; for no amount of care will save kid gloves and leather-bound books from spotting if they are left out in the moist heat.

After all, neither cold nor heat is extreme, but the dampness makes both rather trying to foreigners–that is to say, to non-Japanese. Americans miss their steam-heated houses, and shiver through a Tokyo February as if they were in Rome or Naples. But by a second winter, if they will stay on, they will learn to keep the house well open, wear warm clothing and depend on the sunshine, which never fails on really cold days, for the occasional winter rains are as warm as the May showers are chilly. Even August and September need not alarm anyone used to American summers, for foreign residents pass them comfortably enough at the sea or mountain resorts, only it will not do to undertake much exertion or long journeys; the heat is relaxing, and the rains make the roads heavy or even impassable, while trains are liable to be detained by floods or broken embankments.

Just one caution needs to be writ large–namely, drink no unboiled water unless you know where it came from, and that no rice field has had a chance to drain into it. Remember that the Japanese do not drink cold water, and are consequently indifferent about keeping it pure; even ice is risky; but keeping this rule means health throughout the country at any time of year.

Spring, then, for the blossoms, for weather always uncertain and usually lovely, for that delight of new life felt so strongly in the south, and nowhere more keenly than in Japan; but autumn-October till Christmas–for a prolonged Indian summer, a season of unfailing sunshine and dreamy light, of frosty nights and still days, of rice-harvest and chrysanthemums and brilliant maples. Nine months in the year ladies need cotton or thin silk blouses for the day, and a wrap, not too thin, the moment the sun goes down; even in summer light woolen underclothes are needed on account of the dampness, and after Christmas furs and a steamer rug are necessities for long jinrikisha rides on frosty days.

All ordinary European clothing and personal as well as household goods can be bought in Yokohama or Kobe–not in Tokyo, where you find only such "foreign" things as the Japanese have adopted or adapted for their own use. Prices are about as in America, or even lower for the present, on account of lower duties; so it is better not to burden oneself with extras. Heavy trunks, if brought over at all, had better be stored on first landing, and only such small pieces taken along as can be piled on a jinrikisha and easily handled. In case of leaving from a different port, a shipping agent will take everything in charge and have it put on the proper steamer.

People who wish to be spared all trouble join one of Cook's or Raymond's parties, which go usually in the spring and fall, mostly in round-the-world tours, giving about a month to Japan; or engage a guide on arriving, who will act as courier and plan everything if desired. A month is the ordinary tourist allowance, and it is just enough to get around the more important sights, probably not more hastily than most travelers go through Europe. There is this difference though, that while Europeans and Americans know a great deal about each other beforehand, and their civilization is practically one throughout, East and West have no such common inheritance, no such knowledge of each other's heroes and ideals, and they cannot at a glance understand one another. Therefore, it is well worth an effort to read up a little beforehand, for to those who do not, much of Japan must be quite meaningless, and either "how funny!" or "how absurd!" Books are plenty enough; for instance, Miss Scidmore's "Jinrikisha Days," Mitford's "Tales of Old Japan," Griffis' "Mikado's Empire," Lafcadio Hearn's books, and among the latest and best Mrs. Hugh Fraser's delightful "Letters from Japan" and "The Custom of the Country." These are a few out of many that serve well to beguile cross-continent journey and voyage, while Chamberlain's "Murray" (there is no "Baedeker") and his "Things Japanese" are inseparable necessary companions on the spot, and such works as Rein's "Industries of Japan" and others of the heavier sort become most interesting for reference.

The (London) Traveller for August, 1900, gives an apt piece of advice–namely: "No tourist visiting Japan should fail to put himself in touch with the Kihin-kai, or Welcome Society, which, for a nominal fee, will very materially assist him in traveling and sight-seeing in the islands of Japan. The Society, which was formed in 1893 on the initiative of certain Japanese noblemen and distinguished foreign residents, will supply the traveler with trustworthy guides, see that he is not cheated by innkeepers and others, put him in the way of obtaining genuine objects d'art, if such be his desire, besides, by virtue of its special privileges, passing him into government buildings, Imperial gardens and many other places of special interest where it would be quite impossible for him to gain admittance as a stranger."

The Canadian Pacific steamers sail from Vancouver, the Northern Pacific from Tacoma, the Japan Steamship Company (Nippon Yusen Kaisha) from Seattle, connecting with the Great Northern Railroad, the Pacific Mail, Occidental and Oriental, and Toyo Kisen Kaisha (Orient Line) from San Francisco. All make through tickets or returns in connection with the transcontinental railroads at nearly uniform rates. Accommodations compare very fairly with the average Atlantic lines; some arrangements may be less elaborate, but the quick, silent Chinese and Japanese "boys" furnish a better and far more ready service than the high-minded and high-tipped stewards who rule the other sea. All the steamers of the San Francisco lines now call at Honolulu, making a weekly service between them, and their tickets are interchangeable, allowing you to stop over one or more trips if you wish. The steamers usually stay about twenty-four hours in port at the Sandwich Islands, giving time for a run ashore and a glimpse of the tropics. The voyage by Honolulu is never too cold, but is sometimes too hot, and this fact, as well as the shorter voyage–twelve days against eighteen–sends many travelers to the Canadian route, which is always cool, often cold and–well, just as likely to be rough as any other sea voyage. But of these matters the steamship companies and railroad offices will cheerfully supply all particulars, corrected to date, and present beside a whole library of maps and illustrated folders; while, on the other side, hotel runners meet the steamers and attend to all the details of your going ashore. Indeed, if you permit him, the hotel runner will take you in hand and pass you safely and happily from one to another of his fellows throughout the length and breadth of Japan.

As for the country, the Japanese say it is a huge catfish, with his tail down at Kiushiu and his head up at Yezo, and a backbone of mountains running through, and when he wriggles people say there is an earthquake. Moreover, at the Imperial University in Tokyo, and in caves and on mountains, Prof. John Milne and his clever followers have set their delicate seismological instruments, mapping down every jump and every quiver of the big volcanic heart; and they told us that whereas the earth's crust is never quite still, Japan, being rather new, is one of the thinnest and shakiest parts. However that may be, small earthquakes come very often, and volcanoes are much in evidence, though most of them, like Fuji, are no longer active; and the fish is a very big fish, some fifteen hundred miles from tip to tip, and that without counting in the Kuriles, all ice and fire, or the Lu Chu Islands and Formosa, reaching nearly down to our vexed Philippines. On the other hand, the country is very narrow, nowhere above two hundred miles across from sea to sea; a strip of the Atlantic coast from Maine to Florida, taking in most of the New England States, New Jersey, Maryland, and so on down, would be much the size and shape of Japan. But the strip would have to be sliced up into islands; Yezo at the north, then the main island, Honda or Nippon, reaching from Boston nearly to Charleston, and the rest into five large and any number of small and still smaller islets, with the Inland Sea locked in among them. The upper half of the strip trends north and south; the lower takes a sudden turn near the middle of the main island, and sweeps off to the west and a very little south, so that Nagasaki, in southern Kiushiu, is only three degrees of latitude below Tokyo. Consequently more than half the coast on the Pacific side lies open to the south and the warm Black Current-the Gulf Stream of Asia-while the mountains form a break against the chill winds that blow down from Siberia, and make the west coast dreary and desolate. The result is a climate much like Southern Europe for all the lower half of the country, a little warmer at Nagasaki, a little colder in Tokyo; and only when you get some two hundred miles further north, say at Sendai, the change to more temperate conditions begins. And, in fact, till nearly the middle of the sixteenth century all north of Sendai was pretty much left to the aboriginal Ainu; as for Yezo, it belonged to them and the bears, except for a castle town or two and a few squalid fishing villages, till the government undertook to open the country and encourage emigration, some thirty years ago. Now colonists go up by forty and fifty thousand a year, and Hokkaido, "The North" (literally, "Northern Road"), is new, enterprising, and on the whole prosperous, very American and very unlike the rest of Japan.

From end to end the whole surface of the country is broken up; there is not only the central mountain chain, but peaks, ridges, tumbled hills everywhere. River valleys there are, some wide, and a great deal of lowland near the sea; two true plains only–the great stretch north of Tokyo, and once part of Yedo Bay, and the region south of Mount Fuji–one also in the Hokkaido. There are no towering granite cliffs, no bold and awful heights; thanks to a light soil and abundant rainfall, Japanese landscape is everywhere gentle, varied and lovely, full of wonderful lines and curves–curves, most of them, just a little concave–"eine der zartesten Linien," said Grimm. Such are the lines of Fuji San, the mountain of mountains, that will always get into one's mental background at the word Japan. As for the coast line, not even Greece is more cut and jagged, more deeply folded into promontories and bays and steep-sided inlets.

In such a land everything grows with delight; England is not greener. Mountain ranges and headlands are heavily wooded with chestnut and pine and evergreen oak, and a dozen kinds of maple, gorgeous in autumn; oranges flourish in the south, palmetto and bamboo as far north as Tokyo. Tall bamboo grass roots wherever it can get a chance; where timber has been burnt off the hillsides, and through the northern provinces, there are miles of such reedy waste, empty and desolate; for barely one-seventh of the whole country is actually under cultivation. Rice, of course, is the staple crop, and it must be irrigated; every scrap of ground that can be leveled and have a stream turned upon it is dug over and enriched, and made to yield to the uttermost—green with barley all winter, after the rice has been gathered in, bordered with beans or a bit of yellow rape in the springtime. Wheat is grown, especially in the southern provinces, a good deal of millet, also cotton, flax and various vegetables. Rice, wheat, beans, millet and sorghum are the "Five Staples," Go-Koku, of Japanese writers. Not much fodder is needed, there are so few animals; though horses, of course, there were and are, for the knights in old times, for the rich and the cavalry now. Cattle are used only for draught, and that but sparingly, since the Japanese are not flesh-eaters, and even milk and butter are innovations they have not taken to very much; as for cheese, they feel towards it as foreigners do to daikon, the huge Japanese radish, which grows two feet long and has flavor and scent in proportion. That merry engineer, Holtham, calls the daikon "a most ingenious pickle," for, he declares, after once getting its flavor well over your mouth, you will eat anything to get rid of the taste!

A railroad runs the length of the main island, and a yearly increasing network of branch lines connects it with the west coast and the more important cities, and beyond the Strait of Shimonoseki down through Kiushiu. At the northern end a line of steamers connects across in eight hours to Hakodate and the Hokkaido lines, all well patronized, for the Japanese are indefatigable travelers. The railroad tickets are printed both in English and Japanese, and must be shown at the gate when baggage is checked. Sixty to eighty pounds of free baggage is allowed, and the system of registering is like the European one—that is to say, you receive a paper check, stamped with the number and weight of your pieces, which is of course given up when you claim your goods at the end of the journey.

Except the Hokkaido line, which is on the American plan, Japanese railroads are built and run on the English system, except that many carriages are not divided into compartments, but have long seats down the sides and across the ends. This is more comfortable to the people, who are not used to chairs, and soon get tired of sitting up straight, so stretch at full length if there is room, or drop their clogs and tuck their feet under them. The foreigner may be tempted to envy of a frosty morning, as he taps his boots on the hot-water tin-sole means of heating-and wishes a little warmth would reach his chilly toes. Sleeping-cars are being introduced very gradually, and without them travel at night is an uncertain pleasure. If the train is not full, well and good-blow up your air-cushion, tuck in your rug and join the chorus of snores. Nine journeys in ten there will be room to lie down, but the tenth will not be a restful experience. As to washing possibilities en route, the outlook is at least as good as on European corridor trains, perhaps better. But food for Westerners there is none-no dining-car, not even a station restaurant; instead, men parade the platforms with tea-Japanese, of course, and neat wooden boxes, each with a new pair of chopsticks all top. For a few sen (cents) they will leave you a pot of tea and a cup, or pour hot water on your own brew; the box costs some ten sen, and contains rice and pickles and other dainties, toothsome enough for those to the manner born; but let not the unwary Western traveler set his hopes thereon; he will reach his destination empty and sorrowful, and next time will accept the offer of a chicken sandwich from his hotel.

This is not to discourage any from trying to like Japanese food; but that is an art to be studied with care at a good tea house, not begun on a boxful of rice and cold fish, of which more anon. Let us first consider how to reach the empire.

2

VOYAGE AND FIRST IMPRESSIONS

CONCERNING voyages, for most people, probably "least said soonest mended." After all, it is but a three weeks' affair at longest, made as pleasant as possible by courteous and obliging officers, by cricket matches and chess tournaments, concerts and mock trials, a dance on deck or even a magic lantern exhibition some still evening. There is something almost uncanny about the gay life on board, particularly at night–the bright saloon, the music and the evening dresses, out there in the midst of that great lonely ocean, where in weeks you may scarcely sight another tail of smoke. For the Pacific is no such frequented highway as the Atlantic, at least as yet; birds though there are, beautiful gray and white gulls, and Mother Curey's chickens, and the broad-winged frigate bird, wheeling and dipping like Homer's sea fowl–

"Who through dread troughs of the unharvested brine, seeking his prey, drenches dark wings in the foam."

The steamers which come from the northern ports sight first the lighthouse on a certain mountain island called Kinkwazan, standing in just near enough to signal and be reported, and then run down for another fifteen hours near, but not in sight of, the coast, till they reach the headland of Awa at the mouth of Yedo Bay. On the other hand, the lines touching at Honolulu come in from nearly due east, and their first indication of land is the thickening flock of fishing boats, with high stern and square mat or canvas sails, and the thin line of smoke from the never-resting volcano on Oshima or Vries Island, first and largest of a chain of islands stretching southward from the mouth of Yedo Bay. These islands figure in Japanese history and romance as places of banishment for criminals, usually political ones, the tale often turning on some marvelous escape or on a pardon and recall. They were used for this purpose from the twelfth century quite down to modern times. All are mountainous and wild, and little visited now, supporting only a few villages of fisher folk. Leaving Oshima to the south and round-ing Awa, you steam across a corner of Sagami Bay into the Uraga Channel, and so into Yedo Bay proper. The shores here are low and green, especially to the right, where, except for the bold head-land at its end, all the peninsula is flat and sandy nearly to Mount Tsukuba, sixty or seventy miles north. According to tradition, the creator god, Iwanagi, piled up Awa to keep off the beat of the ocean, and curiously enough the geologists say the story agrees quite closely with the facts, since only the promontory is old, the rest being of recent formation, a part of the great plain north of Tokyo which was once covered by the sea. Westward is a steeper and more broken shore line, backed by the Hakone mountains, rising in blue zigzags beyond Sagami Bay, and above them still the matchless cone of Fuji seems to float out of a sea of mist.

On the left, at the narrowest part of the channel, is the little town of Uraga, which has a good harbor for small vessels; in feudal times it was a place of much more importance than now, because every kind of craft entering the bay had to stop here and be inspected be going nearer to Yedo-now Tokyo-the capital of the Shogun. Under this rule, the guards fired on an American ship, the Morrison, which came over from China in 1837 for the purpose of returning some shipwrecked Japanese, and incidentally in hopes of to trade. But nobody got past Uraga till Commodore Perry landed there in 1853 with the letter from the President of the United States which sprang the first crack in Japan's closed door. The consequences of that opening are visible all along the bay, in the lighthouses, the modern fortifications, the biological laboratory at Misaki–that is on the Sagami side, though–and the naval dock-yards at Yokosuka, just around the corner. The French built these by contract, and rather hoped to keep them; but Japan made a great effort and paid her bill in time to escape foreclosure. The steamer's course bears to the left now along the west shore, leaving half the bay to the north in a wide shallow stretch twenty miles long by some ten across, at the head of which lies Tokyo; and so on by little Mississippi Bay, where Perry anchored, and past Treaty Point and around the turn of the Bluff, with its pretty residences, into Yokohama harbor.

Yokohama, "Cross Strand," is the present town; but everyone knows that Kanagawa opposite was the original Concession. This, however, turned out to be an unlucky choice, for it lay directly on the great post road, the Tokaido, along which the Daimyos were continually passing with their retainers. Prince and page alike were haughty and overbearing, despising the foreigners, who looked down on them and their old-world glory in turn; there were endless encounters and difficulties, culminating finally in the death of the Englishman Richardson. Never mind now who was most to blame; the Japanese government was keenly anxious to preserve peace, and besought the unwelcome guests to remove to a less dangerous situation. For this they had selected the mud flat on the other side of the bay, where indeed was the better anchorage for large vessels, and where they had made preparation by building bridges and stone breakwaters. It was not precisely an inviting place. Black, writing a few years later, describes it as a small, sandy level lying between the sea and a swamp, which separated it from the cultivated fields farther back, and flanked by hills, from which it was again cut off by a tidal creek and an estuary; so that the only way out on the land side was by bridges, provided with gates and a guard of Japanese soldiers; and the foreign representatives feared they were to be shut off from intercourse with the people as effectually as the Dutch had been on the island of Deshima at Nagasaki. But while they hesitated, the traders settled the question by promptly going over to the better anchorage, and the dispute ended in a compromise, by which the Powers were allowed to build consulates on the Kanagawa side if they wished.

Naturally the privilege was not claimed, and the one survival of the old Concession is in the official name of Yokohama, which appears in police notices and the like as "Kanagawa Prefecture." As for the merchants, they settled themselves firmly and built shops and warehouses, and grew and do grow and prosper, some two thousand of them, besides a host of Chinese.

In the harbor craft of all kinds abound, from the latest modern cruiser to a weather-beaten brown sampan, a sort of attenuated dory, guiltless of paint, seemingly most unsteady, but in fact strong and very seaworthy. The men row standing, four, six or more to a boat, lithe, brown figures, in sleeveless shirt and all but legless trousers; they face sidewise, pushing the long oars, swaying out and back to a monotonous chant. Yachts and pleasure boats lie off the Bund; trim launches skim about; tugs and colliers, junks and tramps and liners, an American oil-tanker and a fine coasting steamer, flying the sun-flag, her blue peter at her mast. And the throng on the dock is not less motley; neat military-looking policemen and customs officials, blue-clad porters and coolies–Far East English for all laborers–Japanese tradesmen or travelers in European dress or their own long sleeves, Chinese, Americans, Europeans of every nationality, a Babel of tongues and an epitome of New Japan. The Custom House formalities are precise, but not rigid, and these over, comes the sensation for which the stranger has waited, the first jinrikisha ride. The runner sets down the shafts of his tiny carriage, you step in and take your seat, and he catches up the shafts and is off with a dash. To tell the truth, the first moments are not unmixed bliss; it takes practice to sit easily, and to feel quite sure the whole thing is not going over backward. The motion is rather like a small road-cart, and the runner's height and gait count just as a horse's would; but on a fairly good road, with a kurumaya (jinrikisha man) who runs steadily and holds the shafts firmly and not too high, all goes comfortably enough. Kuruma, "vehicle," is, by the way, the preferred Japanese word, whence kurumaya, "wheel-man," ya being originally "a place," then "the one at a place," "the one who does"–as shinbunya, the newsboy; denpoya, the telegraph messenger. "Jinriki-sha," "pull-man car," as somebody calls it, is a Chinese

combination which has got itself adopted thoroughly in English, but somehow does not seem to please Japan.

It is not ten minutes from the landing-place to the Bund–Far East English again–the drive along the stone-faced water front, where the hotels and club houses are. The streets are even more of a medley than the dock; high, ugly warehouses, the big custom house, the post-office tower, flags flying over consulates half-hidden in trees and shrubbery; beside a bit of the Japanese part, narrow streets of low wooden houses, the shop fronts open and displaying tempting curios, silks and photographs, or again handbags, shoes, hats and "foreign" articles of various utility and universal ugliness. The signs are irregular and very picturesque, part English, droll enough some of it, part Japanese, written in square Chinese character, like the tea-boxes of our youth, or the bold, flowing "grass-hand." There is not much color on the street, since only small children dress in

dashing reds and yellows and rainbow mixtures; such gorgeous rai-
ment is left to professional dancers, men and even young women
keeping to quiet shades, except where girls show a peep of red in
sleeve and petticoat, a bright fold at the throat, and, to make up, a
very riot of color in the wide sash. Jinrikisha men and coolies are
in blue cotton, not a straight gown, but tight-fitting trousers and
belted jacket, often adorned with huge white ideographs, which are
the employer's name or trade-mark; round their heads they tie blue
and white handkerchiefs, fillet fashion–shade of Praxiteles! was this
the realistic version of the Diadumnos?–or wear a round straw hat,
covered with cotton cloth, like a big white mushroom. Children
swarm everywhere, at least half of them carrying babies on their
backs, which does not seem at all to interfere with tag or any other
lively amusement. All is stirring and busy, not shrill like Paris, not
languid like Naples, nor yet anxious and struggling like New York.
A really pretty face in the crowd is rare; stern ones and smiling
ones both plenty; an unkind or crabbed look rarest of all. Then the
jinrikisha spins out on to the Bund, with the bay on one side and
the houses on the other, to the Club or the Grand or the Oriental
Hotel, where everything is of Europe except the faces of clerks and
attendants, and where you may almost forget, if you will, that you
are in Dai Nippon.

3

YOKOHAMA

IT is difficult to deal fairly with so cosmopolitan a place as Yokohama. Speaking broadly, it is only one of a number of European settlements in the Far East, akin to all the rest in that it is like no one country, but is rather a coming together of all the nations under heaven; less English than Hong Kong, smaller than Shanghai, on the whole more American than anything else–particularly on the Bluff, where the pretty houses might belong to any prosperous suburb in the United States. That it is not strictly Japan goes without saying–a good deal less so, at least till lately, than San Francisco's Chinatown is America–since from the time the Concession was granted in 1854 till the Revised Treaties went into effect in 1898, consular jurisdiction held good, and an American or European was legally in his own country–tried, if he sinned, according to his own laws and by a court of his fellow-countrymen. It ought to be not less clear that it is unfair to judge Japan by the specimens of Japanese men and women met with here and in other treaty ports; but unluckily this piece of injustice is perpetrated constantly in print and out of it. This is not the place to enter upon that controversy; see rather Stafford Ransome's chapter on the subject in his much-criticised "Japan in Transition," which, when all has been said, is still one of the most unbiased books yet written. Yokohama makes no attempt at architectural beauty–indeed, the business part could not well be uglier–but it has an air of solid prosperity nevertheless. The town divides naturally into two portions, the original Concession, still known as the Settlement, and the Bluff, which was added a few years later for residence purposes. The swamp of Black's memory has long since been drained and part of it turned into the cricket ground, and the creek and inlet deepened and carried around through the town as a useful waterway for small shipping; while plenty of open bridges replace the two guarded entrances. An odd feature of the place is that the names of streets are scarcely used, though they do exist; instead, each property is known by a number, and if you want to go to the Grand Hotel, you bid the kurumaya take you to Number 20; a well-known girls' school is 212 Bluff, and so on. It follows that the numerals–ichi, ni, san, etc.–are the most useful bit of language that a stranger can acquire; but the fact is a very little Japanese goes a long way in Yokohama. They do say that foreigners calling on the master of a house will turn up a thumb and say, "Arimas'ka?"–"Is he?"–literally, "has?" The little finger and the same remark serves to ask for the lady of the house. "This I have not witnessed," as Herodotus would say. Nor will I vouch for the lady who wanted O yu (hot water), and vainly demanded O my, till her patience gave out, and she cried, "Oh, you idiot!" "And then, my dear, just as soon as I spoke sharply to him, that stupid boy went and got it right away!" Such are the tales they tell the newcomer, just by way of encouragement.

"Yama," hill or mountain, is a far more appropriate name than Bluff for the great ridge thrusting up a couple of hundred feet above the sea, where the residences are. The Creek, as it is still called, faced with stone embankments and picturesque with odd craft, cuts the hill sharply from the level Settlement on the harbor side; the Bund or drive along the seawall ends in a little bridge, and just across there is a small Buddhist temple, cheaply and coarsely decorated. Not far off a tea-house well known to foreign visitors is perched at the top of the "Hundred Steps," which appear in almost every series of views of Yokohama. Other flights of stone steps climb the hill at various points, making short cuts to the houses above, and good macadamized roads wind upward between stone walls and trees, and peeps of gardens full of shrubbery and flowers. The houses, hidden among the mass of green, are of course altogether "foreign-built"–that is to

The Hundred Steps

say, un-Japanese–and possessed of doors, windows and chimneys; bungalows and "Queen Anne" cottages, or more pretentious brick or stone dwellings, elbowing plain little frame houses, or the high fence and big, rambling dormitories of some mission school. There can be nothing regular or monotonous where house climbs above house, and the road zigzags to avoid turning into a ladder, giving exquisite glimpses backward of the sea and the green fields beyond the town, and the Hakone peaks and Fujiyama best of all. If anybody in this part of Japan wants to boast a little of his fine outlook, he will probably tell you he has a view of Fuji from his windows. Stylish carriages roll by, coachman and footmen often in a neat livery of dark blue, tightfitting trousers, like the jinrikisha men's, belted tunic, with flowing sleeves, and white mushroom hat. The master's crest or initial, worked between the shoulders, completes the costume. There are pretty girls on horseback, too, with running grooms ahead, and plenty of jinrikishas dashing down at break-neck pace, or toiling up, pushed by an extra man behind. They say accidents are not frequent; but many residents who love their lives prefer to walk the hill both ways–a practice which must cultivate excellent muscles.

One of the lower slopes, called Camp Hill, is lined with Japanese shops–great places for old stamps and curios of more than doubtful authenticity. This region is part of the old village of Honmura, which was here long before the "Black Ships" came from America; and a guard-house–Japanese, of course–stood here in the sixties to protect the Settlement from over-zealous patriots. Another street near by is the haunt of dealers in second-hand European furniture, which is always plenty in this ever-changing community, where diplomatic officials, merchants and missionaries alike are literally here today and gone tomorrow. One after another sells out and departs, and the newcomers who take their places attend auctions and explore Honmura Machi, well knowing that they will presently shift in turn to other lands or other parts of the empire.

While here, however, this unstable population endeavors to live as nearly in its native manner as possible, in spite of the distance from base. Lane & Crawford's big general store, and the milliners and tailors, and their likes, contrive to furnish European food and European fashions, only a little out of date. There is the cricket ground, where some good games are played; banks and churches of course; a hall for entertainments and public meetings; the various clubs–English, German and the like; half a dozen newspapers, among which Captain Brinkley's Japan Mail is of more than local value; and finally the race-course beyond the Bluff, by Mississippi Bay, which supplies the social event of the year, and is occasionally visited by the Emperor himself. Housekeeping is not particularly difficult. Japanese servants are neat, obliging and generally honest, even in the open ports, and so many fruits and vegetables have been introduced that Tokyo and Yokohama provision shops contain almost everything that Western people are used to, including abundance of game all winter. Mutton, though, if it appears at all, has been imported from Australia or China, for sheep will not thrive in Japan. There used to be two or three sorrowful-looking specimens at the Zoo in Uyeno Park, Tokyo, and if they survive, they must be the last of their race, for the little flock at the experimental stock farm have all been killed and eaten. Some say there is a kind of hard grass that injures them, but the real difficulty seems to be the damp-ness of the climate, which causes foot-rot. This could probably be avoided by care in housing at rainy times, if it became worthwhile. At present the Japanese dislike mutton even more than beef, so it is no hardship to them to do without, and as yet there is no great demand for wool. Milk is more and more used every year, and some very good butter is made at the experiment farm at Sapporo, and at two or three stock farms in the Hakone district; it is put up in one-pound tins and sold at a good price, the demand being always ahead of the supply. Unfortunately, many of the foreign hotels serve the California tub variety instead; it has the double advantage of being cheaper and less eaten.

In summer the whole Settlement is redolent of tea, and the drying and packing firms are at their busiest. From the great iron-shuttered storehouses comes a hum of voices, and through door or window you see scores of girls and women bending over the heated trays, deftly handling the leaves. Many a woman carries a baby on her back, comfortably asleep and no doubt a great deal better off than plenty of babies in other lands; but it seems hard on the mother, who has to bear this additional burden through the long, hot days.

The Japanese part of Yokohama extends across from the edge of the Settlement to Kanagawa and far up the inlet between, in itself a city of over two hundred thousand people. Curio shops are here, and Japanese goods generally, especially in Honcho Dori (dori is lane) and Benten Dori, and the streets near by, all close to the railroad station. Many of the wealthier Japanese, whose business or official duties call them to Yokohama, have houses on the ridge at Kanagawa, or a station or two out along the railroad. Then there is the Chinese part back of the Settlement, and an unsavory nest of sailors' boarding houses, and all the evils of all civilizations together;

while up on the Bluff a number of mission schools are earnestly striving to spread a saving knowledge of the greatest possible good.

Of all the open ports Yokohama has the largest foreign trade, eighty million yen in 1898 against Kobe's sixty million, which comes next–more than half the total import and export of the country, says the last official report. The swamp behind the Settlement was drained and built upon long ago, the old gates and guard-houses taken away, and the yakunin (guards) replaced by dapper Japanese policemen in full "Europe clothes," as Kipling would say. From May to November they look quite too immaculate in their white summer suits to tackle six-foot Irish sailors on a spree; but a Japanese can usually make up in agility what he lacks in weight. After a terrible fire, some dozen years ago, most of the original town was rebuilt and improved. Good water has been brought in from Lake Yamanaka in the mountains, the harbor greatly improved and a pier built, two thousand feet long, where most of the liners come up instead of anchoring. A large dock was finished in 1897. Raw silk, the largest item of export, goes mostly from Yokohama; the next value is silk piece-goods, then tea, which they say is slowly falling off of late years; mats and bamboo wares seem to be on the increase, lacquer and fans about even, and of imports, machinery and woolen goods come in more and more every year.

How the Revised Treaties will affect Yokohama it is too soon to know. They bring foreigners under Japanese law instead of the consular courts, and in return anyone may reside or do business anywhere in the country, Chinese alone excepted. Some Americans and Europeans have gone to the interior, and more will doubtless go; but it is probable that, for the present at least, the difficulties of the language will keep most business people where they can depend on English for their transactions. In any case, it would seem that the place must continue to grow in importance, because large vessels cannot get up to Tokyo, and there is no other harbor so fitted to serve as a seaport for the capital. The surroundings of Yokohama are exceedingly pretty. On one side is the Tokaido, the Eastern Sea highroad, always full of picturesque life, and on the other Mississippi Bay, a beautiful curve between Treaty Point and the promontory above Sugita village. Tomioka, just beyond Sugita, is frequented by Hama people for the bathing, and a little boat runs across from the city in three-quarters of an hour. By the road it is a charming walk or ride, some six miles, first down by the race-course and the paddy-fields, and then along the bay; and there are pretty teahouses by the way, and a side turn to Macpherson's Hill, where the view is exceptionally fine. The plum blossoms at Sugita are famous, and on this warm, sheltered coast they come out weeks before they do in Tokyo–sometimes early in January. Last year, in flower time, one of the papers noted an odd group of visitors at Sugita; they could hardly be called sightseers, for they were all blind! It was a party of Amma, or blind shampooers, as they are generally called, belonging

to the Shampooers' Guilds of Tokyo and Yokohama. Professional massage is reserved for the blind, because it is something they can do, and particularly well. You often meet one of the men on the street, feeling his way with a long staff, and every few minutes blowing two or three shrill, plaintive notes on a kind of penny-whistle. There are women Amma, too, and they also appeared on this occasion, patting the rough trunks and breathing the fragrance with as much delight as those who saw. Indeed, they stayed so late–caring nothing for the gathering darkness!–that the guardians of the place had to fairly turn them out at last.

Spinning along today behind a cheerful and talkative kurumaya, it is difficult to remember that this bay road was built for the express use of foreigners, to keep them away from the Tokaido and encounters such as the fatal "Richardson affair" of 1862, which cost Japan so much. It is not a pleasant story, but so characteristic of the time that I give it in some detail. This Richardson, then, was a Shanghai merchant, who had retired and was spending a few weeks in Japan, on his way home to England, when he and two other gentlemen, Yokohama residents, took a lady out one afternoon for a ride on the Tokaido. They turned up toward Yedo from Kanagawa, and kept meeting groups of Samurai, the two-sworded retainers of some nobleman. Here accounts differ as to the English party's behavior, but while they certainly did not mean to give offence, they seem to have thought they were doing wonders of conciliation in walking their horses past the groups, and disregarding black looks.

By the crests on the knights' sleeves the Yokohama people recognized the retainers of Satsuma, proudest and just then most powerful of the Daimyo, who was openly of the Nationalist party; and at last they came to the guard surrounding the litter of the prince himself, about a hundred men. Now, when a Daimyo passed, it was the inexorable law for every Japanese of less rank to get off his horse, if he had one, and bow down; and at such times quarrels between the retainers over points of precedence were so apt to take place that whenever they could the great lords avoided passing on the highway. Instead of dismounting, however, the foreign party merely drew off to the side of the road and kept on riding, two abreast, taking up nearly half of the narrow way–at least Richardson and the lady did; and it is to be noticed here that she was recently from Hong Kong. The wiser Yokohama gentlemen urged turning into a side road, but Richardson is said to have called out, "Let me alone; I know how to manage these people." A moment later a man came forward and motioned them to dismount; but, misunderstanding, they turned their horses to go back, and at the same instant a Samurai, enraged past control by the supposed insult to his lord, rushed at them and cut Richardson across the side. Others drew and struck at the rest of the party, wounding one of the men severely; but they spurred their horses and dashed through, and three of them rode safe to Kanagawa, after seeing Richardson drop from his horse, nearly or quite dead. His body was "found by the road, with a mat thrown over it–they say by the kind deed of a woman who still keeps a tea-house close by, whom the foreigners call Black Eyed Susan. Of course the uproar in the Settlement was tremendous, and only the clear judgment and strong will of Colonel Neale, the British charge d' affaires, kept the community from acts that must inevitably have brought on war. When pressed for redress, the Shogun's govern-ment had to acknowledge that it could not control the great clans; and the result was that, after much negotiating and vain promises, the English took the law into their own hands and proceeded to punish Satsuma. Their ships bombarded Kagoshima, a town of one hundred thousand inhabitants, nearly destroying it and killing many people, beside losing some themselves; after which the Prince of Satsuma apologized and paid a large indemnity, in the usual manner of such affairs. Luckily the doctrine of Spheres of Influence had yet to be invented, or there is no knowing what might have happened. But the event had one important effect; it convinced Satsuma that the barbarians could only be beaten with their own weapons–a conviction which had far reaching results for the coun-try at large; while the foreigners, on their side, learned some useful lessons on keeping out of danger. Still, there was no real security for them till after the Restoration in 1868 did away with the Jo-i, or anti-foreign party, and made the region round Yokohama free from irresponsible "patriots."

Another pleasant excursion is to Yokosuka, down the penin-sula, either by train–the usual way–or by boat, in about an hour and a half. From a mere fishing hamlet the place has grown to a thriving town, on account of the naval dock-yards already mentioned. These cannot be visited, though, without a special introduction. Already they build torpedo boats and other warlike vessels of the smaller classes, and no doubt some day will turn out the largest; it is only a matter of time. On a hill near by those who have a turn for tombs may visit the grave of Will Adams, the English pilot, who lived here "like any great lord," as he wrote home to his friends. This Adams came on a Dutch ship which put in for repairs at Bungo, in south-ern Japan, in 1600, or fifty years after the Portuguese came, and after the edict expelling foreigners and forbidding Christianity had been put forth, though not yet rigorously enforced. Adams, who seems to have been a man of parts, was sent up to Osaka to answer to "the King," as he calls the Shogun Ieyasu. Perhaps his outspoken hatred of the Spanish and Portuguese won the Shogun; moreover, Tokugawa Ieyasu was a thoroughly practical statesman, and had the true Japanese thirst for useful ideas. Anyhow, he persuaded the pilot to stay in Japan, had him teach navigation and build ships, made him a knight, with estates and servants, and always contrived to keep him from going home to England. His letters lament for his English wife and children; but failing them, he consoled himself with a Japanese, who seems to have made him very comfortable, and who is buried on the hill not far away.

Just before reaching Yokosuka by rail there is a pretty little vil-lage on the sea, Dzushi by name, which is quite a haunt of Tokyo and Yokohama (foreign) residents; certain of the diplomatic corps have built villas there, nestling against cliffs half hidden in wild vines and flowering shrubs. There are two inns also Japanese, of course–one charmingly quiet and the other apt to be full of noisy guests, especially "weekend" visitors from the port. But the favor-ite breathing-place of all is Kamakura, at the station just before Dzushi. Today it is only a seaside resort of one "foreign" and two good Japanese hotels and some cottages; but for the sake of its great past, Kamakura deserves to be considered respectfully and apart.

4

HISTORY-THE DAWN AND THE MIDDLE AGES.

"In the Japan of to-day the world has before it a unique example of an Eastern people displaying the power to assimilate and to adopt the civilization of the West, whilst preserving its own national dignity unimpaired."–Weston, "The Japanese Alps."

FROM Yokohama to Kamakura is almost always the first trip. But before entering upon Japan proper it may be well to say a little concerning Japanese history, else the inevitable names and much beside will be but a weariness and vexation of spirit.

The more the race is studied the more complex its origin seems to be. It is now fairly well established that there were at least two principal waves of immigration–the one from the mainland of Asia by way of Korea, a race not Chinese, and not even closely related to China, and the other of Malay extraction, which came up by the Lu Chu Islands and through Kiushiu. A third race was in the islands already, the Ainu, a few of whom are still left in the far north; but where the Ainu came from or to whom they are akin remains a puzzle. It must have been somewhere in the last dozen centuries before the Christian era that these various elements were engaged in shaking together, through trade and fightings, into the Japanese race. Mazeliere claims that the Malay element is that of the imperial family and the court nobles (the Kuge), and the "Ouralien" of Asia that of the Buke, the military class and the feudal nobles; while the conquered Ainu formed the basis of the peasantry, who till recently were to all intents and purposes serfs attached to the soil. Of course it will not do to understand this neat classification too literally, but it is quite true that the Emperor himself is of the Malay type, having nearly level eyes, short, straight nose, and square chin; while the feudal nobles show usually the long face, arched nose and eyes a little oblique, and the peasants are chunky and round-faced like the Ainu.

Japanese historical accounts begin with the creation and the doings of the gods, leading from these directly to Jimmu Ten-no, the first Emperor, grandson of the Sun Goddess, whose legendary date is 660 B.C. He crossed with his followers in a stone boat from Awa, in the Inland Sea, to the Yamato district of the main island, and subdued the "Earth-Spiders" (perhaps Ainu; perhaps a still older race), slew dragons and set the land in order; and his descendants reigned after him, as they have continued to do, even to Mutsuhito, the one hundred and twenty-first, who now occupies the throne.

So say the Kojiki and Nihongi, chronicles compiled in the eighth century, the earliest written record of events. At least it is certain that by the beginning of the Christian era the races must have settled into one people, under a patriarchal clan government, living in villages, cultivating rice and other foods, and having all the ordinary arts in a more or less primitive degree of development; each clan having its own ancestral nature gods, or Kami, among whom the Sun Goddess stood highest, and the chiefs of the Sun Clan possessed a kind of loose hegemony over the rest. To this vague early period belongs the Empress Jingo, who conquered Korea on behalf of her infant son, the Emperor Ojin; and the Emperor Nintoku, who remitted the taxes for three years, and, while his house fell to ruin, rejoiced to see smoke rising once more from the straw huts of his people; and Prince Yamato-take, who destroyed robbers and ogres, and conquered the Emishi–these were certainly Ainu–to the east and north as far as Sagami Bay; and the Empress Suiko, who established Buddhism. With her closed the age of the gods and heroes, and with the "Nara period" of the eighth century authentic history begins.

It was three centuries sooner, about 400 A.D., that Buddhist missionaries had first come from China through Korea bringing letters and arts; but the new religion did not take hold till late in the seventh century, when there was a great wave of zeal, temples building everywhere and sacred texts copied and images made for temples and private shrines. The old nature gods, the Kami, were turned into Buddhist saints and angels, and with Chinese arts and civilization came the wisdom of Chinese sages, which was to Japan even more than the wisdom of Egypt was to Greece.

Before 700 the Court moved with almost every reign; then it settled at Nara, and remained there nearly a hundred years. It was a time of rapid growth and development; Chinese orders of rank and ceremony were adopted, histories written (in Japanese words, but with Chinese characters) and a new and higher civilization established on Chinese lines, but with the inevitable Japanese modification; for the Japanese, like the Greeks, are always borrowing, but always changing the loan to suit their own intense individuality–a habit which is often very distressing to those who believe Western civilization the only reliable brand.

By the time the Court removed to Kyoto, about 900, the formative stage had been passed, and Heian, "the Peace," was a thoroughly national epoch–a period of great refinement and activity in art, literature and government. To this time belongs Kobo Daishi, Buddhist saint, poet, painter, to whom is attributed nearly every early work of art in the empire, along with miracles and pilgrimages enough for twenty saints. In the tenth century they compiled twenty volumes of poetry written since the "Manyoshiu" collection was compiled at Nara; and the great Japanese classics, the Genji Monogatari, the "Journey from Tosa" (Tosa Nikki) and the "Pillow Sketches" were all written between 900 and 1150. But to this time also belongs the inevitable weakening of the Court circle through luxury and over-refinement, the decline of the Emperor's power and the rise of the great families whose chiefs aspired to rule as Chancellors or Regents in the Emperor's name.

This usurpation of power by the clans is the most characteristic feature of the early Middle Ages in Japan. The Fujiwara came first, getting their daughters married to successive Emperors and obtaining almost entire control of the throne. They were checked for a time by the great Michizane, of the Sugiwara Clan, who became Chancellor and served two Emperors with wisdom and faithfulness, but was exiled on a false charge, and died in half-savage Kiushiu; but after Michizane was out of the way the Fujiwara regained their influence, and kept it till they were finally overshadowed by two great clans descended from ninth century Emperors, the families of Taira and Minamoto.

All the last half of the twelfth century is filled with the strife between these two clans, which is known in Japan as the Gen-pei, Gen being the Chinese (and therefore elegant) pronunciation of the character for Minamoto, and Heiki (H becoming P in composition) for Taira–called also the War of the Chrysanthemums, from the red and white flower badges used by the two sides. Their fightings make up nearly half of the hero stories of old Japan, partly embodied in the drama, partly in long romances, in which the Minamoto warriors are the chief favorites. The struggle began definitely in 1156, when Kiyomori of Taira was foremost in putting down an insurrection in which some of the Minamoto were involved; the Minamoto chief was killed, and Kiyomori put to death nearly all the leaders of the clan, sparing only three children of the chief at the entreaty of their mother, a beautiful peasant girl named Tokiwa. Then Kiyomori got himself made Prime Minister, and married his daughter to the Emperor, getting the same control of the throne as the Fujiwara had enjoyed, beside a great deal more military power than they had ever had. But Kiyomori was by nature cruel and arrogant, and his acts became so arbitrary that all the nobles turned against him; so that when the young Minamoto lads, Yoritomo and Yoshitsune, grew up and escaped from the monasteries where they had been placed, they found it easy to rally their clans and attack Kiyomori. The ex-Emperor–who had become Ho-o (retired), as the usual custom was–having had more than enough of Kiyomori, openly favored the Minamoto, whereupon the Taira carried away the child Emperor, Antoku, Kiyomori's grandson, and kept him in their camp. The struggle was tremendous; the battles went now for one side, now for the other, till at last the Taira were driven south and utterly defeated at Dan-no-ura, on the Inland Sea, hundreds being slain, hundreds forced into the water or sunk with their ships. When all was lost, Kiyomori's wife took her grandson, the little Emperor, in her arms and leaped with him from a boat into the sea. Many of the leaders who survived were afterwards put to death, and the women made servants; the Taira Clan was all but annihilated, and never again recovered its prestige.

During all these years of disturbance, when there was no safety for the weak except under the protection of the strong, the feudal system had been developing just as it developed in Europe under like conditions, save for the strongly patriarchal qualities which it never lost in Japan. To quote Fenollosa, "The wars bred a new race of Japanese-hardy, fearless, cruel. The polite culture of centuries had disappeared in a holocaust of burning palaces; Chinese learning was forgotten; the only faith left was that in self prowess. The new element which now leaped to the front was Japanese character." At the same time a purely military class had grown up, the Bushi, knights or Samurai, men whose sole duty was to fight for the feudal lord to whose clan they belonged, and who in return was pledged to their support. This class Yoritomo did much to establish, by defining their position, duties and privileges, which last were only less than those of the nobles. His first step after his victories was to obtain recognition from the new Emperor, the next to have himself appointed Shogun or General-in-Chief; then he set up a military capital at Kamakura, on Sagami Bay, and proceeded to appoint provincial officers from his own following to administer the empire throughout, formulated the duties of knights and lords, and placed the whole system of feudal government on a firm and orderly basis. An important part of his plan was to strengthen the central power, namely his own-by settling his family and immediate followers in the eight provinces north of the Hakone Pass, known as the Kwanto, in distinction from the Kwansei or Home Provinces south of the pass and around Kyoto. Much of this Kwanto region was still uncultivated, a waste of forest and reedy swamp, and grants of land were made to knights who would undertake to have the country drained and tilled, and drive out the barbarous Emishi, who still lingered about this Northern Gate. There was a general feeling that this district was less sacred than Yamato, and might be fully controlled by a subject without violation of loyalty, since it had never been under the actual rule of the Son of Heaven.

Yoritomo had caused the office of Shogun to be made hereditary in his family, but he had no worthy descendants; his clever widow, Masako, becoming a Buddhist nun, ruled ably from behind the curtain, but the power presently passed into the hands of the Hojo family, who were not strong enough to make themselves Shoguns, but governed as Shikken (Regents) on behalf of a series of puppet Shoguns. The Kyoto Court tried to throw off both Shogun and Shikken, with the result that civil war broke out again, and two Emperors claimed the throne; so that for nearly a hundred years there were two lines reigning at once, one supported by Kamakura and the other always plotting against the Shogunate, all of which naturally made the Rojo so much the more secure. At last a compact was made that each line should furnish an Emperor in turn, an arrangement, however, which did not continue after the first round.

Here the Emperor Go-Daigo appears–a man of some real ability, but vacillating and easily led. As ex-Emperor he made a strong fight against the Hojo, aided by his son, Morinaga, who was a Buddhist priest and won over the monks. The Regent sent an army to Kyoto; Go-Daigo fled, but was captured and imprisoned on a small island. Meanwhile two great generals fought for him, whose names in Japan are synonyms for bravery and loyalty, Kusonosuke Masashige and Nitta Yoshisada, the latter a Minamoto; and with them fought Ashikaga Takauji, who was likewise a Minamoto. They took and sacked Kamakura and restored Go-Daigo, who had managed to escape from his island; but Ashikaga soon began to usurp power, and, persuading Go-Daigo to have his son Morinaga imprisoned at Kamakura on a charge of disloyalty, after some months put him to death. Masashige and Nitta then came against Ashikaga and were defeated. Masashige fell in battle, Nitta killed himself when all was lost, and Ashikaga had himself proclaimed Shogun, set up a

Cryptomeria Avenue

new Emperor and established a family who remained in power till the middle of the sixteenth century.

The Ashikaga period was a brilliant one for art and literature, but it was also a time of degeneracy and gradual decline of the central power, which resulted in another season of disorder throughout most of the sixteenth century. More than one daring Ronin or Samurai who had become masterless put himself at the head of a band of robbers and terrorized half a province, and to protect themselves the feudal lords assumed power and became more and more independent. The most distinguished of these new lords was one Oda Nobunaga, a small Daimyo descended from the Taira family, who suddenly rose to great power. By a series of brilliant victories and combinations he overcame one Daimyo after another, seized or built castles, and at last deposed the Shogun and became absolutely powerful, Shogun in all but the name; but, unlike former generals, acting with the greatest loyalty toward the Emperor, rebuilding the palace and supplying the Court with ample revenues.

It was just at this time that the Portuguese reached Japan–by accident they declared–bringing Western knowledge, and, above all, firearms, which the Japanese seized upon with eagerness and promptly imitated. Nobunaga's victories must have been at least partly due to the new weapons, which he took pains to secure; and, moreover, the Portuguese, and the Spanish who followed, supplied him with another arm which he was not slow to use–namely, a new religion to turn against the Buddhist monks.

Long before this the Emperor Go-Shirakawa had declared that there were three things in the empire which did not obey him– "the waters of the Kamogawa, the dice of the Sugoroku players and the priests of Hiezan." The great monastery on the mountain over against Kyoto, founded along with the city in the ninth century, had become enormously wealthy and powerful; both here and at other temples it had become customary to maintain soldier-monks and to interfere actively and often insolently in affairs of the empire. Nobunaga alone had courage to attack the unruly priests. He laid siege to Mount Hiezan, and in spite of the scruples of his generals destroyed the temples and the monastery, killed many priests and monks who ate meat and broke their vows of celibacy, and, after much fighting here and elsewhere, completely subdued the Order.

This antagonism to the Buddhists was almost certainly the secret of Nobunaga's special favor to Xavier and the missionaries who followed the Portuguese traders to Japan. Many of his followers professed Christianity; Nobunaga even built them a place of worship in Kyoto itself, and during his time there was no change of attitude toward them. Nor is it possible to doubt that many did truly become Christians, according to the degree of knowledge given to them; otherwise the after persecutions would not have been needed to stamp out the faith.

The sixteenth century was pre-eminently a period of brilliant men. Nobunaga's chief general was a marvelously clever adventurer– Hideyoshi, the son of a peasant; a creature so grotesque that he was nicknamed the Monkey; so able that, from being Nobunaga's horse-boy, he rose to the highest military honor, and after Nobunaga's death got entire control of the empire, nominally in behalf of Nobunaga's young son. He could not be made Shogun because he was not a Minamoto, and all attempts to get himself adopted into the family failed; but as Taiko (Regent) he obtained a really higher title. Adventurer as he was, Hideyoshi was no mere soldier; perhaps the peasant-farmer crops out in his new and very excellent land regulations; and he appointed a Council of Elders and made other less important reforms in administration. His great ambition was to conquer Korea, and for this he sent out a large army, which was at first successful, but afterwards all but defeated; and after a good deal of fighting and much loss, the Koreans made peace and paid a nominal tribute.

Hideyoshi gave the first check to Christianity; in his time the foreign priests received a sudden command to leave, according to some because one of them had behaved with want of respect to some great lord, but according to others because the government took alarm at something they heard from the Protestant Dutch and English-who had likewise come to trade-of the temporal power of the Pope and the land-grabbing methods of the King of Spain. For whatever reason it may have been, the missionaries were banished and Christianity forbidden; but there was no great effort to enforce the law except as to exclusion of foreign priests, and the persecutions did not begin till nearly a generation later.

The third great man of the century, and much the greatest of the three, was Tokugawa Ieyasu. He came of a minor branch of the Minamoto family, which had long been in difficulties with stronger neighbors. A Japanese authority declares that as a child Ieyasu was "confined in various places as surety for his family's conduct," which experiences "may have helped to sharpen his naturally remarkable abilities . . .Gradually and astutely he encroached upon the neigh-boring provinces, until finally he found himself the strongest chief-tain in the Tokaido." ("History of the Empire of Japan.") Later, after assisting Hideyoshi to overthrow the Hojo and Odawara, their prov-inces, comprising nearly the whole of the Kwanto, were given into

Ieyasu's charge; whereupon he built Yedo Castle (now Tokyo), and proceeded to establish himself as lord of the whole region north of the Hakone Pass.

After the death of Hideyoshi, his followers held Osaka Castle, his principal stronghold, on behalf of his son, Hideyori, who was still a mere child. At first Tokugawa was apparently loyal, but a break soon occurred, and after some years of struggle the Tokugawa got the upper hand everywhere. He finally defeated the allies at Sekigahara, a little north of Lake Biwa, and shortly after took and partly burned Osaka Castle, Hideyori and his mother killing themselves in the flames. Ieyasu then got the Emperor to appoint him Shogun, and spent the rest of his life consolidating his influence and laying the foundations of the "Great Peace," which lasted, at least outwardly, till Commodore Perry appeared in Yedo Bay.

5

THE TOKUGAWA AND
THE RESTORATION

TOKUGAWA IEYASU'S great work may be summed up in one word–centralization. Nobunaga and Hideyoshi had gained enormous prestige for themselves, but had not been able to establish a permanent government. Ieyasu took up the work where they left it, and organized a system of administration which broke down after two hundred and fifty years, chiefly bemuse it was too rigidly perfect, too inflexible to bear the strain of changed conditions. The problems before him were two: first, to control the other great nobles; and second, to keep on good terms with the imperial court at Kyoto, from which the Shogun derived his authority, and which had greatly increased in influence through Nobunaga's care. Accordingly, after the battle of Sekigahara, he showed himself very merciful, putting to death only two leaders from among the prisoners; but at the same time he confiscated the estates of those who had opposed him, and made a grand redistribution of all the provinces into two hundred and ninety-five Daimiates, greater or smaller, the rank of each Daimyo depending on his revenue, reckoned in koku (bushels) of rice. (The number of Daimyo was afterward increased to over three hundred.) In this distribution Ieyasu carefully surrounded himself in the Kwanto by members of his own family or nobles especially attached to himself, and also placed others of tried loyalty beside those likely to be disaffected, so as to head off any large conspiracy against him. In like manner he protected the road to Kyoto, and at the same time took care to reward special acts of valor or loyalty by grants of land and rank to individual knights. The next step was to appoint a Board of Elders to advise with the Shogun and administrative officers acting under them, also local officers throughout all the provinces–all, of course, being chosen from the nobles who were faithful to Tokugawa. This body of officials formed the Bakufu, or Curtain Government, so named from the tent-curtain behind which military officers consulted. Later the influence of the Bakufu became very great, overshadowing even that of the Shogun himself. It would have been hopeless to attempt to lessen the authority of the Daimyo on their own estates, and Ieyasu's administration accordingly provided for a high degree of local autonomy, subject to certain strict regulations of the general government; but as an offset to this the wily Tokugawa devised the system of compulsory residence at the capital. Ieyasu had suggested this scheme, but it was only completed by his grandson, Iyemitsu, who carried out this and many other details of the first Shogun's system. By it each Daimyo was required to spend a part of every other year in Yedo, and to leave his wife and children there when absent in his province. The time of going and coming was laid down by rule for each prince, and so contrived that neighbors were never on their lands at the same time. Moreover, as a further, check, lords who became too wealthy were apt to be ordered to undertake public works at their own expense. This traditional Tokugawa policy of keeping check on the other nobles seems to have been at the bottom of Iyemitsu's strange exclusion laws, so unlike all Japanese character before or after. The southern clans were the most dangerous rivals, Satsuma and Choshu especially; and it was just these who were nearest the ports of China, from which the strangers came, and who would gain most advantage from foreign trade in wealth and new weapons. Therefore not only Christianity, but all Western learning, was forbidden, and the Dutch and Chinese alone permitted to trade, under humiliating conditions, at Nagasaki. Ieyasu had sent an expedition to Mexico, and sanctioned certain yearly trading excursions of Japanese to Siam and China. These were now prohibited by Iyemitsu, and a later edict forbade any ships to be built over a certain small size, or decked sufficiently for ocean voyages.

These laws were rigidly kept till the opening of the country in 1854, though others, concerning trade with the Dutch and the export of metals, were probably evaded. Toward the imperial court the early Tokugawa professed the utmost loyalty, providing for suitable revenues, rebuilding the palace, and appointing officers to see that all things were properly conducted. The "Testament" of Ieyasu–a somewhat apocryphal document on government–declares that "the duty of the Shogun is to protect the Emperor against all perils which may threaten him in his palace, and to maintain peace throughout the empire. . . . When an Emperor ascends the throne, it is his (the Shogun's) duty to provide abundantly for all the expenses of the coronation." Iyemitsu further formulated the distinctions between the Kuge, or Court nobles, and the Buke, the military lords, who had charge of all practical matters; an of which regulations tended to deprive the Court of any actual power, and made it possible for later Shoguns to treat the Emperor as a mere puppet; and this in turn helped to bring about the reaction and the downfall of the Shogunate. The Buke Hato, or rules of the Samurai, were not less minute, and for any breach there was but one honorable atonement–hara-kiri ("body-cutting")–for which the second short sword was always ready. The Samurai were of various rank, from the Shogun and Daimyo to the "sandal-carriers." The retainers of the Tokugawa were called Hatamoto, and ranked above the retainers of lesser lords. But whatever his rank, every Samurai enjoyed certain privileges common to all, such as the right to a family name and crest, and above all the right to wear two swords, which was the special badge of the class. Everybody besides nobles and Samurai belonged to the "Cho-nin" ("street people "), who might not carry swords, except in the case of a head-man of a village, or other prominent person who for some special service was given the honor of wearing a single one. Cho-nin again were of various ranks, farmers standing first–it was not dishonorable even for a Samurai to engage in farming; then artisans ; and last of all, merchants, no matter how wealthy, for the Code taught that trade was in its nature degrading. Below these were only the Eta, who killed and skinned animals and did the lowest tasks, and whose existence was scarcely recognized

Gate of Nobles House

by law; and the Hinin, utter outcasts, including criminals and disgraced Samurai.

The Tokugawa encouraged formality of every kind as a check on the fierce spirits of the warriors, such, for instance, as the practice of cha-no-yu, or tea-ceremony; and an immense impulse was also added by the study of Chinese, which was revived just at this time. It came about almost precisely as the Renaissance did in Europe, through the fall of the Ming dynasty, and the exile of many savants, who fled from Nankin to Japan, and were received by Tokugawa and Mito and others, just as the Medici received Greek refugees after the fall of Constantinople. Hitherto men who wished for a life of study had become priests; now Samurai were forbidden to lay down the sword, but encouraged to use their studies for the benefit of the State. Ieyasu set the example of appointing scholars to important positions, and it became the fashion for Daimyo to retain Kan-Gakusha (classical students) as advisers and lecturers in their households. Schools for knights were established and patronized by the great lords, and the Buddhist priests, restored to high favor again under the Tokugawa Shoguns, held schools for the common people at nearly every temple. Dramas and novels by the dozen were put out and eagerly read, and repeated everywhere by professional story-tellers, to the delight, and not a little to the instruction, of the unlearned. Samurai, however, were not permitted to go to the theatre. The doctrines of Lao-Tse and Mencius, and above all the iron-bound regulations of Confucius, became the dominating principles of the age. Men strove after a more rigorous stoicism than ever, and women were restricted more and more to domesticity and the "Three Obediences"–to father, then husband, and after them to the eldest son.

Along with Chinese classics, the study of early Japanese history and literature was revived. The Prince of Mito, grandson of Ieyasu, kept a staff of learned men at work for years, compiling a history of Japan, in two hundred and forty volumes; and two great scholars-Mabuchi and his pupil, Motori, set themselves to revive the use of pure Yamato, the original, Japanese language in which the early literature was written, which had been overlaid by a mass of borrowed Chinese words and phrases. The result of these studies was a wave of nationalism and loyalty to the Emperor as the Son of Heaven, and therewith a questioning of the Shogun's right to supreme authority; all of which combined, with the growing social evils and financial difficulties, brought on by luxury and extravagance, to produce a deep current of unrest throughout the whole nation.

This was the internal situation when Commodore Perry arrived with the American demand for treaty ports and intercourse. Such intercourse was undoubtedly most desirable for Japan, as well as for the other nations, and ports of call for fuel and water absolutely necessary, if our American ships were to sail the Pacific; but as to the often boasted peacefulness of the expedition–well, there is something appropriate to the situation in Dean Hole's story of the cowboy in a Western church, who was asked to take up the collection. If I remember rightly, Fighting Bill passed the hat with a revolver on his hip, and the congregation "panned out" handsomely. Commodore Perry likewise didn't shoot; he merely asked the Shogun's representatives to call and see his guns, and told them stories about the Opium War in China and then left, promising to come next year. The country was in a fever of excitement; arms were cast, troops drilled, forts built. But happily the Shogun and his advisers realized the situation and the country's weakness, and in 1854 they signed the treaties. It was the signal for a storm; the Emperor refused to ratify the agreement and ordered the barbarians expelled. The barbarians declined to go, but rather came in greater numbers and made more demands. A Nationalist party arose, the Jo-i, having for its rallying cry, "Up with the Emperor! Down with the alien!" The clans opposed to Tokugawa joined the league, especially the three most powerful–Mito, Satsuma and Choshu. In 1863 a party of Mito Samurai assassinated the Regent Ii Kamon, who favored the foreigners. Everywhere the treaties were used as political capital against the Shogunate.

In 1867 the Emperor Komei died, and shortly after the Shogun resigned, giving as his reason that the state of the country required a single head, and it was time the dual system should be done away. The "Restoration" dates from this time; but the Tokugawa clan refused to submit with their chief. They drew up a paper declaring that the young Emperor was misled by evil advisers of Satsuma and Choshu, and held Yedo against the Imperial forces, even taking the boy-prince, who was nominal Highpriest of Uyeno, and calling him Emperor, carrying him off with them to Utsunomiya and Nikko. It is a terrible record of fruitless bravery. The Tokugawa had more modern arms, but the Imperial name carried weight, and little by little the Shogun's followers were forced back, as clan after clan gave in its allegiance to the Emperor. A last stand was made in the northwest, at Wakamatsu Castle, in Aidzu, and after that fell, all submitted except the few who had escaped by sea from Yedo, and held out in the island of Yezo for a little longer.

In the changes which followed it was not the Kuge nobles or the Daimyo who took a leading part, but the Samurai. Many of their names are familiar in the Cabinets of recent years; others died or were killed during the formative period. Such were Yoshida, put to death by the Bakufu; Kido, who dared propose to his chief, the Lord of Satsuma, the abolition of the feudal system, and who died in Kyoto just before the Satsuma rebellion, which was raised in the hope of restoring that system; Okubo and Mori, victims of political fanatics; Saigo, leader of the Satsuma rebellion, dead in a lost cause; Count Katsu, recently deceased, one of the ablest of all; and again the older statesmen of today, such as Marquis Ito, Marshall Marquis Yamagata, Count Okuma. They threw a dynamite bomb at Okuma in 1889 on account of his too foreign views on Treaty Revision, but he escaped with the loss of a leg. Some day the lives of these makers of New Japan will be written, and the story will read like the wildest romance.

Kido's suggestion about doing away with feudalism was backed by a powerful agent-namely, want of money. Nearly every great lord was at his wits' end to provide for his retainers; so long as they were ready to fight for him, so long must he find them rice according to their rank, and the economic changes, due in part to the opening of the country, made this yearly more and more difficult. Clan after clan took up the new idea. Choshu, Satsuma, Tosa-all the greater ones united in proposing to the Emperor to give up their feudal rights and duties, and in compelling the lesser nobles to do the same. The Samurai were accordingly released from their allegiance, and in the same moment deprived of the revenues which for generations had come regularly without any thought on their part-which it was utterly against all their training for them to think about at all. At first a small yearly grant was made to each; then a lump sum presented, with which they were expected to begin life for themselves. The full misery of those days only Samurai can know. Brought up to believe that the very knowledge of money was something utterly unworthy, their attempts at business were pitiful beyond words. Nearly all lost their entire capital in a few months through sheer lack of what an American would call "business sense." All who could, got into government service in some form or other, many becoming policemen, that they might still serve the Emperor and wear a sword. Hearn has written many sad little stories of that time, which has its nearest parallel, perhaps, in the condition of our own Southern States after the war.

Of course the dire consequences of the changes brought protests from many sides, and the discontent culminated in the Satsuma Rebellion of 1878-9, led by General Saigo, the man who had commanded the Imperial forces in the War of the Restoration—a great, pure soul, set singly on bringing back the old heroic ideals which he saw being swept away. The struggle was hopeless from the first, and when it was over and Saigo had fallen by his own hand, the last clan gave in its entire loyalty.

Since then the difficulties of the government have been financial and social ones; so many reforms have had to be made, so much done to bring Japan to the position she longs for among the other nations, that friction is inevitable, and the marvel is, as Weston says (in the book "Japanese Alps"), that the country can make such radical changes and yet retain its own intense individuality.

The Emperor Mutsuhito, who came to the throne in 1867, gave his reign the auspicious name of Meiji (Enlightenment). In 1881 he promised a Constitution and a representative government, but the country was not yet ready for such a step; and, in point of fact, the Constitution was not promulgated till 1889, and the first Parliament elected the following summer. The plan is based chiefly on the Constitution of Germany, on the ground that Japan's social condition is nearer to hers than to any others; but certain elements have been borrowed from England and some from France. There is an Upper House, partly hereditary, partly elected from the lesser nobility, partly nominated by the Emperor from any class on the ground of learning and ability; and a Lower House, chosen by ballot, the franchise being limited by a considerable property requirement—namely, fifteen yen direct tax for one year in the voter's district, or three years' income tax of the same amount in one place. The Cabinet is responsible to the Emperor and not to Parliament, which can manifest its displeasure only by refusing to vote the appropriations. The Liberals want to introduce responsible Cabinets, but Count Okuma and many other statesmen think the country is not ready–that for the present the Cabinet must, in the main, lead the country, instead of merely carrying out its wishes expressed at an election, as in England. To tell the truth, Parliamentary matters do not work very smoothly as yet, at least in the Lower House; the Upper does better, being more conservative and mature, and also more apt to be in sympathy with the Cabinet. There are parties galore, and they split and combine and play each other off with bewildering facility; but in the meantime the government goes on steadily and quietly, with now and then a conservative movement, but on the whole ever towards greater progress and enlightenment.

A complete system of national education was suggested by Kido, and fully planned out by Viscount Arinori Mori on his return from service as Minister to Washington. The plan is based largely on the German system, with some American modifications. It provides a graded course leading to the universities, which so far are two–Tokyo and the rather recent Kyoto University. Of course, only men are admitted to the universities. The highest school for girls is the Higher Normal, which prepares for advanced examinations for teachers' certificates, and is about equal to the men's higher schools, which prepare for the university. In the boys' schools military training is carried on all the way through, and counts toward the term of service afterward, which is compulsory, as in Germany.

The army has been nearly doubled since the war with China in 1895-6, or rather is to be so increased inside of eight years from that date. It is no secret that the government is straining every nerve to perfect the navy, which must always be the best defence of an island nation, and the people are with it to a man. Besides the ten ships captured from China, which made a fleet of forty-three vessels by the end of the war, seven new armored cruisers have already been added, built in America and England, of which the Fuji and the Yashima are over twelve thousand tons, and more are to follow, with torpedo boats and torpedo destroyers, and all the rest of the horrid train. Along with this policy for the navy goes that of building up a merchant marine, by means of subsidies for large vessels and lines chartered for trans-oceanic trade, such as the Nippon Yusen Kaisha, which sends lines to America, Europe and Australia, as well as to comparatively near ports, like Hong Kong, Bombay and Vladivostok. So far, it is to be feared, these lines have had to let their pride keep them warm, as the saying is; but, if they can hold out, they will surely win a place in time, for the Japanese are born sea-men, and their ships are immaculately clean, the table fair and the service excellent. The Orient Line (To Yo Kisen Kaisha) has already the best ships sailing between San Francisco and Japan.

River Front, Tokyo

THE TOKUGAWA AND THE RESTORATION   57

Since the war with China, the great event has been the Revised Treaties, granted in 1896, first by England, then America, Germany and all the rest, and going into effect in 1899. The principal points are "mixed residence"–i.e., permission to foreigners to live and do business anywhere in the empire, instead of only in the Treaty ports; and, on the other hand, tariff autonomy for Japan, and the doing away of the irritating "Extra Territoriality" and Consular Jurisdiction. Whatever other effects this may have, at least Japan's pride is satisfied, and she is much less restlessly anxious to have her position recognized; and two years have already almost passed without any of the awful experiences of Japanese law predicted by the Kobe Herald and its fellow Japan-haters.

In 1897 the gold standard was adopted, with the yen fixed at fifty cents American money, and silver yen to be redeemed by the government at that rate within a specified time. It was a risky measure, and against the judgment of many thinkers, both Japanese and foreign; but it seems to have turned out well on the whole, and nobody accuses it of the general rise in prices "since the war," which has gone on faster than ever of late.

But of details of policy it seems hopeless to speak; what is true today will be ancient history tomorrow, for New Japan grows like the young child that she is, or like a stalk of her spring bamboo, on which the Japanese Munchausen hung his hat one night, and in the morning found it above the treetops.

6

KAMAKURA-A FORSAKEN CITY

"Representons-nous done le golfe de Sagami et Kamakura, les collines boisees, la ville aux fortes murailles; la baie tranquille, ou glissent les voiles. Au bord de la mer, dans les rues de la ville, quelle activite! pecheurs, forgerons, marchands de toutes sortes, et les processions des bonzes vetus d'or et de pourpre sous la pluie des fleurs, dans la fumee d'encens, et les corteges des daimio revenant de la chasse ou de la guerre." –Mis. de la Mazeliere, "Histoire du Japon."

"Whoso will, from pride released,
Contemning neither man nor beast,
May hear the soul of all the East
About him at Kamakura.
"Yea, voice of every soul that sprung
From life that strove from rung to rung,
When Devadatta's rule was young,
The warm winds bring Kamakura."
–Kipling.

Two little fishing villages, mere clusters of tumbledown huts–that is all there is left of what was once a city of nearly a million people, the sumptuous capital of Yoritomo and the Ashikaga Shoguns.

Going south from Yokohama, the train leaves the main line at Ofuna Junction for the Yokosuka branch, and plunging through short tunnels, and in crosses between rice and millet fields to the long, low "Foreign Hotel," the Kai-Hin-in, or Seaside Sanitarium-a pleasant house, where European ways and wants are understood and provided for. It stands just back from the sea, hidden from it by a strip of slender pines, twisted and slanted by the wind, and beyond these again by irregular sand dunes, grown over with heavy, coarse grass and tangled weeds.

Following a little footpath to the top, the sweep of the bay breaks before you, a perfect crescent, finished at either end by a bold, wooded headland. Tucked away in the shelter of each curve is a little village of gray, thatched houses, creeping almost to the tideline, where rows of narrow sampans lie beached, their long oars inside. The people here, as in most of the hamlets along the coast, combine fishing with farming, the women and children of the family doing a large share of the field work. Picturesque as they are, these villages under the cliffs have a certain wind-blown, weather-beaten look, quite unlike the trim tidiness of the little "Strassdorfer," as the Germans would say, which bead the great Tokaido highway. The old thatch is beautifully moss-grown, but many of the tiny cabins are not even thatched, only roughly shingled–sure sign of poverty in Japan–and their mud-plastered walls are cracked and broken. But the lean, sinewy men and dumpy women look sturdy and cheerful, and the country children are delightful, if not over-clean–fat, round-faced, brown cherubs, with narrow, bright eyes and most beguiling grins, who come straying along the beach with the usual load of babies, in hopes of selling a few shells and bits of stone or coral to the Ijin San (Mr., Mrs. or Miss Foreigner). Here at the tideline something is always going on. One of the most picturesque moments is when the boats come in, and the rowers steer swiftly through the line of surf, and then spring out, bare-legged, into the foam, with garments tucked about their waists, and drag the long, narrow craft far up the yellow sand, while the women flock down to help with the unloading. Dragging the nets is another interesting sight. A dozen or twenty men, more or less clad according to the season, stand on the shore, pulling in line on a long rope. Sometimes they haul and coil away for hours, the brown fishbaskets lying idle on the sand, till at last the great mesh is brought close in and the take can be gathered.

Yet another harvest the tide brings–the great masses of seaweed that are washed up by the spring and autumn storms. It is all eagerly gathered, the women going over the piles and carefully picking out the edible varieties; for the Japanese are very fond of seaweed, and there are several choice kinds much eaten as a relish–and very good they are, too, when you once get used to a flavor of oyster-shells! These special sorts are separately dried and prepared for market; the rest is spread out on coarse mats along the shore, and watched and turned for days. This, too, is work for the women, and the old men who are too rheumatic to go out with the boats. At last, when it is thoroughly dry, it is beaten fine with a flail, sifted through basket sieves and packed down in sacks, to be shipped for fertilizing the fields inland.

To an American, all this manipulation speaks volumes as to Japanese "intensive" methods of cultivation; and, in truth, the entire little plain itself is tended like a garden, and always green or brown or golden with crops. A little of everything in Japan seems grown on these tiny holdings, none of which are more than an acre or two in extent. There is rice, of course, and barley, and a few rows of beans, a little rape, a little wheat, a little cotton, and brown tasseled millet, to be gathered and dried and beaten out on mats by the roadside at the cottage doors.

Quantities of big, mealy sweet potatoes are raised at Kamakura. "Satsuma imo" they call them in Japan, because they really belong to the southern province. They are very cheap, and are considered very plebeian food, only fit for coolies. And last–surely this should endear it to an American heart!–the region is famous for an excellent quality of peanuts. These, too, are dried by the wayside; indeed, everything is spread out at the door, just as in Italy, including the long strips of buckwheat macaroni–o soba, as they call it–and the tasteless rice-flour wafers, which are a luxury of the very poor. Naturally there is dust; but what will you have? They are not princes or Americans, these people, that they should waste good crop-land on such matters.

And all around the quiet plain circle the steep, tumbled hills, dark with heavy masses of pine and fir and the thick-leaved evergreen oak. Summer cottages of foreigners or wealthy Japanese climb the sides here and there; but that is all. The charcoal burners go where once there were barriers and knights in armor guarding every approach, in the days when temples and houses and palaces filled all the level and overflowed up the ravines between the slopes. Yoritomo founded it at the end of the twelfth century–Yoritomo, of the house of Minamoto, eldest of the three baby sons with whom their mother, Tokiwa, fled from the massacre of their kin. You see her often, in Japanese prints and kakemono, trudging through blinding snow, Yoshitsune in her arms, and Yoritomo and little Noboyori clinging to her hands. She it was who gave herself up to save her mother, whom Kiyomori had captured, and by her beauty won over Kiyomori to spare the boys, in an evil hour for himself; for hair-cutting and enforced monastic vows worked no better than at certain periods of European history. Marvelous are the legends of their boyhood, especially of Yoshitsune, "the young bull," as the unhappy monks called him; how, when they brought him the conventual frock, he would none of it, demanding a sword instead; or how, in the depths of the forest, he took fencing lessons from a Tengu, or goblin–a strange, winged creature, which hops on one leg and plays something like the part of a German troll in Japanese folklore. The lads grew up to rally their clan, and presently the fierce old Kiyomori of Taira, dying, desires only "the head of Minamoto-no-Yoritomo to be laid on my grave." But Yoritomo's head stayed fast–and it was no common head either, but one that knew how to take advantage of the storm of hate Kiyomori's arrogance and cruelty had roused; and once in power, he ruled justly and with a mighty hand, bringing peace and order, after the years of tumult. He it was who established the feudal system on a workable basis–"gave it a constitution and a hierarchy," says de la Mazeliere; and he who also established the hereditary Shogunate, that strange "Dual System" which only ended in 1868.

First Yoritomo's military camp was here at Kamakura; then his scarcely less military court. Here, too, he wrought the injustice and treachery toward Yoshitsune, his brother, that forever darkens his name; for the younger was stronger, braver, everywhere beloved, and though he had fought Yoritomo's battles, and in truth won him his power, yet–perhaps for that very reason–the Shogun was jealous and distrusted Yoshitsune. Long weeks he kept him waiting over here across the hills at Koshigoe, not permitting him to enter the city, although he had come bringing a Taira chief who had made submission, refusing to heed his protestations of innocence, till Yoshitsune gave up in despair and went back to Kyoto. Then Yoritomo sent a spy to kill him, and Yoshitsune killed the spy and denounced the Shogun to the Emperor; and so back and forth, plot and counterplot, till at last, a fugitive in the wild Northern provinces, Yoshitsune and his faithful henchman, Benkei, were treacherously murdered by the Shogun's order, or, perhaps, killed themselves when all was lost–no one knows. And here, under the hill, below the Kwannon temple, they set up a stage, that Yoshitsune's beautiful favorite, Shizuka, now Yoritomo's captive, might dance a sacred dance and sing the triumphs of the Shogun. So she came, the beautiful woman, more beautiful than ever, in a wonderful dress; but, instead of Yoritomo's praises, she made a song of her own, and wove it in the dance–how Yoshitsune fought and suffered, and of his innocence and betrayal and death. But the people say their hero could not die; they believed he fled to Yezo, where, strangely enough, the Ainu to this day worship a god by his name. And others say he escaped to Asia, and reigned there many years, being no other than the great Zenghis Khan.

Kublai Khan, though, grandson of Zenghis, comes really and genuinely into Kamakura's history; for a generation after Yoritomo he sent to demand tribute from Japan. Nor was he entirely outside of his rights, for annual gifts had really been given to the Emperor of China in a loose sort of way in the earlier centuries of our era. However, it had been discontinued for generations, and Japan was in no way disposed to renew it. The first set of ambassadors returned empty; the second likewise. It may have been the fourth or fifth legate who was taken down to the shore here and beheaded, as a "demonstration" we should say now.

The invasion which followed was repulsed in the southern island, Kiushiu, and a second still greater one held in check till the Emperor made pilgrimage to Yamada in Ise and prayed at the shrine of his ancestor, the Sun Goddess; whereupon, say the chronicles, a terrific storm arose and all but destroyed the Chinese fleet; and that was the end of continental claims on Japan.

The chief "sight" of Kamakura, in a guide-book sense, dates back almost to Yoritomo's time; it is the bronze Daibutsu, or colossal image of Buddha, so often pictured and described. Tradition says that Yoritomo greatly desired to build such an image, but could not accomplish it, and about fifty years after his death–at the beginning of the thirteenth century–some pious lady of the court carried out his wish.

The figure is an Amida (the Buddha of light and wisdom), seated, the hands in the lap, palms up and thumbs together, in the traditional attitude of contemplation. He sits on a stone platform, in a little gorge under the open sky, in springtime up to his shoulders in cherry bloom, for, after his temple had been twice destroyed by tidal waves, it was not again rebuilt; and for three hundred years he has been one of the "wet gods," as the Japanese say.

Perhaps the best time to see the Daibutsu is under a cloudy sky, or late in the afternoon, when the sun has just gone behind the hills; the absence of shadows, the flatness, so to speak, of the light all going to heighten the motionless calm of the figure. Like all true colossi, he does not seem so very big at first. One has to be told that he is all but fifty feet high; that the "jewel" on his forehead–it is a ball of pure silver–is over a foot across; that his mouth measures three feet and his face eight or nine. A modern Liberty or Victory standing by on the platform might peep-on tiptoe-over his placid shoulder, only to be dwarfed into a fussy, overgrown puppet beside his still dignity.

The image follows closely the earlier types of Nara and Kyoto. The folds of drapery fall straight and barely indicated; all the forms are large, rounded, yet never puffy; the nude parts treated absolutely

without detail. The face is equally typical; the broad forehead, the full child mouth, the eyes, closed all but the narrowest of slits–yet he is not sleepy. Behind those lids the god is alert with an intensity the keener because so removed–the alertness of concentration. This is no repose, rather an immovable, passionless calm, as far from ease as from stiffness or stolidity.

Negation, remoteness, repression. Surely these are the attributes of this great God of Self-Control. What, then, did the maker mean? Did he think only of the Buddha who overcame desire, the example all men should seek to follow? Or did he dream, too, of the Compassionate One, whose love and pity were for all living things? If so, then however faintly expressed, in his heart at least was a glimpse of the world's desire–the All-Pure who yet can care for sin and sorrow.

To climb inside the figure is not a little disenchanting; the effect on one's feelings is like going into a bell-tower as the chimes die away, and seeing all the wheels and pulleys by which the music was made. Still, everyone goes and will go, and perhaps it is worth while, because only so do you get a true idea of the actual size of the statue. There is a low entrance cut in the side of the lotus flower which forms the seat, and through this you pass in and find a ladder, by which to mount into the head, and peer out of a little window into the tops of the cherry trees.

There is also a small shrine inside, dedicated to Kwannon, the Goddess of Mercy, and a tablet inscribed with a sacred text in Chinese characters. The construction can be better understood from here, too. The figure was cast in separate sheets of metal and run together in position, and finally finished outside with the carver's chisel. The inner surface is rough and shapeless, and the whole cavity dusty and unattractive, with a sort of unnecessary ugliness that one resents, particularly in Japan, where most of life is made so scrupulously beautiful.

There is another famous statue at Kamakura, held very sacred by devout Japanese, though in workmanship it is greatly inferior to the Daibutsu. This is a colossal figure of Kwannon, the merciful- the Eleven-Faced Kwannon–who wears for a headdress ten smiling little faces of herself. According to tradition, this figure and another were carved by two of the gods themselves from the trunk of a huge camphor tree; and this one, being cast into the sea, traveled all the way from Yamato to Kamakura, and was brought ashore by some fishermen. The temple itself is large, but not otherwise remarkable, except for its beautiful situation, far up the side of the hill, commanding a wide view. It is reached by three flights of broad stone steps, time-worn and greened with moss and lichens. Noble old trees stand around and behind, and the delicate dwarf maples that put out crimson leaves in the spring; and between the branches you look down on the tiny checker-board of a plain, and the cliffs opposite, and the curving bay, where, as they say, those pious fishermen found the image of Kwannon floating in a halo of marvelous light. The figure is not bronze, but wood covered with gold lacquer, and it seems to glow still in the dim inner shrine where it stands, lighted only by a few pale lamps. They do not show it at all times, but at certain festivals, or in response to special offerings. Artistically a small bronze Buddha in aside shrine is of far more value. It dates from the middle of the fifteenth century, the time of the Ashikaga Shoguns at Kamakura, which was one of the most brilliant periods of Japanese art. Outside, near the entrance, there is a quaint life-sized figure of Binzuru, a very popular deity with the unlettered classes, the touch of whose image is believed to have healing powers. He sits outside, because, although he was one of the "Sixteen Disciples of Buddha"–the Rakan–he once marred his saintship by noticing the beauty of a woman, and may not therefore come inside the temple itself.

Then there is Engakuji, which has a bell eight feet high, the largest in Kamakura, though hardly more than two-thirds the size of the great bells at Kyoto and Nara; not hung in a bell-tower, but, as all Japanese bells are, placed in a sort of open shed, with a curving, pagoda-like roof. Likewise there is a small temple to Emma, the Buddhist god of the lower regions, who judges the dead according to their deeds, sending them blessedness or torment. The image in this temple is said to be a memory portrait made by one Unkei, who died and came to life again, sent back by the dread judge himself to show his likeness to men. It is hideous rather than awful, like the devils of mediaeval Europe. The priests add to the effect by keeping it behind a curtain, which they draw aside suddenly, revealing the squat figure and open mouth, and ferocious eyes glaring out of the dusky shrine.

Also there is Kenchoji, of which Hearn writes with a sympathetic enthusiasm most of us cannot share; for it is old and faded and dusty, the carvings broken and the color scaling away. Only the great "Third Gate" still keeps something of its stately magnificence.

Another and much more popular shrine stands higher on the hill–so popular, indeed, that special trains run to Kamakura on the days of its festival; but it has no interest for the tourist unless on such days, and those who come here at all come to see the grounds at Kenchoji and the fine old junipers. Of course, a Japanese will make a garden of a sand heap or a bulrush swamp, but here at the edge of the hills they have only had to encourage nature–to guard a tall pine here and flood a lotus pool there. Lotus–Buddha's flower– is much in evidence at Kamakura.

A bronze lotus leaf receives the fountain at Kenchoji; the flower is carved, in conventional rendering, on stone balustrades and tomb–stele and lanterns, and Buddhas stand enthroned on the petals; while in July and August the temple ponds are brilliant with the sumptuous great blossoms, rose-pink and white, against the peculiar bluish green of the leaves, which look like weathered bronze.

Many other temples there are among the hills and ravines, survivals of the lost city, all more or less forsaken and dilapidated, and none of any real interest except the one dedicated to Hachiman, God of War, on the far side of the plain from the Daibutsu.

This is still a fine building, though its splendor has been spoiled by the Shinto reformation, which, since 1868, has swept away from many a temple the bronze vases and images and shining brass lotus flowers, and all the rich paraphernalia of Buddhist worship. Yoritomo founded the temple in the twelfth century, and although the main building is a comparatively modern restoration–rebuilt after a fire in 1828–the first Shogun's sword and many other relics connect it with his time, when it was the most important shrine in Kamakura. In fact, Yoritomo may be said to have almost created the worship of Hachiman, which until then had been merely a minor hero-cult, local and insignificant; and in this de Mazeliere discovers another example of the Shogun's shrewd statesmanship; for Hachiman, in the flesh, was the Emperor Ojin-a very remarkable personage, too, being that son of the strenuous Empress Jingo in whose name she conquered Korea before ever he was born. But his significance for Yoritomo lay in the fact that he was the great-grandfather or great-great-grandfather of Minamoto, who founded his clan, and not many generations back of Minamoto-no-Yoritomo himself.

Such a hero-divinity of an ancestor would certainly be valuable to any ambitious ruler; at any rate, Yoritomo unquestionably took pains to promote Hachiman worship, and established it with great pomp in this his new dominion, north of the Hakone Pass, which he and his descendants took care to appropriate to the family in every possible way.

The main building stands back and somewhat to one side of a massive stone-faced terrace, to which a long flight of steps leads up. The colonnade in front, as well as the pillars and beams of the temple itself, are painted with the dull vermilion red which one comes to associate with all Buddhist temples. The carvings of birds and animals have a good deal of interest; but the interior is plain, not to say bare, containing only the simple accessories of the Shinto faith, the mirror and the Gohei, or folded strips of paper. In the porch they usually keep the portable shrines used for carrying images at festival times; the relics are not often shown except at these festivals. Oldest and most perishable of all these sacred memorials must be that court robe of the Empress Jingo, mother of Ojin-Hachiman, which Pierre Loti saw by special favor. In his marvelous language he describes the visit, and the opening of the great chest, the unwrapping, fold after fold, till at last within all lay a shining filmy thing, light as gossamer, so delicate that it seemed ready at any moment to shiver into a cloud of dust. There is something striking, almost pathetic, in the preservation of such a garment for such a woman–if hers, indeed, it was–a sort of reassertion of her womanhood, through accounts must have been spent chiefly in the saddle.

Her grandson, the Emperor Nintoku, son of Ojin, has a little temple below the steps leading to his father's, and a second small building contains an unimportant wooden statue of Yoritomo.

A long avenue of pines, now much destroyed, leads straight up to the temple from the sea. Three high stone torii stand across the avenue–those strange Shinto pylons, whose type-form is two posts and a cross-beam, projecting at the ends, and whose origin goes back out of sight in the dim "Age of the Gods." Something in their loneliness, as they stand apart, makes these particular torii especially impressive.

The temple beyond is almost hidden in the trees, and there are no other buildings near. Seen so, the fine proportions and purity of line–the slight inward slant of the posts, the curving ends of the crossbeams turning a little up–give them a certain severe beauty most characteristic of pure "Yamato" taste, which has strangely little in common with the gorgeous Indo-Chinese influences of Buddhistic art. To the simple cross-beam is added here, and often elsewhere, a second cross-tie-beam, and a supporting block between the two. It is probably a concession to the necessities of stone construction, the original form being wood. Tradition says they were perches for the fowls (tori), brought for sacrifice to early Shinto temples; or that the Golden Crow, the mystic Hobo Bird, rests thereon in his flight toward the sun.

One version is about as authentic as the other, and about as probable; for what this form does suggest inevitably is a Dolmen, the stone uprights and lintel translated into wood, and then, as here, back again into stone. When the archaeologists explain Stonehenge, perhaps they will throw some light on these strange torii.

Modern education in Japan has borrowed from Germany the good custom of sending schoolboy excursions to study history on the spot, and the youngsters sleep in camp on the shore, and tramp Kamakura over, rehearsing how soon Yoritomo's direct line went out in blood, his grandson and last descendant, the Shogun Sanetomo, being murdered while worshiping at the Hachiman temple by a nephew whose father Sanetomo had killed, and who was killed in turn; how the Hojo Regents usurped the Shogun's power and ruled for them as they for the Emperor, and how the Ashikaga branch of Minamoto helped the ever-unlucky Emperor Go-Daigo to overthrow the Hojo, and then took unlawful power in their turn. They hear, too, of Masako, Yoritomo's clever wife, who became a nun after his death, and from the convenient retirement of the cloister directed affairs of state. They go to see the cave where an imperial prince, Go-Daigo's son, Morinaga, was confined, and at last put to death by Ashikaga; and they are reminded that the period of these disloyal Shoguns was filled with treachery and strife, so that in spite of their power and magnificence the memory of the Ashikaga family is held in abhorence. And they climb the western headland where Go-Daigo's faithful general, Nitta, stood and cried to the God of the Sea, for the Hojo had a guard of ships across the bay, and a chevaux de frise at the foot of the cliff, and all the hills were full of armed men. And when he had prayed, he flung into the sea his most precious thing, his sword, "the soul of the Samurai," and Kompira accepted the sacrifice and rolled back the water, and the army passed round the turn of the cliff and took and sacked the city. But the Ashikaga rebuilt it more magnificently than before, and its decline came only gradually with the disturbances of the fifteenth century and the removal of the Shogun's court to the neighbor city, Odawara. Finally, when Tokugawa Ieyasu chose Yedo for his capital, Kamakura was completely deserted for two hundred years, till the Yokohama residents rediscovered it for their own use.

The place is really getting quite crowded now. Besides the hotels, many Japanese, as well as Americans and Europeans, have cottages near the sea or up the hillsides. The bathing is quite good, though the water is hardly cold enough to be particularly bracing, and the beach is soft and shifts treacherously after storms. The country people say that at a certain season–just after the Feast of the Dead, according to the old calendar–the Sea-God claims a yearly victim, and as the fatal time is in August, when wind and currents are most uncertain, it too often happens that some careless swimmer fulfills the tradition.

Summer at Kamakura is undeniably hot, and its devotees are forced to claim that they prefer it that way. Winter and early spring are especially delightful here; the air is warmer and softer than in Tokyo, and the blossoms come early. By the end of March the scent of purple bean-flower steals up from the roadsides, and the frogs pipe all night long in the wet fields; the hills and woods are full of wild-flowers, startlingly like those of our Atlantic coast, while up the sunny cliffs, where the air is heavily sweet with wild pittospo-rum, you may close your eyes and dream of June in Italy.

7

ENOSHIMA

ON a sunny day, if you climb the east cliff from Kamakura to a certain little tea-house perched far up the side, you will find a glorious view of the country round about, and all across the bay to the far shore of Sagami, where stand the Hakone mountains, and above them Fuji San-seeming, as some one puts it, "to bathe their feet in the sea." Lying between Kamakura and this far shore, just beyond the next inlet, is a beautiful little wooded island, green to the edge of its steep cliffs. It is Enoshima-Island of the Bay-the sacred island of Benten, Goddess of Luck.

Everybody goes to Enoshima at least once, and many of the Yokohama and Tokyo "foreign residents" have cottages there, and run down for days or weeks to get the sea air and escape the greater heat of the city. It is an all-day trip from either Yokohama or Kamakura, but not a hard one. In Japan there is always an inn to rest at, and on Enoshima there are three good ones-shoes off, of course!-where chairs and tables and knives and forks are to be had, also omelette and excellent fried or broiled fish, with the never-failing rice. Moreover, those who do not wish to depend on such viands, or venture on an entirely Japanese meal, can bring a lunch from their own hotel and have it nicely served at the inn.

The jinrikisha men will carry it, after you leave the kurumas to cross to the island. Most of these men speak half a dozen words of English, and they will act as guides, carry your purchases, and make themselves generally useful, quite earning the twenty or thirty sen apiece which they are sure to ask for their own meal.

In fine weather it is possible to take a boat and row or sail from Kamakura directly over to the caves; but the usual way is by kuruma over the western cliff and along the beach road, about four miles each way. The road crosses the cliff by a deep cutting, between walls of rock that rise high above one's head, green with moss and ferns, and almost arched over by splendid maple trees, making a gray-and-green frame to the view backward over Kamakura and the sea. A group of weather-worn tombstones stands beside the road, some fallen, some leaning this way and that; and near by is a row of stone images of Jizo, friend of travelers and protector of little children. For the sake of these little ones mothers make funny red bibs, such as babies wear, and tie them under Jizo's chubby chin, where they hang till rain and wind have beaten them to faded rags.

In spite of the deep cut, it is a long climb to the top of the cliff and the slope down to the next beach. This, too, is a crescent curve, backed by high dunes and ending in a strip of sand, which at low tide connects Benten's island with the shore; and just over the sand, between the dark island and a darker headland, if the mists permit, Fuji San sweeps up into the sky, dazzling white or faint as the clouds about its base, and flanked by the blue Hakone ranges, sloping off on either side. At the far end of the beach there is another tiny village of thatched huts, where the men leave their kurumas; for beyond this there is only deep sand or rocky footpaths. The rickety wooden bridge which crosses over to the island is usually washed away by storms two or three times a season; and when this has happened, you are poled over in a sampan, or trudge across when the tide is out, ankle deep in the shifting yellow sand.

At the end of the neck, below the first slope of the hill, a high bronze torii marks the entrance to the sacred island. It is the third and last of three, the other two being on the road which comes directly in from the Tokaido, around the turn from the little village we have just left. About the base of this torii climb tortoises, wrought in relief-tortoises toiling up steep rocks from the dash of curling bronze waves.

They are the companions of Benten Sama, whose home is in the depths of the sea, whose servants are dragons and sea-serpents, and whose worshipers may not harm a snake of any kind. (Luckily there are no venomous ones in Japan.) In golden images and pictures Benten appears as a serene young matron, seated on a rock splashed by the waves; at her feet a dragon bears in his claws the crystal ball which brings in the tide, while she holds the other "tide jewel" which makes the waters recede. She is the friend of seamen, the protectress of young mothers, the bringer of love and luck and beauty; and her sons are Daikoku, personification of wealth, a fat and merry godling, with an immense rice-bag on his back; Ebisu, who carries a fish on a line; Hotei, grotesque and grinning; Bishamon, who gives success in war; Jurojin, good luck; and Fukurokuji, happy old age, whose long head is made still longer by an enormously high cap.

This is the legend of Benten's coming to Enoshima: Long, long ago there was no island here at all, but the river Kashigoye flowed into the sea, as it does now, just behind the point of land which ends the beach, and about the river lay a great marsh, where lived five terrible dragons, who came forth and devoured the fairest maidens of the neighboring villages. And the people groaned and prayed in vain. But one night there arose an awful storm, as if all the demons of sea and air had broken loose, and the people lay shivering with terror; but in the morning, when they looked forth, the wind was still and before them lay a beautiful island, new-risen from the sea, and on the highest point sat Benten herself, throned on a rainbow cloud. Moreover, the dragons departed, never to return; and the villagers drained the swamp and made it into fertile fields, even as it is this day.

The folk of Enoshima seem in no way oppressed by any burden of sanctity resting upon their island; all the year round seems a perpetual holiday, a ceaseless thronging of pilgrims and sightseers coming and going across the sand and under the great torii. Enoshima village clusters against the cliff and climbs it by a single street, which is hardly more than a long flight of mossy steps cut in the rock, and lined with shops and booths for the sale of all manner of sea curiosities–anything that can be found or made to take home as a memento of the pilgrimage. Here are shells and beads, and the strange and beautiful glass sponges found below Benten's cave, and bits of coral or odd stones; there are flower hairpins such as little girls delight to wear, made of delicate, tinted shells; netsuke, carved weights for the pipe-case or other articles carried in the belt; paper-weights; slate ink-stones for mixing the india-ink, with bits of shell or coral bedded in the lid; agate teacups, boxes and trays innumerable; some things fragile, some useful, all having some suggestion of the sea, and all wonderfully dainty and alluring. The shops are served by coaxing obasans (grandmammas) and roundfaced girls, the country type, seldom pretty, but always smiling and good-humored. Flags and blue and white hangings flutter in the wind; wooden clogs clatter up and down, to a rippling accompaniment of voices, till you get past the shops and climb on, by more irregular mossy steps, through deep, cool shade, catching between the branches exquisite glimpses of the mountains and the clear sea far below. Near the top there is a graceful little temple, with curving, tiled roof, Shinto now in faith, but decidedly Buddhistic in architecture. There are three temples in all, the highest standing where Benten first appeared upon her island. They seem deserted now, the pilgrims visiting most the sacred caves below the cliff. Skirting around the side of the island, you come out upon a high point directly over these caves, commanding a wonderful view of the coast far and near.

Little rest-houses are placed here and there, mere platforms, each spread with a piece of clean matting and roofed with rough mats or thatch; and there you sit and enjoy the view, while a smiling old woman brings tea and dry little rice-flour cakes, shaped like scollop shells, and the inevitable box of coals to light your pipe. Everybody smokes in Japan; there are cigars and cigarettes for the progressive, and tiny pipes for the conservative–pipes having a stem as thick as a pencil and a bowl nearly as big as a child's thimble. Three puffs is the rule, and then knock out the ball; but it is usually refilled again very soon.

At the foot of the cliff is the sacred cave, which is neither very large nor in any way remarkable, unless one could trace the supposed likeness to a dragon; a pretty path leads to it, plunging steeply down, ending in some rickety bridges across the rocks just above the tide-line. The cave is rather wide at the mouth, but narrow and low as it runs back far into the hill; more shaky planks, fastened to the ledge, pass into it, and a few guttering candles show little shrines set against the rock, a dim lamp burning before each.

There is no suggestion of danger, still less any sense of awe or mystery; for one thing, there are quite too many people about, pilgrims and holiday-makers, and boys anxious to dive for pennies in the transparent sea outside. In storms, though, the dashing surf about these rocks must be very grand; at such times it is not possible to enter the caves.

In the thirteenth century Enoshima was almost the scene of a martyrdom, but claims a miracle instead. Nichiren, the great Buddhist saint and reformer, had been going about preaching in court and camp, denouncing crime and vice in high places, which so angered the Regent, Hojo Tokimune, that he first exiled the priest and then condemned him to death. They took him out to die on the rocks at Enoshima, but twice the sword turned aside, and the third time broke in pieces. The frightened guard sent a messenger post haste to the Regent's palace at Kamakura to tell the miracle. Meanwhile a thunder-clap a phenomenon less ordinary than an earthquake in Japan—coming from a clear sky, so terrified Hojo Tokimasa that he, too, hurried off a messenger to stay the execution. The two envoys met at a tiny river which flows into the sea half-way between Kamakura and Enoshima, and thenceforth this stream has been called the River of Meeting. Nichiren was released; the Regent came and made prayer to Benten, and after waiting three weeks beheld her in a vision and received forgiveness.

Since the Restoration, Benten Sama has been ousted in favor of three Shinto goddesses; but it may well be doubted whether the common people are aware of any distinct difference. It is likely they feel about it much as so many Italian peasants would if the church of Saint Catherine were to be rededicated, say to Saint Elizabeth and Saint Anne. They believe the divinities of the island bring luck, and they know, in a dim sort of way, that he who prays must not do wrong; for did not the goddess warn that same Hojo, the Regent, that if he and his descendants were unjust and wicked, his line would end in seven generations, and did not all this come to pass? Such things they believe; but in truth they are a simple folk, and for the most part trouble their heads with very little thinking at all.

And so up over the hill again to the Ebisu-ya or the Kin-ki-ro, to lunch and rest on the cool mats, while the sea wind sweeps through the open screens, till it is time to return by beach and cliff to Kamakura again.

8

A JAPANESE INN

THE whole coast southward from Yokohama is full of coves and picturesque nooks, delightful to visit; but there is no full-fledged "foreign" hotel on the sea, except the one at Kamakura. There are plenty of good Japanese inns, though, some of them the very ones in which the Daimyo used to lodge, with their trains, on their periodic journeys to and from Yedo; but it is best to beware of places much frequented by foreigners, for where the globe-trotter goes to play with what he calls "the Mousmees" one will not find anything either respectable or typically Japanese.

Broiled fish (shio yaki) and eggs are to be had at all good inns in Japan, and with these and rice one will not starve for a few days; still, such a limited diet is distinctly unwholesome, and is sure to become most unappetizing in a short time, even if it does not thoroughly upset the digestion. Along the railroad lines there is usually bread to be had, and condensed milk and vile coffee, also "biru," i.e., beer; butter generally gosarimasen, honorably is not, or of a quality uneatable. Generally speaking, therefore, it is not well to go off the beaten track at first without a guide who will lay in a small stock of provisions, and is not above cooking, or at least superintending the operation. Chickens are nearly always to be had, and beef frequently; but to get them properly prepared is quite another thing.

The charges at these inns are very moderate, and it is an under-stood thing that every guest will add a gratuity, called chadai (literally; tea-money), as a present to the house and the servants. The amount is theoretically in proportion to the rank of the guest and the kind of accommodation he has received, and of course a Japanese knows without difficulty what his position requires him to give. A third more than the bill is a fair sum for a foreigner to bestow, when he has been charged the usual rate of seventy-five sen to a yen per day; of course, if he has been charged two or three yen a day, he is not expected to pay chadai at all, and should only give a small fee to the servants who have waited on him, as here or in Europe. If you think you are not being treated as well as you deserve, a rather liberal cha-dai may be given soon after your arrival, instead of on departing, as a sort of indication of your expectations; it is sure to be responded to promptly. Such donations are always folded in a piece of paper marked with the character for "gift;" it is one of those little courte-sies a Japanese never neglects. When you depart, mine host makes little return gifts as remembrances, usually fans or printed towels or tiny teacups, always exceedingly, dainty and tasteful.

Accommodations of a Western sort vary with the number of foreigners who frequent the place in question; at many inns now they have a table and a few chairs, which they will bring out, and knives, forks and plates. At night they will always pile quilts on top of each other till they make quite a soft bed, though bedstead there is none. (I can't remember who it was that said his heaped-up couch always made him think of Hector's funeral pile.) There is only one under sheet, tacked fast (see that it is a clean one), no upper sheet and no blankets; the cover is a huge quilt, its top end padded up into a roll particularly fat and smothering. The hard sausage pillow will not be much comfort to a foreigner, and wise people carry at least an air-cushion, if not sheets and pillows, of their own; towels and soap everybody is expected to bring. Washing apparatus in the bedroom there is none; the Japanese think it a very untidy custom to wash there, and go to bath-rooms in another part of the house; but they will yield to Western eccentricities so far as to give you a basin and jug, in a corner of the balcony opening on your room–never

The Kitchen

inside, on the spotless mats. Indeed, the Japanese are inclined to have a poor opinion of Western notions of cleanliness. Mr. Stafford Ransome relates how he remonstrated with a landlord once on the condition of the "foreign" part of his house, as compared to the immaculate Japanese portion, and mine host explained that it was not worth while to clean up much for foreigners; they were an essentially dirty race, and would not know the difference. Didn't they wear boots into the house? What could you expect of a people like that?

The landlord's argument suggests the notice which used to be posted in the cars of a certain American railroad, "Gentlemen will, and others must, keep their feet off the seats." The rhythmic advice applies precisely to Japanese houses; the thick, soft mats which cover the whole room are chairs, tables, all the furnishing of the establishment, and should be treated as such, and not soiled with dust from the street or cut up with sharp heels. So, however bothersome–and nobody hates it more than a Japanese in European clothes–"Gentlemen will, and others must," put off out-door shoes at the door of every Japanese house.

At some temples, though, and other places often visited by foreigners they keep huge canvas socks to pull over your shoes instead, or the guide will carry your own; and at most shops and wayside tea-houses you sit on the edge of the open room, instead of going inside at all.

Still, in spite of possible discomforts, a stranger is never quite in touch with the country till he has spent a night in a real Japanese yadoya, eaten with chopsticks and slept on the floor; so try my pet inn, which shall be called the Sign of the Pine Tree, because that is not its name, and which is situated on the coast somewhere between Volcano Bay and the Inland Sea.

Many Japanese inns open directly on the street, but the Pine Tree stands back a little in a fenced court, entered by a wide gate hung with metal lanterns. The entrance proper is a roofed space something between a porte cochere and a vestibule; the front part of it is bare beaten earth, the back a raised platform of polished boards level with the floor of the house.

As one approaches the rattle of wheels and the jinrikisha men's shout of "O kyaku san!" (guests) brings a row of maids to the entrance, bowing shiny black heads to the floor, with pretty cries of welcome: "Irashai! O hairi nasai!" ("Enter, honorably enter!") You seat yourself a moment on the edge of the platform, and one of the porters hastens to untie your shoes; he is a slight young fellow in the traditional blue cotton garments, with the hotel trademark stamped in white across his back and sleeves.

A bowing clerk calls the number of the room assigned, say 33, and "san-jis-san!" chant the men and maids in chorus. One takes the shoes and puts them in one of the numbered cupboards in the vestibule; others gather up bags and wraps and lead the way through long, slippery corridors and staircases steep and narrow as ladders to the room.

A stranger may be forgiven if his first instinct is to stop at the door and ask to see a furnished apartment. There is not even a door, by the way; only sliding paper panels for walls, and for window a whole side open to the street or garden, or partly closed with more paper screens thin enough to let the light through. And in the room itself is no stick of furniture, only a thin, flat cushion or two perhaps, and a text or picture in the one raised niche, which looks as if it might do for a seat. The maid hastens to bring a hibachi, literally a firepot or box of burning charcoal, with a small iron kettle on a tripod in the coals. Next comes a round tray holding a teapot and tea jar and five small handleless cups, and kneeling by the hibachi she makes tea, and offers dry little cakes to beguile the time till dinner is ready. Never be in a hurry at a Japanese hotel, or anywhere in Japan for that matter; it is quite useless, and only gets you a reputation for bad manners. Tadaima, which as Mr. Chamberlain says "the dictionaries in their simplicity render as 'immediately,'" means any time at all. It is better to wait quietly, and meanwhile accept the damsel's invitation to the bath, "honorable hot water" as she calls it. First, though, make sure that you have the first turn of the tub, and remember, too, not to enter it till you are as clean as soap and abundant rinsings will make you, if you do not want to be set down as a "dirty Tojin" by those who follow you in the same tubful of hot water. The bath-house, as usual, is far away in a secluded recess of the garden–such a pretty garden, too, all made up of tiny courts and alleys and goldfish basins. Here is a clump of bamboo screening an outhouse; there a picturesque pine and a dash of vivid azalea blossom; a morning glory vine is climbing over a bit of sunny fence, and a willowy nanten bush trails long, dark leaves over a rocky pool. The bath-room is separated from the world merely by sliding paper panels, like those all over the house, but at the Sign of the Pine Tree one is not troubled, like the immortal Orthodocia, by rude fingers poked through the paper walls. On the slatted floor you take your scrub, then enter the scalding water for a soak, which is to be followed by as many pailfuls of delicious well-water as you care to splash over yourself. The inn provides freshly washed cotton kimonos, to take the place of your own dusty garments, and so arrayed you may wander back through the courts and the polished corridors to your own upper chamber, there to lounge delightfully on the soft mats or groan over the absence of chairs, as your mood and your muscles dictate.

The meal is served to each guest on a square lacquered tray, and whether it be breakfast, dinner or supper, consists ordinarily of fish or some kind of omelette, two soups in little covered lacquer bowls, and a small dish of pickles; an empty china bowl for the rice, and a pair of chop-sticks (O hashi) laid across it, completes the set; and the maid sits by to serve the rice from a wooden tub. One of the soups is usually made of fish, with bits of green vegetables floating in it, the other of beans in some form; shoyu or soy is served as a sauce with nearly everything, and many dishes are cooked with it, giving a peculiar flavor not unlike Worcestershire sauce. Everything is daintily and prettily served, the pickles lending a touch of color, which is helped out sometimes by a leaf of bamboo and a pile of white horseradish, grated, just as we use it.

Certain inns make specialties of one or another delicacy; thus Sir Edwin Arnold praises the broiled eels of the Golden Carp in Tokyo, and another house is famous for o soba, buckwheat maca-roni, and another lets you choose your fish from a pool and cooks it while you wait. But a list of dainties would fall coldly on Western ears, even if it included chawan mushi, steamed eggs cooked with fish and mushrooms, and take-no-ko, young shoots of spring bam-boo; or raw fish, carp or tai, fresh from the water and cut in thin, pinky slices, more crisp and delicate than any Little Necks or Blue Points, and so digestible that Tokyo surgeons give it to patients for the first solid food after an illness; or bean-curd (o tofu) and white beans delicately sugared, and plump chestnuts boiled with mashed sweet potato-this last dish should be eaten in November, looking out on a hillside of crimson maples. I suspect the secret of learning to eat Japanese food is never to force down anything one does not like; just taste, and taste again another time, and so get over the strangeness, which makes half the difficulty. It is quite certain that to be really wholesome for any length of time all the elements of the food must be eaten in proper proportion, especially the soups and the shoyu sauce, perhaps even a little of the pickles, which are very many and very, very strange.

Somehow Japanese food never seems to taste quite right unless it is eaten with chop-sticks, or o hashi, to use the prettier Japanese name. After all it is easy enough to manage them safely, if not too gracefully, once one has caught the trick of holding them between the thumb and fingers–they are not to be held one in each hand like a knife and fork. The lower stick should be kept firmly against the third finger, while the top one is held by the thumb and the first and second fingers, and plays on the other like one half of am old-fashioned pair of tongs. It is proper to drink tho soup from the bowl, holding it with both hands, or, taking it in the left hand, to pick out the pieces of fish or vegetables with the o hashi. Soup, broiled fish, eggs or whatever there is should be eaten along with tho rice, not as a separate course, as we should take soup. Of course, the rice is the staple dish, two and even three bowlfuls being eaten at a meal; it is so cooked that every grain lies distinct, yet so sticky that it can be lifted in lumps without spilling a grain. It is quite hard, though, and, by the way, foreigners often find soft-boiled rice a good deal more wholesome. At the inns they will always make this o kai yu, "rice hot water," as they call it, if they are told a little beforehand.

I have a particularly pleasant recollection of one evening at the Pine Tree, when the little nesan closed the shutters on the chilly winter twilight, and a friend and I sat down to what was my first experience of tori-nabe–"chicken-in-the-pan" would be the nearest English equivalent–and this is the way to make it: Take a chicken or other fowl or game bird; cut the meat from the bones in small pieces, and lay it on an iron plate; add several small onions–not great self-assertive Bermudas, but the delicate little Japanese ningi, no thicker than the end of your little finger. Moisten with a liberal allowance of shoyu (soy) and set the plate over the coals in a hibachi; turn the morsels with chop-sticks, and serve from the plate as fast as they brown.

Tori-nabe is a great favorite with students, they say, perhaps because it is hot and savory and comparatively cheap–and Japanese students are always hungry, poor things! But I fear it would not do in America; there would be something wanting, the something that seasons corn roasted in the embers, or trout broiled over a camp-fire. It needs Ume in her pretty Quakerly dress, and the hibachi between us on the floor, and the night wind crying outside. No, tori-nabe in the chafing-dish would not be at all the same thing.

At a feast where sake (rice wine) is drunk it comes first and along with various fancy dishes, the rice being served only at the very end. Sir Edwin Arnold gives one of his pretty descriptions of the way the sake is served, hot, in a tall china bottle set within a wooden stand: "A tiny, delicate sake cup for each guest, lying in a porcelain, bronze or carved wooden bowl of water. . . . Taking a cup in both hands, the kneeling maid presents it to the chief guest, and afterwards other cups to the others, in like manner, filling the cups to the brim, and being careful not to spill a drop. You toss your first cup off, and, rinsing it in the water, offer it with both hands to each friend in succession, saying, "ippai kudasai." He or she takes your cup, lifts it to the forehead, holds it to be filled, drinks, rinses, and returns it; after which you must also drink. The musmee, kneeling before you, keeps her black eyes wide open to notice and fill up all empty cups, or a friend will perform that office for you–the strict rule being that you never help yourself to the 'honorable sake.' "

By the way, asking Sir Edwin's pardon, only Treaty Port foreign-ers speak of the tea-house servants as "musmees," which is a corrup-tion of musume (girl or daughter), a word having none of the impli-cations which Loti and others have tacked on to it. The Japanese say nesan, "elder sister," to these servingmaids, and treat them as the respectable, hard-working girls that they are. If these gentlemen want a toy to amuse them, as is quite too commonly the case, there are geisha to be hired by the hour to sing and dance and make witty remarks like the Columbines and Punchinellos of other lands–but this is quite too large a subject to enter upon. Instead, we will clap our hands and summon the little maid, who will bring in the futon for the beds, close the wooden shutters of the balcony, put up, if it is summer, a green mosquito net on a frame, light a candle in a paper lantern, and leave you to slumber–which you will do more readily if you have brought a package of insect powder, for Japan rivals Germany or Italy in abundance of fleas. Getting rid of noise is hopeless in a paper house, and for this reason the choicest rooms of an inn are at the very top, sometimes in a sort of tower lifted above the merriment of drinkers and card players. These up-stairs rooms, too, are apt to have a window which can be left open, as the wooden shutters at the edge of the balcony cannot well be for fear of thieves. By day this does not matter, for the shutters are pushed back and the whole side of the room is a great window, open to the light and air, or closed by the thin paper shoji, which seem to foreigners so exceedingly inadequate–and are rather so, perhaps, of a frosty morning. The fact is Loti is right; Japan is a tropical country which has moved up North by mistake, and has never found it out.

"Quel pays ou tout est bizarre, ce Japan! Un hiver presque comme celui de France, avec des gelees, des neiges,–et les cycas poussent tout de meme, les bambous deviennent grands comme des arbres; d'un bout de l'annee a l'autre les cigales chantent . . . et tout lem- ond grelatte dans des maisons de papier. Vraiment on dirait d'un pays tropical qui serait remonte vers le nord sans s'en appercevoir; etourdement, sans prendre ses dispositions d'hiver."–("Japoneries d' Automne.")

He caught certain externals with such marvelous sureness, this Loti; strange that he should have so misread the deeper things, even in that very life of the Treaty Ports with which he is so gaily familiar. Well, people generally see what they have come expecting to find, and those who are looking for a toy country of bowing, giggling puppets may possibly discover that–and nothing more.

9

FROM YOKOHAMA
TO TOKYO

"The iron road creeps forward day by day;
    I watch the falling pine trees through my tears.
    Princesses! If you perish for the Way,
    I dare not bid you Live a thousand years!"

THE thought of this little poem is so characteristic of Japan that
I cannot resist quoting it, though it is cruel to spoil with a clumsy
attempt at translation Mme. Shimoda's graceful uta on the prin-
cess-pines (himematsu) which had to be cut down in building the
Tokaido railroad. The dainty terseness of these Japanese verselets is
as untranslatable as the play upon words on which they turn: here
it is To, a road, a way, which may also be read To or Tao, the Way of
Life, the Way of the Gods–and the mysterious, lofty system of ethics founded by the Chinese Lao-Tse. As for the sentiment, a remark
of De Mazeliere's in the Histoire du Japon might have been written
as a commentary on this very poem: "No people has shown such
disinterestedness in sacrificing what they hold dear or individual
to the exigencies of a higher civilization. Leur ideal fut toujours un
ideal de lutte et de sacrifice."

The railroad from Yokohama to Tokyo was the first line built in
Japan, unless we count the little toy road which Commodore Perry
set up and ran with toy engines, to astonish and amuse the people.
The line was finished in 1872, and all the city turned out to see the

first train, which entered Tokyo with flags flying and arches of green across the track, as if it were a national festival–as indeed it deserved to be. Englishmen built the road and manned it too at first, and all its habits and traditions are English born, though Baldwin's, in Philadelphia, have since contributed certain engines of hybrid pattern, neither English nor altogether American. Japan has already begun to build her own; long before now the foreign experts have been succeeded by natives in all departments, and, by this modification and that, the national mark has been set upon it all, as in Japan it invariably is–and ought to be.

The distance from the port to the capital is eighteen miles, and takes fifty minutes by train. It is a pretty ride through a richly cultivated country, with peeps of Yedo Bay on one side and hills on the other, and behind these the serrated line of the Hakone mountains, with Fuji above them. The Tokaido–the old post road–runs nearly parallel to the railroad, part of its avenue of pines still standing; low, thatched villages line it here and there, one house deep between the road and the paddy-fields; the thick roofs, velvety brown or green with moss, crowd down over the little houses, as a man pulls his hat over his eyes, till they are almost out of sight. The ridgepole often supports a flourishing bed of lilies, covering it from end to end; the story goes that in ancient times women used so much lily-root powder on their faces that an edict was made forbidding anyone to plant lilies in the ground, whereupon these daughters of Eve promptly set them on the housetops, and there they stay.

Here and there in the fields is a little shrine in a graceful clump of trees, a veritable sacred grove. Everywhere the country is full of people at work, whole families together, including the usual baby on somebody's back; they are true peasants, owning their little plots, which average two or three acres to each family. Occasionally there is a bullock or heifer to be seen pulling a rude wooden plow, but most of the work is done entirely by hand, with spades or a kind of great hoe or mattock. Hillsides, even though not steep, are seldom cultivated, unless they can be terraced and have a stream turned in, to give water for the rice. All winter long the plain is green with vegetables and barley; in May it is reaped, the dikes and ditches are put in order, and the ground is flooded and enriched and left to lie a little before being dug again for rice-planting. The big mattocks come in play here; the farmers turn up huge clods of mud, let them dry, and then knock them to pieces with a kind of hammer, finally harrowing all smooth. Then one small patch out of half an acre or so is sown with rice, and when the stalks are about a foot high they are taken up by hand, root by root, and set out again in the new fields in rows afoot apart. This is the re-planting Japanese artists love to paint–men and women in huge peaked straw hats and faded cotton clothes, well turned up over heavy leggings, bending in rows knee-deep in the flooded fields. Others bind the uprooted stalks in bundles and carry them on their backs along the little paths between field and field, where rows of beans line the dike-side with their purple blossoms. Here and there a ditch is planted with edible lotus, grown for its long, tuberous root; the bluish leaves and great white flowers show effectively against the vivid green of the rice.

Then the rains come, half June and early July, August and all September; and always the rice must be watched and weeded and enriched, and the water let on or drained off as the sun and rain dictate. Just when the rains are ending harvest comes, and the plain turns gold and brown, and the dike-sides are ablaze with scarlet lilies; the reapers still work up to their knees in mud and water, and hang the sheaves on frames or tie them about the trunk of a slender tree to dry. That is the time of the festival of the first fruits; the cotton crop is picked then, too, and the brown millet tassels dried and threshed. They do not thresh the rice; the grain is combed from the stalks and carefully winnowed–all of course by hand. Finally it is packed down, unhulled, in bags holding each a koku, which is about half a bushel.

This koku measure has a peculiar significance, because in old Japan all revenues were reckoned in koku of rice. This prince or that was said to be a Daimyo of so many koku, according to the average number of bushels produced on his estates, and his rank was graded in like manner. Income was reckoned in this way until after the Restoration.

The revenue given by the lords to their retainers was also paid in rice, each Samurai receiving a certain number of koku monthly. In Tokugawa times this rice was brought down from the provinces and stored in warehouses by the river, from which it was distributed at fixed periods. At first the knights received it in person, idling the hours of waiting at the tea-houses near by; then these tea-houses began to undertake to collect and sell the allowance, and the knights began to think it beneath their dignity to handle the rice themselves. It was a time of extravagance and reckless living, and many a Samurai borrowed on his next month's pay, and when it came found every koku mortgaged to the rice dealers. Such was the state of things when Perry's coming precipitated the Restoration.

These country people are like the peasant type all over the world, short and thick-set, with round, heavy faces, slow of wit and yet shrewd enough about their own business. Some say they are partly descended from the aboriginal Ainu, and it may be true, but generations of toil may well have dulled this man of the hoe without help from a duller ancestry than his fellows. Of course they are true conservatives, very slow to change any of their ways, yet these simple folk along the Tokaido are modern and progressive beside the population in the south and in districts which the railroads have not reached. An excellent place to see them is at one of the temple festivals, such as the monthly matsuri here at Kawasaki, half-way to Tokyo; the crowd is always good natured and kindly, full of child-like curiosity and enjoyment, equally delighted by a beautiful cherry tree and an American mechanical toy. In the old times they came afoot, but now they throng the trains, the men wearing gorgeous red shoddy blankets, in place of the old-fashioned straw rain-coat. This, though, is still in vogue for actual use in the fields and else-where; the long straws are woven in, forming a sort of thatch, which keeps the workman dry and warm even in a heavy downpour.

At these festivals the girls wear their brightest sashes and pret-tiest hairpins, and the children are replendent in red, orange and purple flowered dresses, while Oba Sans and Okami Sans–grand-mammas and matrons–clip about on their high clogs, chattering and laughing and displaying their black, shiny teeth for this custom of blackening the teeth after marriage, once universal, still lingers in the country villages.

At Kawasaki the train crosses the Tamagawa–by the way, kawa or gawa means river–which is here quite a considerable stream. The railroad bridge seems needlessly high and strong, till one remem-bers that Japanese rivers have an inconvenient habit of rising in the September rains and breaking banks and carrying off whatever they can. The Tamagawa has its source among picturesque mountains, some fifty miles west of Tokyo, and as it leaves the foot-hills a great dam and a canal turn aside part of its waters for the city's supply. The water is pure and good when it leaves the river, but unfortu-nately it enters Tokyo in wooden aqueducts, and until the new sys-tem of iron pipes is completed to take their place, perennial typhoid and periodic outbreaks of cholera cannot be avoided.

Beyond Kawasaki the line runs for some distance on an embank-ment between curious pear orchards–curious because each tree has its branches spread out flat on the under side of a bamboo frame, so that you look down from the train upon acres of thin green roof. These Japanese pears are sadly disappointing; they are not pear-shaped at all, but round and brown like a russet apple, and, though fairly juicy, they have almost no taste. Cooked with lemon or cloves, it is true; they make a pretty good compote; but they certainly give color to the saying of the Treaty Ports about scentless flowers and tasteless fruit. It is a clever little proverb, and contains just about one grain of truth to ninety-nine of the other thing.

The next station is Omori, where Dr. Morse made his wonderful find of shell-heaps, like the "kitchen middens" of Denmark and elsewhere, over which there has been so much controversy. Are they relics of the Ainu, who make no pottery now, and have never made any, so far as Japanese history knows? Or do they belong to a still earlier race, the "Earth Spiders" of Japanese tradition, who lived in caves and holes in the rocks? Or, perhaps, were these makers of the

shell-heaps the Koropok-garu–the little blue-eyed Good People the Ainu tell fairy stories about? Nobody knows, and nobody seems very likely to find out; but then life would be very dull for the archaeologists without a puzzle or two.

Omori is famous for plum blossoms; the station lies under a hill which is full of bloom from the middle of February till late March. A path climbs through the trees to a charming tea-house, standing back on a little lawn at the edge of a pine grove; the wide thatched roof, curved up a little at the corners, looks like brown velvet against the green. On the lawn there are benches and a table or two, or you may go inside, where the open screens let you look out across the tops of the plum trees to the misty green plain, spreading away to the bay, a couple of miles off. Farther back there are some wonderful old trees, and another still more ancient grove at Ikegami Temple, a mile or two back in the hills.

From Omori on the fields are more and more given over to market gardens. Naturally the Japanese, not being meat-eaters, make up by a large variety of vegetable food, and there are more greengrocers in some streets than almost any other provision dealers. Far the largest part of the supply is brought in on handcarts from the neighboring country, or carried to the city in baskets slung over a pole. Green vegetables never fail the year round, though some sorts of course belong only to a single season, like bamboo shoots in early spring, or a queer kind of squash in the autumn. Then there are all manner of roots, lotus and radish and lily-bulbs, potatoes and onions; half a dozen varieties of beans; egg plants and gourds and cucumbers; and ginger and herbs for seasoning, besides the tomatoes and cabbages and other things introduced since the opening of the country. It is hard to imagine where all the green stuff comes from, till one realizes what a circle of little villages fringe the edge of the immense city.

Now the railroad draws near the bay, the houses thicken and thatch gives place to tiles. At Shinagawa the train passes through a deep cut in the hills into a closely-built suburb, full of tall factory chimneys and smoke, and sweeps round in a long curve beside the bay, past the line of island forts–dismantled now–which rose so hastily in defiant answer to Perry's demands; past the lovely garden-palace where General Grant and other dignitaries have lodged, and so into crowded, bustling Shinbashi station in the heart of Tokyo.

10

TOKYO-THE CASTLE AND THE CITY

"This big, dreary city of innumerable little houses."
–La Farge, "Letters of an Artist."

SMALL blame to the four weeks' tourist if he loves not Tokyo. Its
stock sights are only half a dozen or so–the Asakusa and Shiba temples, the moat, Uyeno Park, the tombs of the Forty-seven Ronin, a
feast and the geisha's "butterfly dance" at the Maple Club, Danjuro
at the big theatre, or the wrestlers over in Mukojima–this last
amusement distinctly not for ladies–cherry blossoms, iris, lotus or
chrysanthemums "in season," as the caterers say of game. These
attractions are scattered over the length and breadth of a city measuring five or six miles radius every way from Nihonbashi Bridge,
every part of which, to unaccustomed eyes, looks exactly like all the
rest–low roofed, gray, interminable.

The foreign resident, too, finds plenty to growl about–heat and
cold, dust and rain, and, worst of all, the weary jinrikisha rides over
those endless distances. Yet, granting all shortcomings, the great
city exercises a fascination of its own–a charm made up of quaint
lanes and mysterious turnings, of tide-water canals busy with odd
craft, of hills and green hedges and tall trees rising like islands out
of the gray sea of roofs, a glamor of flooding sunlight that is never
glare, of hazy twilights and the firefly dance of lanterns in the dark;

everywhere, and most of all, the picturesque come and go of its streets, the spell of its vivid, throbbing life.

There is a tale of a traveler who rode over Tokyo for three days, and then went away in despair, saying he could not find any city; he saw only suburbs. The fact is, it is not a city really, but rather a bunch of villages clustering round the moat and the castle, which have grown together and melted into each other till nobody can say where one stops and the other begins. Each part has still its own temples, its local guilds, local festivals, local industries, sometimes even special customs of its own–all, of course, coming under the general management of the central city government.

Perhaps this persistent individuality is less strange when one stops to realize what a comparatively recent place it is, after all–that before Tokugawa Ieyasu's time, only a matter of two or three hundred years ago, there was nothing here but a small castle and an insignificant fishing village. Beside Kyoto's record of ten centuries Tokyo is an upstart, a mere parvenue, like the Tokugawa themselves who created it. Then, too, the broken hill-and-dale quality of the ground may have helped to keep the villages distinct, as well as the innumerable creeks and intersecting canals which cut its lower portions.

It must be remembered, however, that though the Tokugawa made Yedo what it was, they did not actually discover the place for themselves; the real founder was one Ota Dokwan, a vassal of the powerful Uyesugi family, whose provinces lay further to the north. This Ota perceived the strategic possibilities of the situation, and built a small castle on the central hill. Later this changed hands once or twice, but was never a place of much importance till it was given over to Tokugawa Ieyasu about a hundred years after. Ieyasu took possession in 1590, and his first care was to strengthen Ota's site by digging the moats deeper and raising the great walls; his next to level part of the neighboring hills and fill the swampy places round about. Under his firm rule Yedo grew rapidly, and was a prosperous city even before Iemitsu's "compulsory residence" law compelled all Daimyo to maintain their permanent households in his capital.

"Easier to take than to defend," Some one wrote lately of Yedo Castle. He was thinking doubtless of modern warfare; for, as compared with the other strongholds of its period–such as Osaka and Nagoya, or Odawara, which was the seat of the Hojo Regents–Yedo was quite as well fortified, and had far the best situation of them all. Had, not has; for as a castle it no longer exists. In 1873 a fire, which started by accident, burned the great keep and all the more important buildings, and only the walls and gates remain around the Imperial palace which has been built on the same site. Six times before this the castle was burned, the first time being in 1601. Ieyasu was then in possession, but did not receive the title of Shogun till a couple of years later. On that occasion, not only the castle, but nearly the whole town was burned, and, according to tradition, tiled roofs were introduced soon after; but for a long time they were only used on the houses of nobles. Shingles, however, were substituted for thatch as being a little easier to keep from catching fire.

Whether strong or not, Yedo Castle never experienced an actual siege. Built at the beginning of the "great peace," no enemy ever came against it till 1869, when General Saigo led one wing of the Imperial army over the Hakone Pass to chastise the rebellious Tokugawa. Saigo encamped on the edge of the city, at Shinagawa, where his master, the Prince of Satsuma, had a yashiki, and demanded possession in the Emperor's name. Prince Tokugawa was in a very uncomfortable position. He had already declared that he would not disobey the Emperor, but his retainers and allies–among them the fierce Aidzu Samurai–refused to accept his order to lay down their arms, declaring the Emperor was coerced by the hated Satsuma. The city hummed with conspiracy, spies were in every household and no one knew whom he dared trust. The man who saved the situation was a Hatamoto, or retainer of the Shogun, named Katsu–one of the most remarkable men Japan has ever produced. Educated by Dutch teachers at the naval school in Nagasaki, Katsu had already been to San Francisco as captain of the first Japanese ship which ever crossed the Pacific–a gunboat of two hundred and fifty tons and one hundred horse power. On his return, his pro-foreign utterances brought on him the wrath of the Bakufu, and he was degraded and afterward confined to his own house; but his brains and courage were too valuable to be spared long. Saigo was his personal friend, and he had many other friends, and even followers, in the Satsuma Clan, besides holding the respect and confidence of his own side.

So, one morning, Count Katsu mounted his horse and rode alone to Saigo's camp at Shinagawa, and the two talked together as man to man. "I believe my old friend is at his wits' end by this time," Saigo is reported to have said, "and only by placing yourself in my position can you understand where I am," replied Katsu, whereupon the general "bursts into a peal of laughter." A few days later Katsu took Saigo up Atago Hill, a mile or two nearer the castle, and together they looked over the vast expanse of the city spread at their feet. "If we cross swords, these innocent people will have to suffer," said Saigo, and he was silent for a little. Shortly after he went back to his chief, Prince Arisugawa, and arranged terms of peace along the lines Katsu had proposed. The city was to be spared, and in return the castle and the fleet were to be given up, and the ex-Shogun to retire to Mito, another head being appointed for the Tokugawa family. The castle was accordingly handed over, but the fleet—a handful of vessels—was carried off by the officer in charge and held for some time longer; and there was fighting at Uyeno Park, and afterward at Utsunomiya and in Aidzu, before the clans finally gave up the struggle.

But though Yedo has never been overrun by an army, as Kyoto was so often, plenty of blood has been shed in the streets, and close to the castle, too. On the southwest side, here the banks of the moat are steepest and most picturesque, stands the Sakurada Gate, and just here, between the inner and the outer moat, a band of Ronin killed the Regent Ii Lord Kamon in broad daylight in the midst of his train. The ostensible reason for this deed—the reason set forth in the explanatory paper which the assassins carried with them—was that, by signing the treaties, the Regent had disobeyed the Emperor and betrayed the country to the foreigners; but there was more behind, and the real motive was well known to be personal hatred on the part of the Mito Clan.

Ataga Yama

This was the cause: During the excitement and alarm which followed Perry's coming the Bakufu felt the need of a stronger head than the Shogun, who was ill and incapable, and they therefore chose Ii Kamon, giving him the title of Tairo or Regent. Ii was perhaps the most able man in Japan, as he was certainly the most strong-willed and daring. He it was who finally signed the treaties with the foreign powers in direct opposition to the Emperor's command–an act which brought on him the wrath of the Jo-i, or Nationalist party, to which Prince Mito belonged; but worse still, he thwarted Mito's plans for the succession to the Shogunate.

Now an unwritten law required the Shogun to be of the Tokugawa branch of the Minamoto family, and if the reigning member had no heir, his successor was chosen from the Go-Sanke, the three houses descended from Ieyasu himself–namely, Mito, Owari and Kii. This choice had now to be made, and Prince Mito wished to appoint a son of his own, but the Regent had no desire for a rival, and secured the succession for a mere lad of the house of Kii. Mito, baffled, accused the Regent of disloyalty in the matter of the treaties, and got a commission from the Emperor to "drive out the barbarians and restore order." To this Ii replied by sending an agent to Kyoto, arresting many of the Jo-i party, confiscating the estates of some and putting others to death. The Prince of Mito was deposed and banished to his own province, his son succeeding him as head of the family.

A few months later, in March, 1860, the Regent started from his own castle to call on the Shogun, riding in a closed norimon (litter), surrounded by about a hundred followers. It was snowing heavily–the muffling, slippery snow of the south–and the knights were encumbered with rain-coats to protect their fine court garments; and besides, during the long peace, military habits had relaxed and swords were not always sharpened, or the knots of their scabbards untied. Just as the procession neared the gate it was suddenly attacked by a handful of men–eighteen in all, one man being from Choshu and the rest former retainers of Mito, who had become Ronin. Before they could be prevented, they cut their way to the norimon, struck down the bearers and either killed the Regent outright or wounded him so severely that he died shortly after being carried back to his castle; this last being the official version. Of the Ronin, part were killed on the spot, the rest taken and required to kill themselves. The young Shogun died soon after, and this time Prince Mito's son was appointed; it was he who afterward resigned the office and returned the power to the Emperor.

A year later the presiding officer of the Bakufu was attacked in the same manner, near one of the moats, and after this it became more and more the custom for impatient patriots to become Ronin and proceed to reform things in their own way. Such a band attacked the British Legation in 1862 and killed two men; the American Legation was burned the following year, and the murder of Mr. Heusken and several other outrages were of the same order. The first real check was an imperial edict, published at the request of

Sir Harry Parkes, just after he and his escort had been set upon in Kyoto, while on their way to an audience with the Emperor. This edict vigorously denounced such acts, declaring them highly displeasing to his Majesty, and it was published everywhere, with a great deal of effect.

In the autumn of 1868 the young Emperor made his first visit to Yedo, returning to Kyoto in the winter for three purposes: first, to perform certain rites at the tomb of his father, the Emperor Komei, who died the year before; second, to marry the Princess Ichijo; and third, "to make his success known at the ancestral tombs." These things accomplished, he came back to Yedo in the spring and settled there, changing the city's name from "Gate of the Bay" (Yedo) to Tokyo or Tokei, Eastern Gate; while at the same time Kyoto became Saikyo, Western Gate or Capital. The city now returned to its former flourishing state, which it had lost when the compulsory residence law had been relaxed and the Daimyos' families departed to the country. All who desired promotion or the new learning now flocked into it, and Tokyo today claims a population of considerably over a million–including the suburbs it is close on two million people–and is always growing.

It all radiates round the hill of Ieyasu's castle, where the palace now stands, with its "inner circle" of the moat, and its "outer circle," and the irregular ring of yashiki, fortified residences of the Daimyo, now mostly destroyed or altered, which stood on the hills about the castle. North and west lie other hills, south and east a wide level, cut by a network of tidewater canals and crossed by the Sumida River, sweeping in a great curve to the bay. Here among the canals throngs the city's trade; and here, just below, at the mouth of the river, where the forest of masts is thickest, lies the Foreign Concession, Tsukiji, till 1898 the only place outside the Open Ports where aliens might reside without being at least nominally in Japanese employ. Of course, this restriction did not apply to the Legations; they are over on the hills near the palace and the residences of Cabinet Ministers and other dignitaries. The American Legation was in Tsukiji at first, but moved away years ago, and its solid stone building, with Uncle Sam's eagles by the doorstep, is now part of the Hotel Metropole.

Tsukiji, by the way, means drawn out, because this and a great deal more of the level region was drained and reclaimed from the bay, as more probably will be some day.

Some day, too–and everybody hopes it may come before long–the main lines of railroad will run into a central station, instead of stopping miles apart, the one away over at Uyeno, in the northeast, and the other at Shinbashi, close to the bay. A horse-car line now connects the two stations, taking rather over an hour to do the five miles. The cars are always very crowded and very jolty, but fairly clean and excessively amusing to ride on. It used to be considered desperately plebeian, but jinrikisha fares have gone up so since the war that more and more well-dressed people take "basha" rides now, and everybody sighs for the time when the horse-car company's franchise will run out and electric lines be laid throughout the city.

The first part of the street through which the cars run from Shinbashi is the "Ginza," a block of hideous brick buildings in foreign style, which are used for shops, and which were put up by government order, for the really very good reason that statistics showed that all the worst fires swept directly across here. It was something in the direction of the winds, no doubt, and the absence of wide canals, always a great protection to this city of wood and paper; and they say the brick walls actually have proved quite successful in checking serious conflagrations in this ward.

But alas, that when Western civilization first reached Japan, the most rampantly atrocious architecture was at its height! It seems as if the evil touch could never be done away. Scarcely anywhere, unless in a prosperous modern German town, could one discover such horrors of building as here in Tokyo. The Japanese are quite aware that they are hideous, but so they think is everything foreign. What would you have? Modern conditions of life require modern offices and banks and school-rooms and such things; so up they go, and well if they do not come rattling down again at the next sharp earthquake. Nearly all the chimneys in Tokyo did in the shock of 1894, and since then almost all the chimneys in the city finish with a pipe above the roof line, which is the dangerous part. If that breaks off, at least it will not crush in the roof.

Amid the general hideousness, it is fair to note the Houses of Parliament as satisfactory, if not excessively beautiful; and many school and college buildings are suitable and useful. The new Bank of Japan is excellent, and the War and Navy Departments, on the edge of the parade ground, are perhaps the best of all, being thoroughly solid and dignified. One longs to send a few dozen Japanese architects to study in Italy, and learn the secret of making beautiful brick and stone buildings, strong enough to bear earthquakes, and low and big-windowed and wide-roofed for southern suns.

Of course, these foreign and semi-foreign buildings are a mere handful compared to the mass of houses in the city. Away from Tsukiji and the Ginza and the various government buildings, you may go miles without finding a single chimney. Street after street is lined with small, low houses, each consisting of a shop in front and two or three tiny rooms behind; or again there are rows of dwelling-houses standing a little back, and having a close fence and gate in front.

The castle hill is the crowning height of a group which abuts on the Musashi plain, last spurs perhaps of the Hakone mountains-steep, crumpled hills, with sudden valleys between, like so many hills in Japan. The palace is Japanese in general plan, but has glass instead of paper for the outside sliding screens, and a steam-heating plant, and in the reception-rooms much gorgeously ugly European furniture. But the beautiful garden is pure Japanese-a space of lovely trees and rocks and shrubbery and running streams, all hidden safe behind walls and belts of pine, and higher, too, than anything around, unless possibly some part of the British Legation, on Kudan Hill. To this garden the outside world penetrates only at stated times and by special invitation; but the beauty of the moat is free to all-"the most beautiful thing in Tokyo," Miss Bacon calls it.

There are two "circles," so called, though they are anything but regular in form, the inner moat surrounding the castle proper and the outer inclosing the open space about it, where the yashiki of the Daimyo used to stand. This irregularity of the moat is a large part of the charm. Sometimes the banks are low, and the gray walls rise direct from the water, crowned by plastered ramparts and many-storied gateway towers, dazzling white and gabled with overhanging black-tiled roofs; here a wide, shining stretch runs straight away for half a mile, crossed by curved wooden bridges, and willow-fringed along the road on the outer side; and here again are rows of cherry trees. Then a sharp turn, a mass of Cyclopean masonry, and the narrow ribbon of water bends away between green banks, rising ever higher and higher, and walls swept over by long, drooping arms of pine. They are verily walls for giants, built of polygonal blocks, ten, twenty, thirty feet long, uncemented, fitted into the bank at an even slope, and nowhere cracked or jarred out of place, after nearly three centuries of storm and earthquake. On the west, where the sides of the moat form almost a ravine, flocks of water-fowl congregate in winter, swimming in the stream, and resting among the pine branches far up on the palace side, as safe and tame as in some utter solitude. Once the lower reaches of the moat were gorgeous with lotus, but the doctors decided that they made the water stagnant and unhealthy, and a few years ago they were all cleared away. The pond below Uyeno Park is the chief place for lotus blossoms now, and a little pool near the Shiba temples.

On the wide level east and south of the castle, still between the inner and the outer circle, there is now a large parade ground, and smart modern buildings have been put up for various official purposes, as well as some dwelling-houses, private or official. The favorite residence quarter is on the hills to the west and north, and here are charming lanes and hedges, or streets of houses, turning their blank walls to the road and their faces to the pretty gardens hidden behind. Out this way the city grows fast, and will still faster when there is better means of communication. On one of these hills is the Aoyama Palace, where the late Empress Dowager lived in state, keeping up the old court customs to the end. The Crown Prince's palace is out this way, too, and the Nobles' School for boys, and the Peeresses' School; and not far off the admirable Red Cross Hospital, very dear to the tender-hearted little Empress, who often visits it with her ladies. The Peeresses' School was founded and endowed by the Empress, who attends commencements and watches over its welfare, as if she were the president of aboard of trustees. The

Charity Hospital, near Shiba Park, has also a share of her interest and her visits, and she insists on seeing and speaking to every one of the inmates, that no one may feel neglected. Probably few great ladies in the world live busier or more useful lives than this gentle, retiring woman, who never neglects an iota of the duties of her position, or forgets to be sympathetic toward those about her, and who, with it all, hardly knows the meaning of the word health.

A little farther round is the materialistic, germ-hunting, Herbert Spencer worshiping Imperial University, with its various departments of law, medicine, science, arts–for this last, Chinese and Yamato literature are the "Humanities." It is up to date all through, and always carrying on original investigations, that now and then run across some item of world-wide interest, such as a plague bacillus or an earthquake theory. At first the leading spirits were naturally foreigners, such as Verbeck, Hepburn, Morse, Lyman, Griffis and a dozen others; but they have been gradually replaced by native professors, trained first at home and then in the universities of Europe and America, till now there are left only a few foreign specialists, who could not well be spared.

The University stands in what was once Kaga Yashiki, the fortified palace of the great Daimyo of Kaga, inclosing trees and spacious grounds. The professors living here when the University was first opened tell how pheasants nested in the hollows, and how the first token of a coming earthquake was their startled cry as they rose from the ground, moments before the faintest tremor reached human perception. Except the trees, there is little of old times left in Kaga Yashiki. The buildings cover most of its lawns, and instead of sworded knights, it is haunted by energetic professors with degrees from all over the world, and flat-capped, blue-coated students, spectacled and serious, who live, too many of them, in the cheap, wretched boarding-houses of the Kanda district, close by–Tokyo's Latin Quarter. The Student Y. M. C. A. is striving to help them, both in body and soul, and there can be no more valuable work. The latest returns show about thirteen hundred students enrolled, chiefly under the three practical schools of law, medicine and engineering. A reading knowledge of some one European language is required, German being chosen for the medical course, French and English for the others.

Viscount Mori, who gave the educational system its modern organization, based it partly on the American and partly on the German plan. All schools lead by graded examinations to the University (either Tokyo or Kyoto), and certain degrees and licenses may be taken by passing government examinations without attending University courses.

There are three grades in what we should call the common schools, generally translated primary, secondary and middle school; above these come the higher school, of which there are six in the empire, corresponding nearly to the German Gymnasium, or an advanced high school in America, and preparing students to enter the University, just as the Gymnasia do. Naturally the girls have less offered them than the boys; their highest school is the Girls' Higher Normal, in Tokyo, which admits only after rigid examinations, and even so has not room for all who come. All teachers in government schools must have government certificates, and the Higher Normal cannot turn the girls out fast enough to meet the demand for teachers in the higher grades. It is true their ranks are more apt to be depleted by marriage than in some parts of the world.

There are some twelve hundred schools of all kinds in Tokyo, among them one of the eight new schools for languages which were lately established throughout the empire, and which offer courses in Chinese and Korean, as well as in English, Russian and other European languages. English is taught from the middle school up, but as a general thing that is the only European language given outside of the special schools. Then there are several great private schools, such as the one at Waseda, on the edge of Tokyo, which is under Count Okuma's patronage; and Mr. Fukusawa's, which has probably influenced Young Japan more than any other single agency–and this influence is largely on the side of material progress, of what Americans mean by Success. Besides all these, there are the mission schools, one or more for nearly every mission, usually holding government licenses and conforming to the prescribed curriculum. Many are valuable institutions, with fine buildings and good endowment; and others, like the Ragged Schools held in some parts of the city, are doing incalculable good in the quietest possible way.

Perhaps the greatest charm of Tokyo is its greenness; the trees are everywhere, planted and preserved with that instinctive delight in them so universal in Japan. Often in riding about the city one comes upon some splendid bole, most frequently maple or live-oak, standing by itself in a little open space, and hung around with those ropes and knots of straw which are always in Japan the token of things divine. There may or may not be a temple near by; it would seem that the mere bigness and beauty of the tree roused a feeling that is not quite worship, but rather a vague sense of supernatural presence. It is the same sense that belongs to all "sacred places" in all lands; a Japanese does not hallow the ground by building there a temple, rather he sets a shrine in the holy place–even as the Hebrews did, and the Greeks and all Aryans.

In Japan the graves of ancestors share this reverence with the tombs of heroes and great men; the greater the hero, the longer the tradition, so much the more the sanctity of the spot. Thus it comes about that while Tokyo has temples innumerable, it is too recent to possess many which are of more than local renown. Only the temple at Asakusa goes back for its foundation to the centuries when Yedo was an insignificant village; while the tombs of the Shoguns glorified Shiba and Uyeno, as the graves of the faithful Ronin do Senkakuji. Besides these, the most important are the two Buddhist Hongwanji, Monasteries of the True Vow, which are very wealthy and influential. The Shinto temple on Kudanzaka is fast becoming a sort of Pantheon and Westminster Abbey combined–a place of national rites for departed soldiers and great men. The little park beside it offers wrestling and horse-racing as attractions at festival times.

One thinks of Uyeno now as a kind of Central Park, a place for walks and drives and museums and exhibitions more or less educational; but under the Shoguns, when Tokyo was Yedo, what is now the public park belonged to a magnificent monastery and group of temples, founded by Tokugawa Ieyasu to protect his castle on the northeast to the "Devil's Gate," the quarter on which demons were considered to be most rampageous. Several Shoguns were buried there in after years, and the high priest was always an imperial prince–not that he had any real power; he was maintained there for the sake of prestige, and as a check on the Court at Kyoto. All this gave Uyeno immense political power, which was constantly exercised for the benefit of the Tokugawa, its patrons.

In 1868, when the often-mentioned struggle broke out between the Imperialists and the Shogunate, the Prince-Abbot was a mere lad, of course entirely under the control of the priests, who made use of him in every possible way. He it was whom the rebellious Tokugawa finally proclaimed Emperor, and carried off northward to Nikko–of which also he was nominal abbot–when the clans made their last desperate stand. Meantime the great fight took place at Uyeno; the non-combatant townspeople were warned to keep out of the way and given time to remove their goods and their sick, but the monastery could not be saved; the great temple took fire from a shell and was burned, with all its beautiful contents. There is left only a wonderful carved gate, and the shrines of the Shoguns–one of them is very ornate and beautiful–and a high wooden torii before an avenue of stone lanterns leading to the principal shrine. As for the young Prince Kita Shirakawa, the sometime high priest, he was speedily pardoned and sent abroad to study, and served afterward as an officer in the army, dying of fever while on duty in Formosa, during the war with China. Stamp collectors know his face, for it is on one of the memorial stamps put out in 1895, the portrait of his cousin, Prince Arisugawa, being on the other.

After the Restoration the Uyeno temple grounds were turned over to the government and made into a public park. The Imperial Museum stands on the site of the main temple, and contains–besides birds and animals–some interesting collections illustrating more especially the life of feudal times. There are arms and armor, and the ox-cars and lacquered norimon or litters in which nobles used to ride; these last were a good deal like sedan chairs, only that of course the inmate sat on his heels on a cushion. The owner's mon or crest was on the sides, and the poles and other parts were fastened with metal beautifully chased. There are some good kake-mono in the museum, and a good deal of pottery, also a beautiful life-sized portrait statue of an old priest, brought here from Nara. The wrinkled old face is tender and benign as one of Fra Angelico's Dominican saints. A reference library, art school and school of music are all close by. Besides these, three or four temporary-look-ing wooden buildings are used now and then for exhibitions of art or industry, and there is a zoological garden, scenic railroad, and a panorama of the taking of Port Arthur–this last exceedingly popular. It is all very good and very improving, but one cannot help rather resenting the bare, ugly buildings in this beautiful spot; it is a high, broad hill, heavily wooded, looking over the lotus pond at its foot to the vast city stretching away into pearl-colored haze.

Asakusa temple lies over near the river, where a tiny golden image of Kwannon, the Goddess of Mercy, was found in the sea half a dozen centuries ago, when the sea came all the way up here. It is far the most popular shrine in the city; the long flagged walk leading up from the gate is lined with shops and booths and penny shows, and thronged always with a double stream of people pouring in and out. The temple itself is built up high on a timber founda-tion, and has a gallery all round where children play and pigeons flutter; inside it is full of glitter and flashy ornament, utterly unlike the quiet dignity of what is left at Uyeno, or the sumptuous splen-dors of Shiba. The original image is so very sacred that its shrine is never opened; a small gold statuette of the goddess does duty on fes-tival days. At all times there are worshipers before the altar, mostly women and old people, with palms together over a rosary; bowing and clapping their hands as they murmur over and over again the sacred formula, Namu Amida Butsu-Namu Amida Butsu to the continual clatter of thin copper rin tossed on the slatted offering box. At one side of the high altar is a pathetic wooden figure of Jizo, rubbed almost out of recognition by the hands of sick people, who touch the image and then the ailing part, whispering a prayer to the All Merciful.

Near the temple at Asakusa there is a small park which is one of the most amusing sights in the city, for it is always full of peep-shows and jugglers and trick monkeys, and peddlers of jumping-jacks and tumblers and paper butterflies, and sidewalk "fakes" of every kind, together with a motley crowd of gazers all agrin with delight. A huge, clumsy observation tower rises close by, popularly called the "twelve-story;" its pinkish wooden octagon makes a landmark for miles across the flat region along the river.

To give the rulers all the credit for Tokyo's prosperity is to forget two things, the river and the tides. To all the lower part the tide is as necessary as ever it is to Venice; sweeping through miles of narrow, twisting canals, washing their stone-faced embankments, it brings the clean salt smell into the most crowded parts of the city, and carries an immense number of flat barges, loaded with produce from the country. The river is navigable for small boats far up across the Musashi plain, and by it, too, come down boat-loads of fagots from the mountains, and piles of bags filled with charcoal, and again timber for building and great bundles of bamboo poles. In certain streets near the river the tiny yards are stacked full of these overgrown fishing rods, which lean against the houses and quite overtop their low roofs. Such neighborhoods are inhabited by carpenters and cabinet-makers–for the Japanese do use some furniture, after all. There are chests of various sizes, metal-bound and tightly locked; little writing desks, with drawers for paper and ink-stone; and, most frequently of all, the small bureau or tansu, made as a rule in pairs of two drawers each. These tansu have handles at the sides, so that in case of a fire the drawers may be picked up and carried out without difficulty. In good old pieces the wood is beautifully grained and polished, and the metalwork finely wrought.

Morning and evening the narrow channels of the bay are thronged with square-sailed junks coming and going, with here and there a schooner or a little steamer plying to one of the villages lower down. Small steamboats run up and down the river inside the city, calling at the bridges, now this side and now that; the fare is a penny or so, and the accommodation a tiny cabin, with a matted floor on which to sit. There are pleasure boats, too, and sampan ferries crossing to the Chiba side or to Mukojima.

Five bridges cross the Sumida, some iron, and some picturesque wooden ones, like Ryogoku-bashi, which sweeps over in a
noble curve, supported on a maze of posts and rafters. The famous
Nihon-bashi, by the way–the point from which distances are reckoned throughout the Empire–is not across the Sumida at all, but
over one of its canal-like tributaries. Adzuma-bashi is counted the
finest of the Sumida bridges, and it is the highest up the river of
all; near it and above are many resorts of pleasure seekers, more or
less reputable–Asakusa on the city side, and the famous Yoshiwara
beyond, and on the other bank Mukojima, of cherry-blossom rev-
elry, and a mile or so farther up the beautiful iris fields of Hori-kiri.
Eko-in, where the annual wrestling matches are held, is a mile lower
down on this left bank, close to Ryogoku-bashi. Naturally the entire
quarter is a poor one; the streets are crowded and houses small,
dirty and ruinous. In these districts a three-roomed dwelling seems
quite palatial; many are built in a row like a train of cars, each tene-
ment being three mats large, that is to say, nine feet by six. Mere
hovels they seem, but at least there is plenty of light and air. Such
houses rent at three or four sen a day–equal to two or three cents
of our money–and this rent is collected daily, for the people would
never get together a whole month's bill at a time. It would be no
use to bring in the sheriff to sell them out, for they own nothing
but a few broken cooking pots and some dirty bedding, and even
these sometimes go to the pawnshop in the morning and are taken
out at night.

From Asakusa and Adzuma-bashi it is a good five miles right
across the city to Shiba, where as at Uyeno the temple grounds
have been taken for a public park. Nothing could be more unlike
Asakusa; except on a few special days the stone courts are almost
deserted, and the steep wooded slopes might be far away in some
mountain solitude, so still it is, though the city lies about it on
every side. Far up, where only children come to play, a single tomb
stands on a pebbled esplanade; stone lanterns flank the open space,
and behind them against the dark trees single-flowering camelias,
pink and white, scatter a carpet of petals among the stones. The
crows call in the pines and kites wheel and pipe overhead, and the

city's noises reach only in a far off murmur to the Shogun's resting place.

The temples are under the hill, skirted by an avenue of pines leaning every way, their sweeping branches carefully propped in winter, lest sleet and snow should break them. The original main temple was burned in 1868, in revenge, it is said, because of the Shinto "purifying" done here, as in other places, in the first zeal of the Restoration. It was rebuilt on a smaller scale, and seems rather overpowered by the great two-storied red gate, which escaped the fire-very fortunately, for it is beautifully proportioned and altogether a noble specimen of timber architecture. Like others of its type, the chief characteristic of this gate is the heavy overhanging roof of black tiles, the corners of it slightly curved upward in the Chinese manner, which rests on a complicated structure of cross-beams and

Gate of Temple, Shiba

brackets. The gate is almost without decoration except the dull red coloring, and the whole effect is plain and almost severely dignified. Far more ornate is the second small entrance farther along the road, the corner posts of which are clasped by splendid golden dragons, and which in every part is carved, colored and gilded most lavishly. The smaller temple buildings and many of the treasures were saved from the burning, and the interiors are full of brass and bronze and gold, lacquer and embroidery. Seen in the shadow of the trees and wide roofs, the warm half-light subdues the splendor and all but conceals a certain over-gorgeousness, a crowding of color and detail, which is not felt at all in the temples of Nikko.

The five-storied red pagoda stands on a little terrace half way up the south slope of the hill. It seems almost too much shut in by great trees, yet, even so, the impression of it is exceedingly fine, finer perhaps than that of the pagoda at Nikko, with which one involuntarily compares it. These pagodas are marvels of strength and elasticity; story rests on story in a maze of wooden beams and braces and brackets, and however the ground may heave under them the parts play upon one another like the timbers of a ship. But there is still another safeguard; inside hangs a huge beam, a sort of pendulum, swung from the top like the tongue of a bell, and this is the secret of the pagoda's safety; however far the top may sway, the swinging beam steadies it and it maintains its poise.

Up on the hill above the temples there is a semi-foreign restaurant, which never seems to be much patronized by anybody, in spite of fine trees about it and a very pretty view across the bay; and farther up still is the exceedingly popular house called the Ko Yo Kwan, or Maple Club, which is a favorite place for giving little dinners that often have more than a little political significance. The Maple Club geisha have the reputation of being the best dancers in Tokyo, and tourists usually come here to see the "butterfly" or the "maple dance," and to try a Japanese feast. Everything about the house is strictly in Japanese style; under no consideration whatever will the proprietors consent to lay carpets and permit the use of chairs and tables. They say if they yielded once every party of officials would demand it, since nobody hates the bother of taking off his shoes more than a Japanese in European dress, and the character of the house would be changed and spoiled forever.

There are no shops or shows at Shiba, only a few fruit and cake stands in front of the great red gate; instead, people go shopping just across the road at the Kwankoba–that is to say, the bazaar. There are many of these Kwankoba in Tokyo, but none so large or so good as this in Shiba. It is simply a good-sized wooden building, divided up into aisles which zigzag back and forth through the entire space, so that when you begin to go through you must go on to the end, or else turn back by the very same lanes to the beginning again. The spaces on each side of the aisles are lined with shelves and rented to merchants of all manner of goods, china, wood and metal, quilts, household wares of every kind, dress materials, sashes and neck-pieces, shoes (Japanese ones of straw or wood), stationery, toys, lacquer–in a word, whatever is used in Japan. Every article is marked with its price in Japanese letters, and all is spread out temptingly in full view, which is not the case in the ordinary shops. Each dealer is quite independent of all the rest, paying rent for his own particular space as if it were a separate house, though the same kind of goods are apt to appear near together. The Shiba Kwankoba displays everyday Japanese life in a nutshell, and is very interesting merely to see, as well as a capital place to shop for Japanese articles.

It is a couple of miles farther, between a long ridge and the bay, before you climb a hill to one of the most intensely national shrines in all Japan–the graves of the Forty-seven Ronin. The story has been told and retold till one hardly dares repeat it, how one lord deliberately provoked another into drawing his sword in the precincts of the Shogun's Palace–a crime punished by death; how the dead Asano's chief retainer secretly organized a band of his fellows, now become Ronin (masterless knights), who scattered to abide their time; how, to throw the enemy off his guard, this chief, Oishi Kuranosuke, drank and gave himself up to the lowest life, till even a former acquaintance kicked and spat on him as he lay in a gutter, calling him a miscreant too cowardly to avenge his lord. And when at last the enemy ceased to fear, the band broke into his yashiki one snowy night, overpowered the retainers and invited him to an honorable hara-kiri–invitation which he had not the courage to accept. So they killed him, and took his head, and, marching as in a religious procession, came to the hill and the little grove where their lord lies. At the well below they washed the head, offered it reverently at the tomb, burned incense one by one, and then went quietly to the authorities and gave themselves up for the inevitable death penalty. The law took its course, in spite of universal approbation of the deed. All the knights killed themselves duly, and were buried on the hillside near their lord. The last act of the tragedy was the coming of the man who had insulted Oishi in the ditch. He told his shame and sorrow, burned incense and killed himself at Oishi's tomb, and so was judged worthy to lie beside the band.

All this happened something over two hundred years ago, near the close of the eighteenth century. Everywhere about the place are signs of reverent care. Great pine trees shade the walled inclosure, incense smoulders unceasingly and visiting cards by the hundreds are laid upon the tombs. In the tiny chapel below relics are kept–the armor which they wore, swords and spears, and writing materials such as Samurai carried, effigies of the band, Oishi himself, and among the rest Oishi's fourteen-year-old son.

That was, that is, Japan. Loyalty, absolute, unhesitating loyalty, the one virtue and the one duty for which, if needful, all personal interests and duties must become null and void. That is what a Japanese today all but worships in those heroes of his–the ideal he desires to realize in his own life toward Japan and the Emperor. Taken as an attitude of mind, it may help to explain some things in Japanese life, which, from a Western point of view, are childish–or worse.

11

TOKYO STREETS

THE streets of Tokyo are a never-failing source of amusement. Like all Southerners, the common people almost live in them, with a naive unconcern about privacy or its absence, quite unlike the retiring ways of the upper class. There are no sidewalks; the road is simply macadamized, and everybody strolls serenely down the middle, moving out just a foot or two at the kurumaya's frantic "hai-hai!" as they dash past. One never quite gets over wondering why the runners do not kill somebody, but accidents are really very few; still, they do not trust horses in the thick of it without a betto or groom running ahead, and now and then picking up a baby or turning an old crone gently out of the way. Even the widest streets always seem crowded, there are so many old people, and so many children with babies on their backs. If the family supply of real babies gives out, the tiniest girl has a doll tied on her shoulders, so that she may learn how to hold it and be ready for a small brother or a neighbor's child. The poor little baby heads tumble around till one feels sure they must fall off; but nobody seems to mind, baby least of all. Playing tag, hop-scotch and swinging on a see-saw are among the amusements practiced any day by five and six-year-olds, plus a bundle anywhere from a week up. The small morsel half sits on the hump of its sister's sash, half rests on a wide band which passes under the little thighs and over her shoulders, and then back and around again, leaving the child's arms and bare feet quite free. In winter the sister slips her wadded haori on over baby and all, and it peeps out atop, like a little Eskimo from its mother's hood. They seem to sleep most of the time, as babies should, and it really is a fact that they very, very seldom cry.

Often one sees a group of these frowsy-headed, barefoot youngsters settle by the roadside, squatting on their wooden clogs, and fluttering and chirping like so many brown sparrows. They are probably playing ken ("fist"), which is a form of one of the oldest games on earth–the game the Italians call Moro. Yet another version of this came to us from the north of Ireland in our childhood; you hid your face in Susan's lap, and she held her fingers over your head, saying:

"Roly, boly, trumpty chase,
The cow goes through the market place;
How many horns stand up?"

The Japanese say that their game of ken came from China, but though it is played both there and in Korea, it probably came to Japan with the first migrations of the race as part of their original civilization. It is true that one variety did come from the Chinese during the period of trade intercourse at Nagasaki in the seventeenth century, and became all the rage. In this form the two players put out their hands at the same moment, each calling out a number, which he guesses to be the sum of all the fingers held up by both. At drinking parties, one who makes a wrong guess must drink a cup of wine. This ken was so popular in the early part of the eighteenth century that tournaments were held in arenas fitted up for the purpose in imitation of the wrestlers' ring, and umpires sat all day to judge the contests; but it is hardly played at all now.

The other kind has four varieties, in each of which there are three positions of the hand or body to represent some instrument or animal. The four are the "snail," the "stone," the "fox" and the "tiger ken." The "stone" is one of the easiest and the most commonly played; in it only the right hand is used. The closed fist means a stone, the flat open hand is a piece of paper, and two fingers spread apart stand for a pair of scissors. The scissors can cut the paper, but the paper wraps the stone, and the stone again can dull the scissors, which means, of course, that A conquers B, B rules C, and so back again. This and the "snail" are the children's favorites, and the kuruma men very often play a round of "stone" to decide their turns, instead of pulling straws.

The "tiger" game is more elaborate; it is based on a classical Chinese drama, in which the hero goes into the forest with his mother. A tiger attacks the woman, but it is killed by the man, who bows to his mother, as a dutiful son should. This play needs the whole body, and accordingly the actors come out from behind a screen; the tiger goes on all fours; the man raises a clenched fist, and the mother hobbles like a bent old woman leaning on a stick.

"Fox ken" is very popular, and it is above all the geisha's game, which they must learn to play both gracefully and so swiftly that one can hardly follow their motions. In the "fox" all the positions are made with the hands; the two raised on either side of the head are Reynard's ears; the right hand put forward closed means a gun, which a hunter carries; and the two hands laid primly on the knees represents a village headman. This headman is bewitched by the fox (Japanese foxes are generally enchanted, and they play more tricks than Brer Rabbit), but the hunter kills the fox; and then in turn must bow to the headman, his superior in rank. They say a young geisha often sits playing fox ken with her shadow on the shoji, to learn the quickest and prettiest gestures; but the game is rather beyond our little street sparrows.

For half the day the schools claim a large proportion of the children in Tokyo and elsewhere, but for the poorest even the pittance needed for books and materials is more than they can afford, and their schooling is very brief. Boys get to work early in life, either at the family trade or in some shop, while the little girls help in the house or take care of a neighbor's baby, if there is none at home. Many little shops make what they sell, and the children help in the work or run errands for customers, besides minding the place when the older ones are busy.

There are an immense number of second-hand shops in Tokyo, some dealing only in more or less artistic wares–"curios," as the phrase is–and others selling all manner of odds and ends of clothing; household goods, broken or not; even straw and old baskets and boxes, which are broken up and used for fuel. These shops often club together and hold an auction of such things as do not sell quickly enough. The very poor often do not own warm clothing for the day or quilts to sleep on, and are forced to hire from the pawnshops, taking one out and putting the other back in the morning and evening. Many of these poor creatures have no proper habitation at all, but sleep in a cheap inn, and spend the whole day out of doors, working or peddling things for sale.

The shops stand open to the street, under a sheltering projection of roof; the more pretentious ones hang strips of cotton cloth in front like a curtain, each strip stamped with the house-sign or trade-mark, ya-jirushi–picturesque ideographs in bold strokes, white on navy blue or blue on white. Others are all open, showing piled-up crockery, brooms and sieves and wooden-ware, clogs and sandals, piece goods, tea jars, fruit or vegetables, or whatever. The floor is raised and matted, and the buyer sits down on the edge, without needing to take off his shoes; the dealer, seated among his wares, pushes forward a hibachi of coals, not for warmth, but to light the tiny pipe which every man and woman carries at the girdle; three little puffs will do, as an aid to the bargain. If you are considered an important customer, sometimes they serve minute cups of tea. All Tokyo is full of such small shops, where the owner often makes what he sells; here again the village life persisting in the vast city, one wonders for how much longer now.

There are great firms, too, which have been established for generations, such as the salt-fish house in Nihon-bashi, where people give New Year orders for gifts of fish to be delivered on demand– sometimes not for months or even a year or two later. Then there are the great silk shops, like Dai Maru Ichi and Ichigaya's–these also are in Nihon-bashi, the busiest part of Tokyo. Far down the street you can hear the din of these big shops; as soon as a customer lifts the curtain, the whole force of clerks and errand boys shout in chorus Irashai!– "Please come in!" You ask for something; the clerk who is waiting on you repeats the order, and "Hai !" chant all the boys again while one dashes off to fetch what is required. Repeat da capo, till the customer departs in a perfect storm of arigato and sayonara and matai irashai–"honorably come again!"–the livelier the trade, the merrier the noise.

All this uproar is in the large first room on the street, but up stairs and far within, where the choicest goods are kept, all is dignity and quiet; room after room, matted and speckless, piled with rolls of silk and crapes, like some "Arabian Nights" tale of royal gifts. Here the guest is seated, of course upon the floor, and roll after roll is laid out–brocades, gorgeous obi (sashes), flowered under-robes, heavy kaiki and close habutai, sumptuous gold thread and delicate gauzy chirimens, embroideries and colors and textures past dreaming of. A morning at Ichigaya's is distinctly educating to the senses, and as distinctly dangerous to one's bank account.

Such a firm carries immensely valuable stock, and keeps most of it not in the shop, but in go-downs, which are fairly fireproof. Go-down, by the way, is the universal Far East English for storehouse; Hearn says it is a corruption of a Malay word, gadan; the Japanese word is kura. They are quite a marked feature of Tokyo scenery, these black-roofed, dazzling white go-downs; they are comparatively small, high and narrow, the thick plaster walls sloping out a little at the bottom, the windows very small and high up, tightly closed by thick iron shutters. Well-to-do private families use them, too, for it is a thoroughly characteristic Japanese habit to keep most of one's possessions shut up out of sight, and produce them, a few at a time, to please and honor a guest–a custom handed down probably from early, uncertain times, and perpetuated by earthquakes and fires till it has become a cardinal point of social aesthetics. A sharp earthquake, though, is rather hard on the go-downs; it is apt to crack the plaster, and then, if a fire breaks out before they are mended, good-by to the careful stores.

Fires were much worse in the old days than now, when nearly all roofs are tiled–a luxury formerly allowed only to nobles' residences–but they are still bad enough, sweeping sometimes three or four hundred little houses in a single windy night. The modern fire companies are very active and efficient, with all the means at hand, and the new fire-engines exceedingly useful; but the great difficulty is an insufficient water supply in many parts of the city. Watchmen are on guard night and day on the picturesque fire-lookouts–tall ladders at the street corners, each with a bell and a craw's nest for the watch. If he sees anything, he strikes the bell, one stroke if it is far away, two strokes nearer, three for his own ward; and if it is close by, the hammer clangs fast and furiously, warning everyone to rush out and help or save themselves. "Kaji ga, Tokyo no hana da," says the ominous proverb–"Fires are Tokyo's flowers."

Naturally there are more fires in winter, when everybody has open charcoal braziers standing about, and worse still, glass kerosene lamps for the long evenings. But February and March have the worst record of all; it is then that the northwest winds sweep over the city, and then, too, that wells are low and woodwork dried, after four nearly rainless months.

From all accounts, the firemen of feudal times were a much livelier set than they are now. Inouye thinks it was the spirit of the place: "The people of Osaka and Kyoto, living as they did by pure trade or hereditary callings, were naturally frugal and did nothing merely for show. The case was different in Yedo. It was a new city, and the people, gaining their livelihood through the luxurious habits of the Daimyo, came in time to imitate their extravagance. In this respect the fireman was among the greatest sinners; he took pride in squandering money, and considered it a shame to let a day's earnings remain over night in his purse. It was and is still, for instance, reckoned a luxury to eat the first bonito of the season. The fireman regarded it as worse than dishonor to be prevented by want of means from tasting it, and his wife, sharing her husband's spirit, would pawn everything, even the very clothes on her back, to enable him to buy the fish. It was also one of the fireman's greatest pleasures to pick quarrels, and brawls became a necessary element of his life. He was also invariably tattooed in gorgeous colors, the beauty of which was his constant boast. As a preliminary to a scuffle, he would slip his clothes off his shoulders and make his oppo-

nent sick with envy at the sight of his wondrous tattooed figures.
. . . His favorite attitude was to sit awkwardly, one heel upon the
other, with a towel on his shoulder." Doesn't this sound like Patsy
at Donnybrook fair?

> "If ye're in for a row or a raction,
>   Just tread on the tail of me coat!"

In these degenerate times the force is under the control of
the regular city police, and indulges in nothing unseemly, beyond
an occasional spree at New Year time. The men used to be much
more numerous than now; there were sixty-four companies in all,
forty-eight for the city side and sixteen across the river, which taken
together comprised over ten thousand men. Each company had a
standard bearing its own crest, and these the firemen still keep and
use at certain times; their fees and suits were provided by the ward
to which they belonged.

When not on duty, the firemen used to be appropriately
employed in helping to build houses, by working the heavy pile-drivers with which the foundation stones are rammed down, or taking
the place of a steam-crane in hoisting up roof timbers. Often today
you can hear the monotonous chanting as a band of such men pull
and let go, pull and let go, over the foundations of some new dwelling. It is said that in old times firemen were sometimes guilty of
encouraging fires, in order that there might be more building to do,
and the citizens took care to keep them in a good frame of mind by
frequent gifts; indeed, even the Daimyo seem to have been afraid
to interfere with them, if we may believe the story of a fight early in
the century, when over three hundred firemen set upon sixty-three
wrestlers in the precincts of a temple. The judge in charge of the
case found it so "difficult and inexpedient" to decide against either
party that he "promised to give judgment after fifty thousand fine
days!" (Inouye, "Sketches of Tokyo Life.")

Ekoin, where the annual wrestling matches are held, owes its
origin to one of the worst fires Tokyo has ever known. It happened

in the winter of 1657, and is called "the fire of the long-sleeved robe," on account of the following romantic story:

A young girl of good family once went cherry-viewing with her father and mother, and as they returned, a handsome youth passed them, in the dress of a temple page, wearing very long sleeves. The girl lost her heart at the first glance; she sickened and pined from that day. To comfort her the mother bought a long-sleeved robe of the same pattern the page had worn; but though the daughter kept it by her and would not let it out of her sight, she grew no better and presently died. The family brought the dress as an offering to their temple, and the priest sold it to a dealer in second-hand garments. A young girl bought it; a few months later she died, and the dress came back to the temple on her coffin. Again the priests sold it; again it was bought by a young girl, who died within the year. By this time the priests were very properly frightened, and they made up a bonfire and threw in the unlucky robe, when, to their horror, a gust of wind caught the thing and bore it, all flaming, against the side of the temple. The whole street caught, the fire leaped over the river and burned its way all across the city, going out only when there was nothing more to burn.

Two more fires, within a couple of days after, destroyed the palace and miles of houses; the prison gates were opened, but a warder closed one of the city gates against the prisoners and cut off not only these, but hundreds of citizens, who were caught by the fire or trampled to death. There were so many unclaimed bodies that a special burying ground was made for them on the far side of the river, and a memorial temple built, where masses were said for these unknown dead; hence its name, Ekoin, temple of mass-reading. More than a century later the wrestling matches were moved here from another temple–the same at which the firemen and wrestlers had their fight–and there they have been held in January and May ever since. The contests here determine a wrestler's position for the year, though he goes touring through the provinces all the other months.

These wrestlers are a class quite by themselves. In feudal times their position was considered so important as a part of the art of fighting that they ranked next to Samurai, and were patronized by Daimyo and knights; but since the Restoration their prestige is much reduced. Weight counts for a great deal in their mode of wrestling, and they eat meat and otherwise endeavor to make themselves as large and as coarse as possible. On the street their dress and way of wearing their hair make them look like women–fat, repulsive wenches–towering head and shoulders above all ordinary Japanese. In the ring they wear as nearly nothing as possible; the umpire, on the other hand, is arrayed in the kilted trousers and stiff sleeves of a knight in full dress, and carries a war-fan, with which he directs their movements. The rules are said to be very exact, and of course there must be a great deal of skill exercised, as well as mere bulk.

The workshops add much to the liveliness of Japanese streets, for they are usually entirely open, or screened at most by a short sudare, or shade of split bamboo (such as we use in America for porch curtains), or a hanging of knotted ropes, which does not pretend to conceal anything whatever. Carpenters, joiners, smiths, umbrella-makers, the old pot-menders, the rice-pounders, lifting and dropping great hammers on the unhulled rice-they are all there in full sight as you walk or ride by. You may watch the saw and the plane, pulled instead of pushed (which works backward, we or they?), the workman sitting or standing, the wood held firmly by a flexible bare toe, that has never known anything more binding than a cotton sock.

Toward noon the eating houses are busy, and kuruma men and coolies stand about them eating queer morsels spitted on sticks, or munching big, smoking sweet potatoes from one of the bake-shops where they cook these "Satsuma imo" all day long. Then there are plenty of itinerant food dealers, more even by night than by day; one variety of "hoky-poky man" gets quite inside his booth, putting his head between the cross-bars, and walks it off down the street hissing and steaming, apparently quite of its own locomotion.

One of the most picturesque figures is the flower peddler, hanaya, trotting along with his portable shop, consisting of a pair of bamboo frames slung on a cross-pole, which the old fellow rests on his shoulder, a stand before and a stand behind. They each have three or four shelves, where the flowers are set in little tubs or piled in bundles, and each corner has a bamboo flower-holder or dainty branch tied on at exactly the right angle. Then there is the vegetable man, his two baskets likewise slung on a pole over his shoulder, and full of roots and greens; and the fish man, who carries sets of shallow wooden tubs fitting into each other in layers; and the bean-curd man, and the macaroni man, and a dozen others, not forgetting the street sprinkler, a ragged Danae bearing a couple of perforated pails. There are a few horses, led, not driven, in small two-wheeled carts; a few cows and bullocks, which wear a mat roof over their backs for rain or too hot sun. Almost everything comes to town in tubs or baskets on a pole, or in two-wheeled carts, kuruma, with a man or woman in the shafts and one behind, heavy loads, too, very often; Hoo-da, hoi-da! Hoo-da, hoi-da! they call and answer as they toil up the long bills.

When the sun goes down and the roof-outlines blur in the faint mist, and the after-glow fades in the moat, the rule is that everything on wheels must carry a light, and down the long streets they flash out one by one, between irregular rows of lanterns bearing house signs, the glow of Rochester lamps in open shop fronts, and here and there soft squares of radiance through some closed shoji. Street lamps flash out occasionally, and there are electric lights on the Ginza and near the stations, and at other important points; elsewhere there is darkness only accented by the house lights, and a bobbing vista of kuruma lanterns going off to pin-points in the distance.

A Mr. Matsubara, who lived among the poor to study their life, gives in his "Darkest Tokyo" a vivid picture of one of the poorest quarters at sunset. "A crowd of people are hurrying home to supper, some with pickaxes, others with lunch boxes, others wearing clothes wet with sweat, and still others in coverings of rough straw, worn for carrying heavy and dirty burdens on their shoulders. They are the laboring class, who have exchanged their labor of the day for copper, eighteen sen each. Next comes a laborer pulling a cart; with him is his wife, who carries their baby. Then come two girls of about thirteen or fourteen years of age; one has a musical instrument, and the other carries a (dancing) fan in her hand; they are counting the money they have earned. Then comes an old man who sells bamboo tubes for tobacco pipes, another who mends shoes or sells candy, and still another who has been round the city buying empty bottles or picking up waste paper.

"On the streets which lead into this quarter, fishmongers spread their fresh fish, grocers display on a board egg-plants, cucumbers, potatoes, or lotus roots. Others sell salted salmon, dried codfish, cuttlefish, mackerel and other kinds of fish. On the other side of the street is a man selling pickles. He keeps in his shop pickled radish, egg-plant and plums. There before a grog-shop a man is selling roasted meat, cuttlefish and popped corn, which scent the air. There are many others selling old shoes, old furniture, or old clothes, to supply the needs of the poor." ("Darkest Tokyo," by Iwaguro Matsubara. Translated in the Japan Evangelist, 1894.)

At night the business streets are more than ever full; summer and winter, the lower classes seem to do all their shopping after dark. This is largely because things are cheaper then than earlier, and then, too, there is the money from the day's wages with which to buy. One authority estimates the ratio of buying among the poor to be as three is to seven in favor of the evening. "The prices of vegetables are settled at market about eight o'clock in the morning, but at ten they are worth twenty per cent less, and about an hour later some sell at half-price." Old clothes and umbrellas vary, he tells us, not with the hour, but the season; umbrellas worth eight rin (tenths of a sen) in December fetch three or four sen in the spring. At matsuri–festivals–too, night is the gayest time; the chief street of the ward is hung with red and white lanterns, and chains and arches of lights crossing from side to side; while the roadway is lined with booths, where the showman shouts himself hoarse before his gaudy curtain, and stalls for candy and flower hairpins, and all sorts of catchpenny odds and ends; and the batter-cake man is there, and the vender of toys and charms, and all the droll creatures who belong to fair time everywhere. The crowd is perfectly orderly and good-natured, curious of strangers, but not unpleasantly obtrusive–and it is certainly the best tubbed crowd in the world! The light-fingered

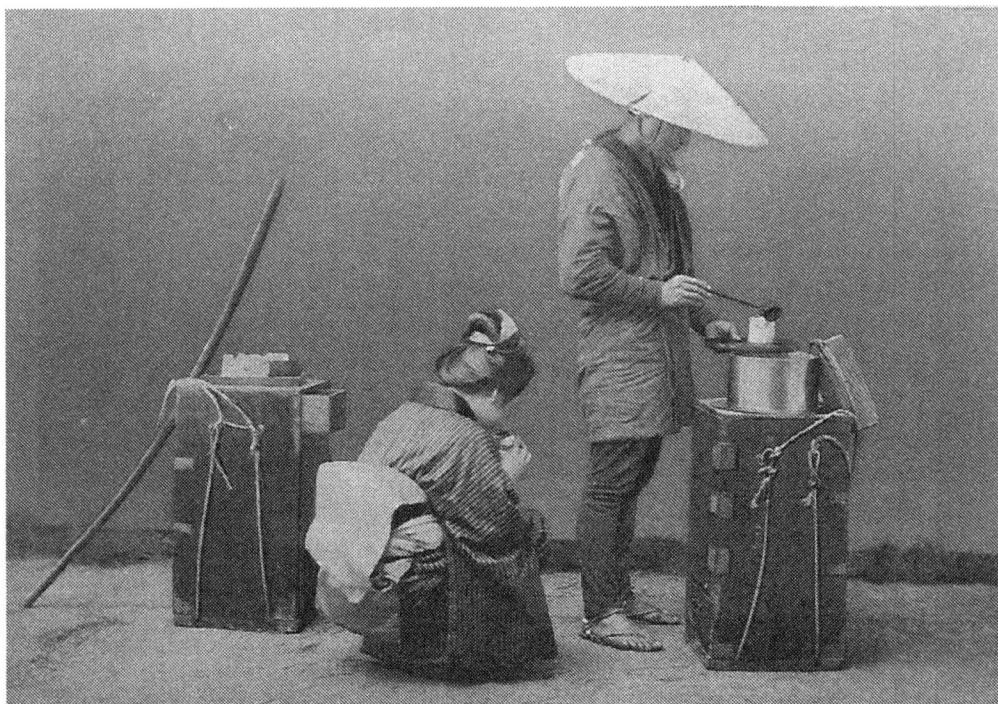

Street Vender

gentry are there, though, and they are exceedingly skillful at finding pockets and watches; they do say a Tokyo thief will steal the very geta-clogs-off a man's feet. This is the way it is done: A pin on the end of a stick pricks the victim's instep ever so softly; he slips his toe from the thong and lifts his foot to rub it–and instead of his good new geta an old one waits the returning toe. Repeat at a due interval, and when somebody gets home at night he will be unpleasantly surprised.

Less elaborate, but even more fascinating than a full matsuri are the en-nichi, or flower fairs, held also at night, and two or three times a month in each quarter of the city, on the Day of the Bird, Day of the Monkey, and so on. Toward sunset the dealers begin to arrive, pulling flat two-wheeled carts loaded with plants, some in pots, more having the roots tied up in straw; they prop up the body of the cart at the side of the street, and set out the plants on and around it in a splendid mass of bloom. Others spread mats beside the roadway, or set up booths as at a festival, laying out all manner of wares; here a china merchant sits on the ground among his bowls and tea-pots; there is a basket maker, or a second-hand dealer displaying tastefully a few old candlesticks and platters and books and imitation bronzes; sometimes, but very, very rarely, some bit of real value. As it grows dark, tins of kerosene, mounted on pointed sticks thrust into the ground, flare wildly among the flowers; a dense crowd gathers, walking up and down, admiring, criticising, bargaining; three or four times the real price is asked, then a few sen—cents—paid at last for a budding plum tree, or a chrysanthemum all over snowy balls, fit for a prize show in America. Sometimes dwarf trees are most in evidence, pine, maple, quince, or plums, white and red, which planted together signify the Gen-pei, the War of the Reds and Whites; or there are great satin-petaled peonies, or azaleas, camelias, magnolias, dwarf Wistaria vines, purple or white. All through the year there is a succession, from the first yellow ranunculus, the New Year "Flower of Happiness," round to the autumn nanten berries which foreigners substitute for holly at Christmas time. It is a graceful thing, this nanten, "heavenly bamboo," as the name means; it grows into a tall shrub, with slender branches and racemes of scarlet berries, and dark, glossy pinnate leaves that do look very like bamboo. It is hardy all around Tokyo, and it seems strange that such a pretty thing should not be well known abroad.

Before we leave the city, here is a quaint bit of old Yedo, the tale of "The Knightly Waste-paper Man."

This person—I follow Dening's translation—was a Samurai who, for some offence, had been forced to leave his lord's service and escape from the province. Reaching Yedo quite destitute and surpassingly ignorant of the world, he and his young wife would have fared badly, but for a wandering knight who saved them from robbers on the road and put them in charge of a kind-hearted tradesman, named Chohachi.

After a polite interval, Chohachi goes to the Samurai and gently inquires what can be done to make the pot boil; how would he like to start a fencing school? Shindo is very sorry, but, like too many knights in those degenerate days, he has lived a life of ease, and has little skill as a swordsman. Well, then, he might teach writing–favorite resource of knighthood out at elbows. Alas! that will not do either; our young gentleman confesses himself a hopelessly poor writer. Naruhodo! What ever can this graceful, charming piece of incompetence be set to do? Clearly it must be something of the simplest; and after much thought the trader provides the knight with a couple of light baskets on a pole, and a pair of long bamboo chopsticks, renames him Chobei (Shindo is quite too fine an appellation for such a business) and sends him out to buy up old paper.

On the first day poor Shindo-Chobei stole through the streets, meditating on the fleeting nature of prosperity, till he got entirely lost and had to pay a man to take him home. Chohachi laughed and scolded, and told him he must learn to call out what he wanted, or how was anybody to know? So, to get used to the sound of his own voice, out went Chobei to an open space, where there were no houses in sight, and cried "Old paper" to the four winds, till the street gamins pelted him for a madman.

Swallowing his laughter, Chohachi patiently explains and exhorts once more. "Try the little back streets; fine people don't sell waste paper! Gossip a bit with the old women and put them in a good humor, and then say, as you go off, 'I suppose you haven't any old paper today?' Go every day and get them to know you; that's the way."

So once more off went Chobei, this time down the lane, where women scrubbed and children played in the dust and bent old crones chopped daikon on the doorsteps, just the way they do now. One and all Chobei greeted them most politely in the only language he knew:

"Good morning, madam! An augustly beautiful morning! I trust you and your honorable family enjoy good health. This is the first time I had the honor–I am one Chobei, from such a street, and I beg the favor of your acquaintance. Got any old paper?"

Of all this courtly discourse, the good dames took in only the last sentence; but, on the whole, they were rather tickled by so much elegance, and though they thought him rather mad, "the Knightly Paper Man" became quite an institution and did a thriving trade; so that under Chohachi's careful management he kept his wife and little daughter very well.

In the rest of the tale, to Western ears, the morality seems strangely mixed. One day Chobei found an old friend begging on the street; it was the knight who had helped him to escape from his province, and who had now been banished by his lord on an unjust charge, and was living in dire poverty. Chobei and his wife decided that honor required them to make a suitable present; but twenty-five gold rio was the least that could be thought of, and the only way to get such a sum was to sell their only daughter. This, with many tears, they proceeded to do, and Chobei went off with the money to his friend, Bun-yemon. The friend, however, utterly refused to accept such a gift, and when it was pressed became very angry; still, Chobei managed to slip the packet into a tobacco-box and went home.

When Bun-yemon found the money had been left in spite of him, he scolded his wife roundly for not watching better; but, as they had no idea where Chobei lived, she urged her husband to take it as a loan and redeem a valuable sword which he had pawned; he could then sell the sword for a much larger sum, and pay the twenty-five rio back as soon as he found Chobei. This Bun-yemon finally consented to do; but unluckily the pawnbroker's clerk, balked of the sword, which he had fully expected to get possession of, accused Bun-yemon of stealing a hundred rio from his master. Bun-yemon was arrested, and his wife confined to her house and closely watched.

Now Yedo, under the Tokugawa, was governed by a Machi-Bugyo, or City Minister, who was also the supreme judge, and had under him twenty-five officers for the different departments of the service; and these again directed a hundred and fifty lesser officials. At the time of our story the Machi-Bugyo was the Lord of Echizen, who was, and indeed still is, considered the greatest judge Japan ever knew. To him Bunyemon's wife determined to appeal. A fire in the neighborhood gave her a chance to escape, and finding the

Machi-Bugyo on horseback, overlooking the firemen, she caught his rein and told her tale. The details of the case are too complex to follow, but the Lord of Echizen was judge, lawyer and detective, all in one, and by a series of clever maneuvers he sifted out the truth and got the guilty clerk's confession. Dening quotes the sentence, which, as he says, is "a curiosity from a modern point of view."

The guilty clerk was put to death. Besides his plot against Bun-yemon, he had robbed his master and killed the master's son. The pawnbroker was fined a hundred rio, on the principle which prevails everywhere in the East that the master is to be held largely responsible for the man. These gold pieces were given to Bun-yemon, with the order to use twenty-five in redeeming Chobei's daughter. As for Chobei, he was praised for sacrificing his child to serve his benefactor, and the daughter for obeying her parents, and both received small rewards. The money for this last came out of fines paid by the clerk's accomplices; altogether a very pretty game of virtue rewarded and vice punished, according to Eastern notions of vice and virtue.

To complete the general happiness, Bun-yemon's lord restored him to office, and Hanshiro, the errant knight who helped Chobei when he first came to Yedo, so pleased the Shogun that he made him a Hatamoto (retainer of the Tokugawa), with a revenue of five hundred koku.

12

A JAPANESE HOUSEHOLD

"When I am gone away,
Masterless my dwelling
Though it appear,
O plum-tree by the eaves
Forget not thou the spring."
   –Trans. Aston.

"BIND the rushes together, and lo, a house wherein man may dwell; scatter them, and they are once more but a part of the reedy waste."

I do not remember who he was, the Japanese sage who thus tried to express his conception of the human soul and its relation to the great All, and indeed I fear the saying has stayed by me, not for any half-comprehension of the pantheistic philosophy, but for the sake of the picture it evokes–the memory of wide moors, clothed to the edge of the horizon with tall, waving suzuki grass; and of some group of low huts clinging to the fringe of the waste, mere shells of mud daubed about the woven reeds.

Such a shelter, most probably, was the primitive Japanese house, modified and improved a little, it is true, by memories of Malay campongs raised on piles in that far south from which the divine ancestors came. The after changes, one and all, have been dictated by necessity of material or of climate, as must always be the case with a really vital architecture.

For after all, when everything has been said, a Japanese house is the fittest thing for Japan. Everybody knows them by this time from the specimens at world's fairs and Japanese villages–the low roofs projecting over narrow porches, the straw mats on the floors, and movable, half transparent walls–picturesque affairs of wood and paper, so slight and small that nobody in America can take them seriously, or quite believe that the real, lived-in thing is just like this. If people actually do live in such toy things–why then the Westerner concludes that the whole of Japan must be a toy land, a huge joke altogether.

Certainly a Japanese house is quite different from all our ideas of what constitutes a dwelling. Western architecture thinks of a house as four walls roofed over and pierced with openings for light and entrance; in Japan the conception is simply a roof on supports, filled in with walls or not, just as you wish, for the walls are a mere matter of convenience, and not structurally necessary in the least. One realizes this best after watching Japanese carpenters building, for they go at it almost roof first, and apply walls and openings afterward, according to requirement, very much as Americans build a modern fireproof sky-scraper.

The first step of all is to level the ground carefully, not digging it out, for there is to be no cellar. Then where the supports are to rest they set a foundation of round stones, pounding them in solidly with heavy hammers like pile-drivers, so that they shall not wash or give. No part of the building is set into the ground; each of the uprights rests on one of the large round stones, being hollowed out a little on the under side, so as to fit over the stone like a shallow socket. When this foundation is ready, the horizontal beams of the roof are laid foursquare on the ground, the uprights of the gable, the ridgepole and rafters, are all placed and made fast, and the whole roof-frame raised by many hands and with much chanting, till the props can be slipped under in their right places. These supports are then braced with cross-beams, and it remains only to thatch or tile the roof, and fill in an end wall or two, and the thing is done. No, not quite; the wooden outside shutters count as part of the house, although the inside screens, which serve as partitions, are generally counted furnishings. The whole building is simply a strong elastic frame, which rocks together like a ship when the ground heaves, or even slips a little on the foundation stones, while the heavy roof keeps it from jumping about to a dangerous extent. So long as the timbers have not rotted, such a house can stand even a severe earth-quake without damage beyond shedding off a shower of tiles which last it is pretty sure to do, because these heavy tiles are not fastened in any way, but simply laid in abed of sticky mud, and a prolonged shake is sure to send them flying.

Even the tiled houses keep a memory of the primitive thatch in the prominent ridgepole, which is often made of white tiles instead of black, apparently for a purely decorative purpose; and in the backward slant of the gable ends, which makes the roof slope four ways, like the little reed shelters.

A typical Japanese house is oblong, and more often one story high than two. The entrance is at the side, and not in the middle of the side either, but near one end; there is a little vestibule; a space of bare earth, closed usually on the outside by a slatted sliding door, and here you drop your shoes before stepping into the house proper, the floor of which is a foot or two higher. Most often it is the gable ends of the house which are filled in with lath and plaster, while along the sides run narrow balconies, called roka, floored with bare polished boards. Within these are the rooms proper, their floors completely covered with the tatami or thick, soft mats, which are about as springy as a gymnasium mattress, and serve for chairs, tables, in a word, all the furniture of the house.

The rooms near the door are least honorable; the guest room is farthest back, or in an "upper chamber," opening always on a gar-den, if it be only a few feet square. Passing through into such a guest room or zashiki, you find yourself in an oblong apartment, having at one end a kind of alcove in a plastered wall, two sides closed by sliding screens of thick paper, painted or stamped with some deli-cate design, and a third side open most of the day to the balcony and the garden. The floor of the rooms is sunk a little, so that the surface of the mats is just level with the sill of the balcony. In this sill, and in the beam directly above it, there are double grooves, and in these slide the screens or shoji, each panel six feet high and three wide, made of the lightest possible framework, so light that it can be lifted and taken out at a moment's notice. Like grooves run between the rooms for the fusuma or thick paper screens, which take the place of partitions, and the fusuma, too, can be lifted out easily, throwing the whole house, if you like, into one large room. The shoji screens next the balcony being intended to let in light, are covered with what we should call tissue paper; it is a good deal tougher than ours, but tears quite easily, and has to be frequently replaced; and meanwhile the neat housewife mends torn places with decorative strips or stars of the same thin paper, called hanshi. Hearn, in "Shadowings," quotes a pathetic little poem, supposed to be written by a mother who has just lost her child:

" Mi ni shimiru Kaze ya ! Shoji ni Yubi no ato."

"Oh, body-piercing wind! That work of little fingers in the shoji!"

At night, or when the house is to be closed, the wooden storm-shutters (ama-do) are pushed out along their grooves at the outer edge of the balcony; when the last is in place a bolt is put up, and everything is as secure as an eighth of an inch of pine plank can make it. Don't fancy there is an earthquake at day-dawn; it is only the maid rolling back the shutters to their niche at the end of the roka; and till she does there is all but no light. That is the weakest point of a Japanese house; it has no windows, and at night you are shut up in a box-though luckily not a very tight one.

Occasionally an upstairs room does have a window, and if so it is usually worked in some decorative way into the space beside the tokonoma, or ornamental alcove at the end. This tokonoma is said to be the raised seat where the Emperor would sit if he made a visit-at least, that is one explanation often given of a thing nobody quite understands. Others say the tokonoma represents a primitive raised platform to sleep on, such as the Ainu sometimes have in their houses; if so, it has certainly shrunk. It is a shallow niche, lined with wood, its wooden floor raised a foot or more above the rest of the room; the lining and floor and the upright beam or post beside it are the finest timber the house can afford; the post is often a trunk barked and polished, with all the marks of the limbs left in place–suggesting the post of the bed in his fair palace which Ulysses described with so much pride. The place just in front of the tokonoma is the most honorable seat, the place offered to the chief guest–and to be accepted, of course, only after due pressing. All the woodwork of the tokonoma, and in the rest of the house, is untouched by paint, and exquisitely polished by sheer rubbing; the ceiling of a well-built room is beautifully grained, the markings perfectly matched together. They do not waste thick boards on these ceilings, but use pieces almost as thin as paper, tacking them down to the rafters on their upper side.

The tatami or mats are each three feet wide and six feet long and about two inches thick, each piece bound at the end with black cotton cloth; all rooms are made in proportions to fit them, as an eight-mat, ten-mat, twelve or four-and-a-half mat room. When the mats are laid, covering the entire floor, and the shoji and fusuma are in place, the house is felt to be furnished; the rest is luxury or ornament. There may be a few low chests of drawers, a writing stand ten inches high, a hibachi (box for coals), and some thin, square cushions to sit on; in the tokonoma one flower vase, one kakemono or hanging scroll; no more.

It is bare, assuredly, and not at all comfortable to European muscles; but to the eyes, perfectly restful, perfectly harmonious. The proportions are always in multiples of three, the color low-toned, delicate, leaving all accent to the flower and kakemono, which are to be enjoyed without distraction–and changed, by the way, as the mood or the season changes. The scheme has certain positive advantages over the fatiguing complexity of Western life.

The rest of the needfuls of a house are few; there must be a shi-chi-rin, or stovelet for cooking–one is almost forced to use Japanese words where there is no English equivalent–the hibachi being only for warmth, or merely to boil a kettle, on a little iron stand set among the ashes. They say the shichi-rin, "seven rin," gets its name because it burns only seven-tenths of a sen's worth of charcoal; one sen–worth half-a-cent–being till lately a day's allowance for one fire. Then there must be quilts to sleep on, and pillows, which really are small blocks of wood with a little cushion atop, or else a bag of buckwheat chaff–this last is not at all bad either; men use it because nowadays they have no elaborate hair-dressing to save, as the women have. All this bedding is rolled up by day and kept in deep closets, closed like the rooms by sliding thick paper screens. Dishes there are, of course, and trays on which to serve them; basins, tubs, hot-water cans in the bath-room, and pots and cooking utensils generally.

Washing Day

The kitchen is worth looking at, especially in some fine old house in the country. A considerable part of it is usually lower, and floored with beaten earth, like the vestibule, and there tubs of water stand and rough work is done; the rest is raised and matted with tatami, while in the middle a square pit filled with pebbles and ashes serves for hearth. A kettle hangs over it by a chain, and around the pile of coals they broil small fish, leaning them against iron spits thrust into the ashes; this is the crisp brown shioyaki, which even foreigners can enjoy without reserve. An opening in the roof–a sort of little window, directly over the hearth–does duty for chimney, and carries off at least part of the charcoal fumes. These open fires are wonderfully little unpleasant; of course, the secret is that all the house is open through the day, and at night the fire-box is carefully taken out of the sleeping room, besides having the coals well buried in the ashes, for fear of sparks as much as gas. Still, every now and then the papers tell of some tragedy caused by a shut room and a burning hibachi.

After living with these open brasiers for awhile, one begins to realize what the "purity" of the hearth fire meant to the ancients on our own side of the globe; for in Japan, as well as in Greece or Rome, it is the height of impropriety to throw anything impure into the fireplace, even a match-stick, for that would burn with a smoke, or lie unconsumed among the clean white ashes. With the hibashi, "fire-sticks" or tongs, there is a neat little brass scraper, a thing half way between a shovel and a comb; and this is used to rake the ashes into four even furrowed slopes, from the fire to the sides of the hibachi.

Occasionally a storehouse is turned into a dwelling one of those kura or go-downs, with immensely thick, white plastered walls, which are so striking a feature of all Japanese cities. To tell the truth, they are pleasanter when converted into a "foreign" than a Japanese home, for the small windows do not suit a life without stoves. On the other hand, they are far better than an ordinary Japanese house for our way of living; the fact is I can't myself conceive of anything much more thoroughly uncomfortable than a house of paper walls filled with European furniture–and worst of all, rocking-chairs! The missionary women who struggle to make a home-like place out of one of these houses, curtaining yards of glass storm-shutters, enduring tables that wobble on the soft mats, and wrestling with those rockers that are continually poking through the fusuma into the next room–well, they surely have their reward somewhere. There is just one kind of purely Japanese house that lends itself well to doors and windows, and that is the tile and plaster form so much used in the Yedo yashiki, but now little seen; in general principles it is like the other houses, but the walls are filled in with tiles set on edge in a thick body of plaster, the black edges making slightly raised diamonds in the white surface, and the effect is very decorative. There are long blocks of such walls in Tokyo still, remnants of feudal days, but in a few years they will probably all disappear.

Private houses generally turn a blank side to the street, or at most a graceful oriel window screened by a wooden grill. When there is space to spare, the dwellings hide behind walls or bamboo fences or hedges–those high green hedges which are the charm of Tokyo lanes, showing only a line of roof, or through an open gate a peep of shrubbery and a gray rock or two. Raising flowers is no part of the duty of a Japanese garden; a tree there should be, a stone lantern and some rocks, a little lake, a little hill; and the arrangement of it all has an artistic symbolism which everybody understands. If the space be but a few feet, then the tree must be dwarfed, the hill becomes a mossy stone beside a goldfish basin; or tinier yet, at the tabi-maker's or the charcoal-seller's door you may see it all in a shallow flower-pot–an eight-inch pine tree, toy lanterns, toy bridges, or a green china frog by a pond as big as a saucer. On the other hand, where space allows, there is no dwarfing at all, and trees and shrubs are cleverly disposed to keep out prying eyes, for no Englishman has a greater horror of being overlooked than an upper-class Japanese, or a more thorough conviction that his house is his own.

His own; that is to say, his as the head of the family. After all, this is the most radical difference between Eastern and Western life, that in the West the individual is the unit, in the East the family. That is why people say the Japanese do not know what privacy means; the truth is, they both do and do not–they have certain reserves which would never occur to an Anglo-Saxon, and they are perfectly open and out spoken about many things which the West thinks good to conceal. That is the point of view. But family life in Japan is something absolutely sacred, something no outsider may so much as look into; it is not considered good form even to speak of such matters. On the other hand, once within the household, there are no reserves at all; there hardly could be in a paper house; nor is there need when all feel themselves but parts of a whole.

For it is necessary to remember that when a young man marries he does not merely take a wife to suit himself and her alone; he brings home a daughter to his parents. There will be in the household his father and mother, perhaps a grandfather, very likely young unmarried brothers and sisters, or a brother's widow, or perhaps his own widowed sister come back to her own people. It will be his duty as future head of the house wisely to direct all its affairs, to look after all its helpless members, to defer in all things to his parents, and to decide nothing of general interest without a family conclave. The young wife, on her part, will have the brunt of the housekeeping, and besides doing her best to please her husband, she must in all things be useful to his parents. How many American girls would get through the first month of such a life?

In truth it is not too easy for a Japanese girl. As the saying goes, "Mother-in-law and young wife living together in peace is one of the seven wonders," and the crowded households are at least partly responsible for the high rate of divorce, which is said to be one-third of all marriages. Confucian ethics allowed seven reasons for which a man might return his wife to her parents–send her back, as it were, like a piece of goods taken on approbation. The seven are disobedience to her husband's parents, not having a son, unfaithfulness, jealousy, contagious disease, talkativeness and thieving. But "if while she was taken from a home, she has now no home to return to, if she has passed with her husband through three years' mourning for his parents, or if her husband has become rich from being poor," then he may not divorce her. (S. Motoda, in "The Far East.")

Another circumstance Confucianism requires a wife to accept patiently, if her husband demands it, and that is the presence of another in the household. On this question we shall perhaps best understand the Japanese way of thinking by remembering the customs of the Hebrew patriarchs; for a Japanese mekake stands to the true wife almost precisely as Hagar stood to Sarah. Like Hagar, the mekake is regarded as a "handmaid;" she is always of inferior rank, and in every way subject to the wife. The training of her children is not in her hands, but in those of the true wife, who alone is mistress of the house. Under feudalism the number of mekake a man might keep was limited by his station, which prescribed his retinue and the kind of establishment he was entitled to; a prince had four or five, and the Emperor himself was permitted twelve. On the other hand dissipation was denounced: "He alone can rule his family who ruleth himself; and he alone can rule a nation, whose family is in right order." Sometimes the Karo or chief retainer was called upon to protest against the conduct of his lord; if the rebuke was accepted, well; if not, the Samurai took his own life. It is recorded of one Daimyo that he went aside on an expedition to visit one of his ladies in waiting, and remained drinking and carousing long past the time that he should have left. In this difficulty, two of the knights killed themselves at his door, and thus recalled their master to his duty.

Uchimura, in "Japan and the Japanese," cites Yozan, lord of Yonezawa, as an example of right feeling. "The lady to whom he was wedded in her minority by his parents, according to the then custom of the land, proved to be a born imbecile, and her intellect was never above that of a child of ten years of age. Her, however, he treated with genuine love and respect, made for her toys and dolls, and comforted her in all ways, and for the twenty years of their wedded life he never showed the least dissatisfaction with his fate. His other consort (at a time when no one questioned the right of concubinage, and all other Daimyo had four or five, he had but one) was left in Yonezawa, while they lived mostly in Yedo, and was never allowed the dignity he attached to his imbecile wife."

I do not mean to imply that this custom either is or was a universal one; it never was so at any time in Japan, being rather permitted than approved; and modern law does not recognize the institution at all. For instance, in future only the son of an Empress may succeed to the throne. One in a thousand households was the official estimate five years ago; and the number lessens yearly, because nearly every case is a survival from the old regime. It is one of the things which are passing away, and one can only trust that for this, as well as others, a genuine acceptance of the principles of Christian ethics may take the place of the old ideals which have been so suddenly cast down. Failing this, it is to be feared that, for a time at least, many things must be worse rather than better for contact with the letter of Western propriety.

The patriarchal custom of sons living with the parents is likewise bound to pass with the changes now going on in society. Whether as a system it had most of good or evil, need not be discussed; but just here comes in the value of Japanese training in self control, in pleasant looks and pleasant speech, in knowing just what to do and how to do it—in other words, etiquette. All those little things that every child must learn so carefully are only the best and smoothest way of doing needful things; for instance, try to open a sliding screen, to get up from the floor with a tray in your hand, and see if you are not a convert to Japanese rules for those motions, at any rate. And the little daily observances, the little bows and little set phrases, all help the domestic wheels to run more evenly. For in spite of all difficulties and drawbacks, in many a Japanese household there is peace and happiness, and a deep, quiet affection.

Here are some of the things specially enjoined on young girls:

"How to sit down.–Bring both hands and knees together; quietly kneel; sit low, putting one toe over the other and keeping the hands in the lap.

"How to rise.–Leave the right hand in the original position; raise the body with the fingers of the left hand on the mat, rise first on tiptoe, and as the body becomes erect, bring both knees and feet together.

"When a tea cup is set before her, she should take it up with her right hand, and, holding it in both palms, drink the tea in three swallows and a half.

"When a plate of cakes is presented" she should first take out a sheet of paper (ladies should always provide themselves with clean paper), then select a cake and put it on the paper with chop-sticks. Then she may break it into two pieces and eat one piece with two fingers."

A woman should move gently, with hands hanging straight and head a little down; in walking her tight, narrow dress compels her to turn her toes slightly inward, and she should slip her feet smoothly along the floor. They tell a story among the foreigners of a child whose American teacher tried to make her sit up straight and enlarge her chest; after repeated lectures the little girl at last burst into tears, exclaiming, "I don't know what to do! You are all the time telling me this, and when I go home my mother says, 'Don't throw back your head in that rude, forward way,' and between you I am scolded all the time!" Such a thing might easily have happened often in the early days of mission schools; now, the Japanese schools themselves teach a light kind of calisthenics, and the missions go to great pains to have Japanese good manners taught by specialists in etiquette.

Many things are possible to a Japanese woman, because her code has taught her to regard marriage less as a means of personal happiness than as a duty. "Marriage," says the (Chinese) Li Ki, "is intended to be a bond of love between persons of different sur-names, with a view in its retrospective character to secure the services in the ancestral temple, and in its prospective character to secure the continuance of the family line. . . There is nothing so deplorable and shameful as the neglect of the worship of ancestors and discontinuance of the family line." Marriage therefore is simply an act of filial piety, which Confucianism regards as the highest of all virtues, the basis of all morality.

An American once asked a Chinaman if he thought he could do a certain piece of work, and the man answered, "I have been a bricklayer for seven generations, and I ought to know how." Not my father and my grandfather before me, but I–a bit of the whole, a mere link in the chain. Certainly the Oriental notion of the solidarity of the family is beyond the wit of younger nations to grasp.

The etymology of the Chinese word Ko (filial piety) is rather enlightening. It is said to be made up of two characters, "old" and" son," one written under the other, so that literally it means a son bearing his parent on his shoulders, like a Chinese version of Aeneas and Anchises. From this conception of their relation, the custom of a man's becoming "inkyo" (retired) follows naturally enough; as soon as the son is able to support his father, the latter may enjoy ease and leisure, and it is the glory of the son to let his parents speedily enter upon the inkyo life. Though it is a selfish custom on the father's side, Japanese writers think that the responsibility has a steadying effect on many a young man, making him study or work more diligently and avoid evil habits.

Most of the filial piety stories have a Chinese origin; I am not sure though where one of the prettiest comes from, that of the poor woodcutter, all whose efforts failed to bring in enough money to buy sake for his old father. As he went home sorrowfully, he stopped to drink at a waterfall, and found it had turned into wine! You often see him in pictures, kneeling by the stream, and joyfully filling a gourd such as pilgrims, and picnic parties carry.

Naturally the choice of a wife is theoretically left to the parents, but the fact is that in actual practice in Japan both man and girl have a very distinct say in the matter. A missionary once said jokingly to one of his evangelists, "I suppose a lot of you young fellows will be going to the X commencement (naming a large girls' school) to pick out your wives," and the young man answered quite soberly, "I am not going myself, but M. and N. are."

Still, though it is proper to look and decide pretty much for themselves, "premature affection between the two contracting parties is considered improper," says Motoda. "Marriage must begin with respect, and after marriage love begins," he quotes from the Confucian law; and again:

"How do we proceed in hewing an axe-handle?
Without another axe it cannot be done.

How do we proceed in taking a wife?
Without a go-between it cannot be done."

Much of this rigid Confucianism was introduced only a couple
of hundred years ago, along with the great revival of Chinese influence in the early Tokugawa period; before this Japanese women
enjoyed a great deal more freedom and influence, especially in
the brilliant eighth and eleventh centuries. But in the seventeenth
century the "Mirror for Women" was published, and, with the
"Greater Learning," became the guide to women's conduct almost
to the present day. About this period a Daimyo wrote to his grand-
daughter on her marriage:

"In thy youthful womanhood, it is very natural that thy mind is
often taken up with matters of dress; but forget not the frugal habits
thou hast been taught. Devote thyself to silk-worm raising and other
womanly industries, and at the same time feed thy mind with books
of poetry. Seek not culture and enlightenment for their own sakes;
the aim of all knowledge is to lead us into virtue. Serve thy parents
with all fidelity. With obedience to thy husband in all quietness,
may your prosperity know no end!"

Gentle as she was to be, a Samurai woman yet carried a short
sword, and was carefully taught how to use it if there were need. A
young girl once told me that she remembered seeing her mother
and grandmother practicing fencing at the outbreak of the Satsuma
rebellion, that they might be ready, if called upon in their husband's
absence, to defend their lord.

Of such stuff was the Countess Hosokawa, whose husband took
the side of Ieyasu in his conflict with Hideyoshi's son Hideyori.
Hosokawa, going to camp with Ieyasu, left his wife at their residence near Osaka, Hideyori's stronghold; and here she was visited
by a messenger who summoned her to appear with her children
at the castle. She at once understood why; they were to be held as
hostages, in hopes of getting Hosokawa to the other side. Either
her husband would be tempted to betray his honor, or she very well
knew the disappointed followers of Hideyori would not hesitate to
crucify her with her children. She sent for the Karo and her lady-in-

waiting, and begged them to save the boy and girl; they declared it was hopeless. The Countess therefore wrote a letter to her husband explaining the necessity, knelt before the family shrine, and when the soldiers were announced, cut down the unconscious children and thrust the dagger into her own throat. Her story, altered in names and detail, is a favorite on the Tokyo stage.

The simplicity of daily life in Japan impresses all foreigners, but most of all Americans, supplied as we are beyond others with material helps to existence. The newcomer hardly knows whether to pity a people so devoid of what to him are the commonest necessities, or to envy the Oriental his freedom from wants. And, whether we should like it for ourselves or not, it is certain that this simplicity is a large part of Japan's fascination for strangers.

In one of these quiet households day begins with the clamor of the wooden shutters rolled back along the balcony, sometimes before the sun is up; for, as in all southern countries, the people are early astir. Schools begin at eight in winter and seven in summer, and even this is a concession to modern ideas; Samurai boys were often sent to their teacher breakfastless in the dawn. First of all, the children must present themselves to their parents, slip down before them with foreheads to the mat, and say "O hayo, Otot' San; O hayo, Oka San "–Good-morning, father, mother. Even the baby learns to put his fat hands palms down, and bob his funny round head, with its stiff black crown of hair. He says "chichi" and "haha" for father and mother, and the rest all call him "bot' chan" till he is quite a big boy. His sisters may be O Yuki Chan (Miss Snow) and Umeko (Little Plumblossom)–Chan being the childish version of San.

Though there is no dining-table, the family generally take their meals together, sitting in a half circle round the room; on festival days they use the guest room, and at such times there are special dishes served in little bowls set by each one's tray. A New Year favorite is a thick sweetish bean soup, in which float lumps of sticky mochi, the indigestible pounded rice dough the Japanese are so fond of; and a dish which appears many times a year is a mixture of rice and red beans. Peas should be offered to a person going on a journey, because the name (mame) means also good luck, prosperity.

In most non-Christian homes, a little food and a little drink are daily placed before the name-tablets of the ancestors on the god-shelf, and here too the offering varies with the season. It is very bad to stick one's chop-sticks upright in a bowl of rice at dinner, because they are placed so in making offerings to the dead. For the same reason a Japanese will not pour cold water into a basin and add hot; and he dislikes camelias, because their heavily falling blossoms make him think of heads tumbling off!

At the end of the meal the children bow and say go-chiso sama "an honorable feast;" and in like manner each member of the family bows, more or less profoundly, and murmurs "sayonara" before leaving the room. Then the mother looks to her housekeeping; in these modern days she does not always raise silk or spin, but she cuts and sews, and prides herself on her pickles, and overlooks everything, even if she has many servants. The routine of life is varied by endless demands of social etiquette. When a child is born, there are certain ceremonies for the first day, and again on the seventh night, when the baby is named and formally dressed for the first time; a boy's left sleeve must go on first, and a girl's right. Any event among the neighbors calls for gifts and messages; at weddings, funerals, starting on a journey or returning, certain gifts must be sent and duly acknowledged by return gifts, either at the time or afterward. For many occasions there are particular cakes, which have a more or less symbolic meaning; fish, salt or fresh, is a favorite for congratulation. The way the gift is wrapped and tied, the kind and pattern of the fukusa or covering which is placed over it, and which is to be returned, all show to the initiated just what is intended. Callers also bring gifts sometimes; but this custom is going out. Of course, the first thing when a guest arrives is to offer something to eat and drink, usually tea and cakes, or sake at New Year time. The wife must see to all this; she must have the care of the children's health, education, morals; their clothing and her husband's, as well as her own. She is house-mistress in the truest sense, responsible for all and controlling all. She directs the servants, men as well as women; she watches over the children's morning greetings; the tadaima ("just back"), when they return from school; the pretty phrases exchanged when anyone goes out or comes in; she is at the door, with the household, to say O kaeri ("honorably welcome") when the master of the house comes back from even the briefest absence. A survival perhaps, this last, from the days when a man kept literally the Samurai injunction, "Leaving thy house, leave ever as one who may not return."

13

IKEGAMI-A TYPICAL BUDDHIST TEMPLE

"Earnestness is the path of immortality (Nirvana), thoughtlessness is the path of death.

"If a man would hasten towards the good, he must keep his thoughts from evil.

"Let no man think lightly of evil, saying in his heart, It will not come nigh unto me. Even by the falling of water-drops a water-pot is filled; the fool becomes full of evil, even if he gather it little by little."–From the "Dharmapada," Max Muller's translation.

IF one should look over the map of Europe and trace the position of the great mediaeval monasteries and cathedrals, they would be found for the most part to lie in or near important cities. Of course in many cases, as in Protestant Germany or Switzerland, the monastery has been laid down, and the town has fallen to ruin, or has been outstripped by newer neighbors; but taken broadly, it is safe to say that where the Church established herself, the world followed. Look now at the map of Japan. Leaving out the religious establishments–and it is true they were very numerous–at Kyoto and Tokyo, places which owed their existence to the State and not to the Church, the principal Buddhist foundations are at Nara, which was the former capital, and with its neighbor, Hori-uji, the first home of Buddhism in Japan; at Osaka, at Miidera on Lake Biwa, and at Ikegami and Nikko. Of these, Nara retains importance chiefly from force of association with the past; Hori-uji owes its modern existence to the fact that the best tea in the country is grown on the hills round about; Miidera has always been a small place; Ikegami lies by a tiny village in the hills near Tokyo; Nikko is far away in the heart of the mountains. Only Osaka is and has always been a great city, a centre of national trade.

One cause of this striking difference lies in the fact that the monasteries of Europe were almost always situated on or near the great trade routes, while those of Japan as frequently layaway from them; but this in itself points back to a radical difference of aim.

Whatever their after shortcomings, the religious houses of the mediaeval church were certainly founded in a missionary spirit; their object was to reach the people, and both in their choice of sites and in their schools and charities the founders labored to that end. In the East it was otherwise; the primary purpose of a Buddhist's religious life was contemplation, and the more complete his retirement from the world the better. That the monasteries became centres of learning was natural; but schools for outsiders, and especially for the lower classes, were a secondary consideration–an after growth. Therefore it was that a mountain solitude was the fittest abode for these seekers after the Way, as it was also their most frequent choice.

Buddhism came to Japan in two distinct waves of influence, the first from the latter part of the fifth century to the end of the eighth, when missionaries came from China and Korea to the islands; and the second from the beginning of the ninth century, at which time many Japanese went to China to study, and brought back the learning of the East, much as the early Greeks brought the wisdom of the Egyptians. At this later period the teaching of the northern school of Buddhism had reached China from India, and this so-called doctrine of the "Greater Vehicle" is that which finally prevailed in Japan.

But not in a single form. The sects of Christianity do not greatly surprise the Japanese, for they have eight or ten themselves, and as many sub-sects. Of these, one of the latest, and also the most wealthy and influential, is the Nichiren, named for St. Nichiren, its founder; and the greatest temple of the sect is the Hon-monji at Ikegami, near Tokyo.

The easiest way there is by train to Omori station, on the Yokohama line, and from there by kuruma, a mile and a half back into the country; but the prettiest and by far the most interesting is to ride the whole distance, perhaps six miles, by delightful lanes and by-ways out from Tokyo. The general direction is west, first by Shiba Park, and then over the long ridge and into a narrow valley, flanked by wooded hills. You have left the city now; the little road might be an English lane, winding between green banks, or stone walls, where clumps of tiny fern grow in the chinks, and under arching trees; then it skirts the rice fields, which fill all the level space of the valley from edge to edge, and so by more ridges and valleys farther away into the heart of the hills.

Everywhere there is the sharpest contrast between slope and level; the valleys are divided into little squares, watered and cultivated over every inch, but the moment the hill begins, it is as if one stepped from a garden into some forest wilderness. Under foot are violets and wood flowers, mixed with thick stems of the low, wild pieris Japonica, which creeps and roots along the hillside, and lifts its coral blossoms only a few inches from the ground. A tangle of white brier rose is overgrown with long streamers of akebia and wild gourd, and on the open slopes bluebells and dead-nettle and a host of summer field flowers, strangely like our own, are struggling with the greedy knot-grass. In early spring, when the fields lie fallow, all the valleys are carpeted with slender purple trefoil; and down among the leaves one may find the dainty white marsh violet, with blue-veined petals and a faint, delicious fragrance.

Two or three miles out the road leads through a pretty village called Meguro, which is famous solely for the graves of the lovers Gompachi and Komurasaki. If I tell their tale with little sympathy, it is because I was never able to feel much for those misguided persons, particularly for the man, who seems to me as cowardly a young cut-throat as ever got his deserts.

This Gompachi, then, was on his way to Yedo to seek his fortune, when at an inn a pretty girl woke him in the middle of the night and told him that a band of robbers, who had kidnapped her, were going to kill him in the morning. Of course, the knight disposed of the robbers and took the girl home; but, though she was exceedingly pretty and her parents were more than willing, he would not marry a merchant's daughter, and went on his way lamenting.

Arrived at Yedo, he soon spent all his money among kindred spirits, and was quite penniless, when one day he discovered in a famous new beauty of the Yoshiwara his forsaken Komurasaki. It was the old story of parents reduced to want and sacrificing their daughter as a last resource. Gompachi vowed he would buy her freedom, but having nothing left, took to highway robbery. He wasted all he stole, and stole again; and was presently caught and put to death. When the girl heard it, she went to his grave and killed herself there, in the hope that in another life she would join him and be happy. There is nothing to be seen at the tomb where they are buried together, but those who are so moved may turn aside and visit it on the way to a worthier shrine.

Though now so near the great city, at the time it was founded and for three hundred years after Ikegami fulfilled all the requirements of solitude and removal from the world; for Kamakura was then the Shogun's capital, and the region north of the Hakone pass was still barely more than half colonized. Even now, as one rides through the little village of thatched cottages strung along the narrow lane, and enters the pine wood about the monastery, one might easily imagine oneself leagues from any city. The whole wood is very still and lonely; the only sounds are the wind and the birds in the branches, and far off, the dull, steady beating of the drum as the serving priest drones the mystic formula, Nammyo-ho-renge-kyo, "I put my trust in the Law of the Wonderful White Lotus." The village is quite out of sight below; a long flight of stone steps climbs the hill under the trees, and at the top is the entrance proper, a typical two-storied red gate, within which is the temple court, a large open space, fenced in and strewn with pebbles, as such courts usually are.

This Ikegami temple group is uncommonly interesting, because it includes nearly all the different buildings which belong to a typical Buddhist establishment–the Founder's hall and main hall, the bell tower and drum tower, pagoda, revolving library and holy water cistern, besides the treasury, reception rooms and priests' apartments. The two principal buildings face the entrance; they are the main temple or Shaka-Do, hall of Shaka, as the Japanese call Sakyamuni (Gautama Buddha), and the Founder's, dedicated to Nichiren, the patron saint of the place. This last is the larger of the two, and contains a life-sized image of Nichiren in a beautiful lacquered shrine. High up on the wall are pictures of Buddhist angels, and all the half-Hindu appointments of Buddhist ritual are in place–the lamps and embroidered hangings, the drums and gongs and low reading stands for the priests, set before the altar on the matted floor. Tall brass vases hold great gilded lotus flowers, and the lotus is carved on the lanterns and worked on hangings and cut into the stone coping beside the steps, even more lavishly than at other temples, for Nichiren's special doctrine was the worship of the Lotus Sutra, the Book of the Law of the White Lotus. A great stone lotus flower supports the curious stone tope, with a bronze roof, which holds the relics of the saint–a tooth and a handful of ashes; though he died here, his bones were carried elsewhere.

In the drum tower near the entrance a priest is almost constantly beating the drum, and reciting the sacred formula of the sect, the invocation to the Lotus Book. All the buildings are of wood, their heavy tiled roofs resting as usual on a bewilderment of rafters and cornices. Behind the Shaka-Do stands the revolving library, which contains a complete set of the Buddhist Scriptures; it is not exactly a prayer wheel, but the theory of it is that whoever will turn it three times, reciting a suitable prayer, may obtain as much merit as if he had read through the entire collection of over six thousand volumes, a task quite impossible for any single individual; "moreover long life, prosperity, and the avoidance of all misfortunes shall be his reward." (Chamberlain). The credit of the invention belongs to a certain Fu Daishi (St. Fu), a deified Chinese priest of the sixth century, from whom it was copied in Japan.

Priest

A small roofed gate at the back of the temple enclosure leads to the priests' apartments, students' dormitories, reception rooms, etc., which make a considerable group of buildings. All monasteries have rooms for the entertainment of guests and pilgrims, a feature made necessary by their remoteness from towns, if by no other reason. The reception rooms intended for guests of rank were built of costly wood, and the sliding screens were often decorated by the greatest painters of the time, especially by masters of the Kano School, which followed the religious traditions of Chinese art. Indeed, it is chiefly by these decorative works that foreigners are obliged to estimate the painters of Japan, for the movable pieces, kakemono and gaku, are kept hidden away in the treasuries of the temples, and can very seldom be seen by anyone.

The annual festival is held on the 12th and 13th of October, the anniversary of Nichiren's death, and draws immense crowds from the city, as well as from more distant places. Sometimes over twenty thousand pilgrims are said to attend. A second lesser festival takes place in April, beginning on the 22nd, the birthday of the Founder, and lasting five days.

Nichiren is the same reformer saint who so narrowly escaped being martyred at Enoshima. He was born not very far from there, in the province of Awa, across Yedo bay, in the spring of 1222; so that by one of those curious parallels of history, the Japanese St. Dominic entered the world just one year after his European prototype went out of it. The father was living as a poor fisherman, but both he and his wife were of good birth, and had been exiled for some political offence. Many wonderful things are told of the child's birth and babyhood; his mother dreamed that he was the child of the sun-god (Nichi), and in remembrance gave him the name Zen-nichi-maro (Good Sun Boy), which he afterwards changed to Nichiren, Sun Lotus. They say, too, that a clear spring burst forth in the fisherman's garden for the baby's first bath, and a white lotus bloomed three months out of season. Moreover, the date of his birth fell one day later than the birthday of Buddha, and the year was the beginning of the third millenium after Buddha's entrance into Nirvana, the period of the Later Law, at which time the great teacher had prophesied that a light should appear to the east of India. Before he was well grown, the fisherman's son had come to believe himself predestined to be that light.

At twelve the boy was entered as a novice at a neighboring monastery, and took the vows four years later; but he was profoundly dissatisfied with the teaching of his abbot, and still more with the multiplicity of the sects of which he was told—desiring to know which among them all was the true law of Buddha. Besides the so-called "Eight Sects" of the ninth century, the twelfth century had added two more, the Zen, and the Jodo or "Pure Land" sect.

The Zen was imported from China, where it originated several hundred years earlier. Its distinguishing doctrine was belief in a sort of telepathy, in the power to transmit thought without words from one mind to another properly attuned. Hearn gives the story of its origin his unfailing poetic touch: "When the Buddha was preaching upon the Vulture Peak, there suddenly appeared before him the great Brahma, who presented a gold-colored flower to the Blessed One, and besought him to preach the Law. The Blessed One accepted the heavenly flower, and held it in his hand, but spoke no word. Then the great assembly wondered at the silence of the Blessed One. But the venerable Kasyapa smiled. And the Blessed One said to the venerable Kasyapa: 'I have the wonderful thought of Nirvana, the Eye of the True Law, which I now shall give you.' So by thought alone the doctrine was transmitted it Kasyapa; and by thought alone it was transmitted to Ananda; and by thought alone it was transmitted from patriarch to patriarch, even to the time of Bodhi-dharma "-which last saint was he who sat so many years in meditation that his legs dropped off, and he was reduced to the shape of the delightful red tumblers which Japanese children buy at fairs and stand on their heads, to see them turn a somersault and right themselves again.

The Zen doctrine appealed strongly to the educated classes; who delighted in its exercises of mystic contemplation. The Jodo, not less mystical, was directed especially to the common people. It was a doctrine of salvation by grace, derived from the "Mahayana" books, a series of three Sutras concerning Amida and the Paradise of the West. . It taught that works were of no avail; whoever put his trust in Amida was united to him, and after death would enter into Paradise, the Pure Land, there to live a mystic life of holiness till at last he was worthy to attain Nirvana, the state of perfect blessed-ness. Worshipers repeat over and over the formula, "Nammu Amida Buddha"–I commit myself to thee, great Amida–in a long sing-song chant, sometimes accompanying it by ringing little hand-bells; from this phrase they got the name of Nem-Butsu or "Call on Buddha" sect. The Monto sect hold this doctrine in the most advanced form; their foundations are called Hongwanji, monasteries of the True

Vow, and, with the Tendai and the Nichiren, they are the most powerful sects in Japan today.

While fasting and meditating over these difficult problems, young Nichiren believed that he received a direct inspiration through a sentence in one of the sacred books–"Trust in the word, and not in man." This he considered must mean that he was to put his trust in the written law rather than anyone's interpretation of it; and of the four great Sutras, or Books of the Law, he finally chose the last in order, which contains the teachings of the last eight years of Gautama Buddha's life. In this he believed he should find the essence of the whole body of instruction, "the principle of all things, the truth of eternity, and the sacred meaning of Buddha's life and his entrance into enlightenment."

The next step was to study the great Sutra more fully, and for this he set out for the large Tendai monastery on Mount Hiezan, near Kyoto, and there spent ten years examining texts and commentaries. During this time he had dreams and visions of his future work; in one of these he saw all the deities of the country floating over him and promising protection, bidding him go forth and destroy the darkness of the land.

There must have been much of the fanatic, as well as the mystic, in Nichiren's character. It is said that he became particularly inflamed against the Jodo sect, because once when going through a village he saw a party of children playing rudely with an image of Shaka. Greatly horrified, he went to the father of the older ones and rebuked him for permitting such wickedness; to which the man replied, that Shinran (the founder of the chief sect of Jodo) taught that they should put their whole trust in Amida, and, therefore, the other images could be of no possible consequence. Still further appalled by such blasphemy, Nichiren retired, and from that moment preached vehemently against the pernicious doctrine. His is the one sect in Japan which is intolerant towards the rest; it was also the one which Nobunaga especially hated and did all he could to suppress, and which after his time took a leading part in the persecution of the Christians.

At the age of thirty-two, Nichiren was ready to begin his public work. It was at this time that he took the name by which he continued to be known, and at the same time also he framed the sacred formula which his followers recite, Nammyo-ho-renge-kyo. Armed with this, he returned to his native province, visited his parents, and announced that he would preach at the local temple on a certain day. Naturally, the neighbors flocked to hear him; and what they heard was unmeasured denunciation of all they were accustomed to believe. "Know that Jodo is a way to hell; Zen the teaching of internal hosts of evil; the Shingon a heresy to destroy the nation, and the Ritsu an enemy of the land. These are not my words; I found them in the Sutra. Hark to the cuckoo above the clouds; he knows the time and warns you to plant. Now is the time for planting the Lotus Sutra, and I am the messenger of the Blessed One sent you for that purpose."

But for the good old abbot, his former teacher, Nichiren would have been put to death for a blasphemer then and there; as soon as it was dark he sent the fanatic safely out of the province. Nichiren went straight to Kamakura, the Shogun's capital; built a straw hut on a bit of waste ground, and began preaching in the streets–a thing hitherto unknown in Japan. He made disciples as well as enemies, to an extent that alarmed the authorities, and he was banished for a time, but returned to repeat all his offences; adding prophecies of dire evil, and especially of foreign invasion, something which Japan had never known, but which actually came in the Mongol expedition, under Kublai Khan, a year before Nichiren's death. About this time a party of swordsmen set upon him and his disciples in a lonely place, and two were killed in defence of their master, who escaped with a cut on the head. So far his office protected him, but after this he was arrested and sentenced to die at Enoshima, escaping through the Regent's fears. Instead, the Regent exiled him for five years to Sado, a wild island on the dreary west coast, with the result that the neighboring province of Echigo became one of the strongholds of his sect. After this the authorities gave up opposing him, and his followers began a round of visits to other temples in bands of twenty or more, beating their drums and reciting the lotus formula in a droning sing-song. It is hard to imagine how any other creed survived such an onslaught of sound.

His teachings thus spread, the reformer retired to Mount Minobu, near Fujiyama, and meditated and received disciples for the rest of his life. In his last months he went on a visit to Ikegami, and died there in the house of a disciple, being just sixty years old.

The great temples and fine apartments at Ikegami are of a later growth; at Minobu, as in the days of strife at Kamakura, the saint contented himself with a straw hut. The best time to visit Ikegami is in March, when the plums are in blossom; on a sheltered slope below the monastery there are some wonderful old trees, gnarled and twisted as the Japanese love to see them–rivals of the famous "Creeping Dragon" trees at Kameido, in Tokyo. The priests have also a wonderful collection of dwarf trees, some over a hundred years old; one has a trunk a foot thick, and grows in an ornamental porcelain pot only a few inches larger; another taller one bends down its branches like a weeping willow, set with stars of fragrant white flowers. The red plum blossoms very early, and can be persuaded to take on marvelous shapes, but it is less esteemed than the pink or the white, because it has no fragrance.

Later in the year the monks have a fine display of botan, the great satin-petaled bush peony, as different from a common garden "peony" as a tea-rose from a brier. The flowers are sometimes eight or ten inches across, and of all shades, from snowy white through rose color to the deepest velvety maroon, dark as pansies almost. It is a very delicate flower, and will not bear the slightest wind or rain on the petals; the gardeners shelter the plants with bamboo screens, and guard the foliage as carefully as the flowers, massing them when the time comes in open sheds, where the colors are placed to blend and foil one another as if in a picture. There is a fine botan garden in Tokyo, but they say no one has such flowers as the monks at Ikegami.

(Author's note: Since this chapter was written, a fire broke out in the students' dormitories, where a number of young men were working late preparing for examination; it was a windy night, and though fire engines came from Omori, they were useless, because there was no water except in a small well. A large part of the buildings were burned, but the treasury was saved, and most of the works of art in the temples. Even if rebuilt, much of the charm of the place must be lost for the present.)

14

OJI MAPLES

NORTHWARD from Tokyo the hills send out long ridges which stop suddenly, as if cut off, on the edge of the rice fields. Once these ridges must have been cliffs washed by the waves, in the prehistoric time when the sea came up here and extended for miles to the north and east, over the great level which is now known as the Musashi plain. When the coast rose and the sea retreated, there was left a vast reedy morass, where the wild Emishi (Ainu) used to hide; for which reason the Japanese called them Reed-men. It may have been somewhere hereabouts that Yoshiiye of Minamoto, grandfather of Yoritomo, had his famous encounter with the Emishi. I once saw the scene represented on a double folding screen; a few sweeps of the brush had transformed the smooth, brownish surface of the paper into a vast plain shrouded in mist, through which a tall plume of suzuki grass showed here and there, just as you may see it any day if you take the early train from Uyeno station, only now it will be rice-stalks instead of rushes that rise through the mist. On one panel two or three knights reined in their horses on the edge of the plain; on the other, a flock of wild fowl flew restlessly hither and thither. That was all; but to a Japanese eye it told the whole story; how the great general Yoshiiye led an expedition against the rebellious Emishi, and how the land seemed all open and safe, so that the knights were riding gaily down from the hills in the morning sun. But Yoshiiye marked the troubled flight of the birds, and bade his men wait while he sent scouts forward to see what had disturbed

Uyeno Park

the wild things from their feeding grounds; and they searched and found an army of barbarians, with short bows bent, hidden in the low mist. So Yoshiiye fought and slew them, and subdued all the region for his lord.

Oji, a few stations out from Uyeno, has pleasanter and less war-like associations. The station lies under a great hill, called Akusa, which for two or three centuries has been a favorite resort of flower lovers. Perhaps the place was chosen for some fancied resemblance to Takao or Arashiyama, the fashionable flower-viewing hills near Kyoto; for however the Shogun's court might dominate the Emperor's in actual fact, the newer aristocracy long looked to the old for literary and social precedents, much as Berlin followed Hanover thirty or forty years ago. At all events, the Yedo people planted on Akusa a grove of cherry trees, which are beautiful and much visited still, though the view across the plain is grievously spoiled by a large paper manufacturing plant, established just under the hill by the government in one of its efforts to promote modern methods of industry. It is not a very bright example of the benefit of subsidies, for there are two private factories side by side with the government one, which are said to be far more prosperous; however, between them, they succeed in making a great deal of cheap paper, and the city is slowly but inevitably growing out this way.

A reprint from an old picture in the "Official History of Japan" shows "A picnic on the Akusa hill in the flowery season;" except for the two-sworded knights, in their wide hakama (kilted trousers), it might have been photographed last April, for the same figures are there; the little girls in bright dresses running races on the grass; a party of picnic revelers seated on spread blankets, surrounded by lunch-boxes and sake-bottles; a coolie, with blue cotton head-kerchief, tied on like a nightcap, is in the act of dashing a pailful of water over a comrade, who seems to have drunk quite as much as is good for him. Ladies in neat, tight-fitting kimono and handsome sashes pace demurely by under their paper parasols, and a pair of strolling samisen-players are trying to attract the gentry, while down the path comes a paper butterfly seller, surrounded by a crowd of delighted children. The little Inari temple still stands there, and beyond the pines, on the edge of the hill, is the same beautiful view of Fuji San that charmed the visitors of Tokugawa days.

But the maples, even more than the cherry-blossoms, are Oji's glory; and mercifully the mills are below the gorge of the Takigawa, where they grow. The little river furnishes the water supply for these mills, but it is conceivable that they have been set where they are purposely, to be out of the way; for the Japanese do not yet wantonly destroy a beautiful spot. Indeed, to spoil the upper part of the Takigawa would be to ruin valuable property, for in spring and autumn and almost all the year the maple garden brings endless custom to a couple of flourishing teahouses, which own and maintain it for that very purpose.

November is the month of maples; in the old calendar, when it was the ninth month of the year, it was called Momiji-dzuki, "red-leaf month," or sometimes "time of branches"–of course, red ones. The rain of November, which comes seldom and sparingly, was called dew showers, or showers of red, because the autumn rains were supposed to dye the leaves, momiji means any kind of red leaf, whether maple or oak, or whatever; but the maple is the choicest of all the changing leaves, and so carries off the honors of the name.

Sometimes maples are planted so that the sunset light shall brighten them; but at Oji the right hour is early morning, when the sun slants through the branches and turns the leaves blood-crimson, like a hand held up to the light. Oji station is five miles out from Uyeno, on the main line north; till the mills came it was the merest village, nestled among tea plantations on the edge of the plain, but it is growing quite a suburb now. It is only a little way from the station to a gate leading into a bit of wood, through which the path winds to the edge of a narrow ravine, clothed on both sides with maples; some are large forest trees, others slender, graceful things, only ten or a dozen feet high, all apparently growing just as they please among light underwood. Across the river a grove of bamboo soars far above the other trees, the feathery tops always swaying a little, even in the still "maple weather;" a little farther up a curving bridge crosses the stream, and the fallen leaves float under it with the current, just as in a Japanese picture. That is the marvel of it all; the whole scene "composes" like a picture–no rock, no branch out of place, yet with such an innocent air of having "just growed" that you can hardly believe (though you know it perfectly well) that every twig has been trimmed, trained and brought to this easy artlessness by the most consummate art.

But that is just the theory of Japanese gardening–to render nature at her best, in some one mood appropriate to the place. The Japanese gardener loves best to choose some famous locality, and to suggest its features in his composition, tuning all to some given key, whether stern, or gentle, cheerful, pensive. One style he thinks suitable for the dwelling of a philosopher, another for the warrior, the statesman, or the man of affairs; and there are minutest rules for all this occult symbolism.

It is a very old art in Japan, this landscape gardening, and probably has borrowed very much from still older models in China and Korea. Most of its laws have come down from the cha-no-yu (tea ceremony) devotees of the period of the Ashikaga Shogunate, in the fourteenth century, and though they vary widely in detail, the ideal of all is the same. A Japanese writer on the subject says: "In laying out grounds, the general features of a view may be sublime, beautiful and tranquil, according to the style of buildings to which the garden is to be attached. The idea of a garden demands cleanliness" –by which I understand him to mean neatness, freedom from undergrowth or litter. "Pleasing verdure among the trees, fresh mosses around the fountain, should be set in such a way as to show ideal beauty. Calmness is required also, but care must be taken not to render it monotonous. Foliage should be kept green and dewy, without being too dense. A grove that casts gloominess over the surrounding scene may have its place in a certain corner of the garden, but it is not appropriate in a conspicuous spot, the chief aim of a garden being to give delight and comfort. Care is needed to avoid a crowded air in small gardens, and in large ones a scanty and insufficient look." He quotes an old authority on the art: "For a particular view from the drawing-room or library, plan a garden to suit the building, and for villas and pavilions design a garden as though the building was placed there for the sake of that particular bit of wild landscape." ("The Far East," 1897.)

In laying out such a design the first step is to place the "chief stone," or "chief tree," which is to be as it were the keynote for the composition; the next is to arrange the height of the artificial hill, if there is to be one, and the width and shape of stream or lake, and finally reach the placing of subordinate trees, stones and masses of green. "According to most authorities, it is proper to begin with the front and then work up the background, leaving the middle distance, as a painter would say, until the last. The idea of such a place is a panel picture, to be viewed from some one point. The stones are thought of as the frame on which the whole is built up, and so their placing must come before the planting of trees. "The ancients believed in having stones nine in number, four straight and five flat ones, as a charm to drive away evil spirits. However, putting aside that Buddhist superstition, this form is to be complied with; for, without these nine stones, a garden will not look formal."

A flat garden–that is to say, one in which there are no mounds–should depend rather on stones than trees, and a well and stone lantern are important features. These quaint, graceful, stone lanterns, which are such characteristic ornaments of Japanese gardens, are borrowed from the temples, where both Buddhists and Shintoists use them freely. They are hardly intended to illuminate anything, though at the temples, and even in private gardens, lights are sometimes placed in them at certain festivals. An opening like a crescent moon is a favorite device for the side, or the hole may be flower-shaped, or plain round or square. The form of the lantern varies, from the slender tope, with lotus petals around the base and upper corners curled back, to a funny, low, flat thing on four legs, rather like the hat of the "Grand Panjandrum himself, with a little round button on top." A stone basin for washing the hands is often placed in the garden; it may be elaborately carved, or merely hollowed out of a large rough boulder, propped on another stone. A dipper hangs beside to pour the water over the hands; paper to dry them everyone is expected to carry.

Private gardens, though tiny, are often beautiful specimens of the art. In a word, a landscape is thought of as a picture, and follows out all the rules of Japanese composition, which are, chiefly, simplicity and restraint, and the subordination of all the parts to a dominant idea.

The most artificial specimens are generally to be found near the smaller temples, where space is restricted and trees have been proportionately dwarfed or trimmed to fantastic shapes; and planted among bristling rocks which suggest the haunts of hermit saints, like those seated meditating beside lonely waterfalls in religious pictures of the Kano school.

One of the quaintest of these is the famous Wistaria garden at Kameido. It is in the enclosure of the temple of Tenjin, God of Writing, who in this life was Sugiwara Michizane, the faithful prime minister of the Emperor Uda. The thousandth anniversary of Michizane's death falls in 1902, and a society of the hero-deity's admirers are said to be preparing for a grand celebration, part of which will doubtless be held at Kameido. It is a queer, rambling old place, adorned with a big stone tortoise, kame (whence the name), and quaint figures of the cow on which Michizane rode during his exile in Kiushiu. Fish-ponds fill half the space, and beside and over them are bamboo trellises, on which the gardeners have trained the Wistaria vines into a roof, making all the flowers grow inside and the leaves on top. Instead of having short, full bunches, like the wild vines on the mountains, the flowers trail down a stem three to four feet long, and when the wind blows all the stems sway and tremble together like a wavering purple veil. Between the ponds little paths and bridges lead from one pavilion to another, and matted platforms are built out over the water, where people sit and admire the vines and feed rice-biscuits to the fat, lazy carp, which seem to have just enough energy to stir up the water and keep it always turbid. Of course, there are plenty of stalls all about for the sale of omiyagi souvenirs–small pottery tortoises, and monkeys and pigeons, and paper toys, and cakes, and children's hairpins, made of tiny bunches of Wistaria between dangling scraps of tinsel. The temple itself is not particularly remarkable; in front of it there is a queer round bridge, something of a feat to scramble over on wooden clogs, and they who cross it honor Tenjin–just how is not apparent, except that he is an energetic divinity, who approves of overcoming difficulties. Near by is a plum tree, grown from a slip of the one which flew over to the exiled Michizane from his garden in Kyoto.

Perhaps it is the muddy water, or the clatter and dust of many wooden shoes, and the cheap toys and tinsel; somehow, in spite of the beauty of the Wistarias, there is an air of tawdriness and artificiality about Kameido; the very flowers seem forced and unnatural, like wild birds caged. One likes better to think of the vines as they grow in the Hakone mountains or about Lake Chuzenji, where the real monkeys swing on the long cables looped from tree to tree, and the flowers cluster freely in short, sturdy bunches.

But where there is plenty of space there is seldom any distortion or unreality, as on the hillsides at Nikko, for instance, or at Count

Okuma's beautiful home, Waseda, which has wide lawns like an English country seat; or at the finest of all, Mito Yashiki, which is an ideal specimen of landscape art in Japan-or indeed anywhere.

These Yedo yashiki were very complex affairs. The space, which was several acres, was enclosed by a solid row of houses on each of the four sides, broken only by the great gate and its flanking lodges and a smaller entrance on another side for the lesser members of the establishment and visitors of low rank. These houses stood on stone-faced embankments, and were commonly built of tiles set edgewise in a bed of plaster, as I have described elsewhere; and though by no means fireproof, they were much less combustible than an ordinary Japanese house. The openings on the side toward the street were small and closed with bars. The hollow square formed by these buildings contained the residence of the Daimyo and his chief retainers, and the gardens, target range, fencing ground, and so forth, while the enclosing houses were occupied by the lesser Samurai. This was the Kamiyashiki, or castle of the prince himself, and, besides this, most Daimyo had a second or even five or six residences for his numerous retainers in Yedo.

While the greater part of these yashiki have been cut up or allowed to go to ruin, that of the Prince of Mito has happily remained untouched, at least as far as the grounds are concerned. After the Restoration the place was made over to the imperial government, and the buildings torn down to make way for the arsenal; but the park was spared and is kept in order out of sheer love of beauty and reverence for association. It is used now and then for garden parties among the military and naval set, and foreigners are admitted to see it on certain days and by special permits obtained through their respective legations, and are conducted through in state by one of the officers in charge of the arsenal.

The grounds were laid out, they say, by one of the Chinese scholars who fled to Japan after the downfall of the Ming dynasty, and were received and patronized by the Prince of Mito and others, much as the Medici entertained refugee Greeks from Constantinople not many years earlier. This was Mito Komon, grandson of Ieyasu, and ancestor of that Mito Nariaki whose clansmen killed the Regent Ii

Kamon no Kami. Komon, by the way, was that very Prince of Mito whose historical and literary studies and writings had so much to do with bringing on the agitation on behalf of the Mikado's rights, which brought about the fall of the Shogunate; and, besides refugee Chinese, he maintained a host of Japanese savants, both in Yedo and at his provincial capital at Mito, fifty miles northeast of Yedo, employing them in giving lectures and in researches for his great history, the Dai Nihon Shi. He was also one of the first to establish the clan-schools for the education of young Samurai, which sprang up during the seventeenth century in nearly every province.

There is no dwarfing at Mito Yashiki; trees centuries old grow about the slopes, and they point out one group of silvery pines, with that rough, mottled bark like a turtle's back, which Japanese artists paint so lovingly, and tell you that nothing is known of them but that they were well-grown trees when the Chinese expert planned the grounds three hundred years ago. Deep woodland paths wind over the hill, where ferns grow among the rocks as if they were far away in the Hakone mountains. Following the sound of water you come upon a little stream falling in a cascade among overhanging trees and vines and passing into a clear lake; beyond lies a lovely little meadow, bordered with iris, and in the midst of the meadow stands a great drooping cherry tree, which hangs down its branches like a weeping willow and clouds them in April with a gray-pink veil of bloom. But the charm of the garden is not intended only for the eye; to a Japanese every part of the landscape offers a picture, a suggestion, from some scene of history or romance, for each turn and rock and bridge is arranged to represent a well-known spot, as the officer who conducts visitors will explain to those who have ears to hear.

A little boat is tied at the landing by the meadow, and the tea-house on the slope stands ready for a chanoyu party, as if the Samurai and the sages had departed but yesterday. Save for a far-away beat of steam-hammers, the place is absolutely still. The uguisu warble in the thickets, the dragon-flies skim across the lake, and sparrows twitter under the eaves where the knights used to lay aside their swords to write poems and drink tea. You cannot guess how

Palace Garden, Oji

far you have wandered among the winding paths, or dream that a
hundred feet away the hill you climbed under the sighing pine trees
drops a sheer wall upon one of the busiest streets in the city. But
that is Japanese landscape gardening in its perfection.

Of course, all this handling of the ground as if it were paint and
paper, implies an unlimited amount of human labor at command.
Griffis gives an example of the way it could be done, as late as 1870,
and indeed one marvels at the transformations effected even now,
when the cost of labor has increased enormously. A friend of Mr.
Griffis, who was in the agricultural department, was looking for a
site for a model farm. One piece of property offered was part of an
ex-Daimyo's yashiki, which had been allowed to go to waste till it
was so overgrown with trees and bushes that the American refused
it, saying it would take years to bring it to a fit condition. "The

Japanese officer in charge immediately and quietly hired eight hundred laborers to clear and smooth the land. They worked in relays, night and day. In a week's time he showed the American 'a new site,' with which he was delighted. The actual energy of eight hundred pairs of arms developed a wilderness into leveled farmlands within a week." ("The Mikado's Empire.")

Of course, the advantage to the Japanese was that a comparatively useless piece of land could be sold to the government at a fancy price.

I have strayed very far from the banks of the Takino-gawa and the delighted crowd who are admiring "Tatsuta Hime's dress." Tatsuta Hime is the Goddess of Autumn, and the turning leaves are the brocade which she dyes and weaves. So a poet cries sadly:

"My wandering tread
Doth rudely tear
The carpet red
Of rich brocade
On Mimura spread."

Another, still more considerate, will admire from afar rather than mar the beauty of Tatsuta, which is here both a river and a goddess:

"Tatsuta's bravely arrayed
With autumn's brightest weaving;
If I should cross the stream,
Princess Tatsuta'll be grieving
Over her rent brocade."

At Oji, as at all such places, little platforms are dotted down here and there at the most attractive points, where picnic parties sit to drink tea–there is always an old woman on hand with a tea-kettle in Japan. Here and there a group of students or a scholarly old gentleman are adding to the supply of poems fluttering on some favorite tree, or seated apart, with chin ecstatically raised, give themselves up to the thrills of composition. There are many conventional phrases and similes which can be made use of to help out the muse on such occasions. Thus deer and maple are always paired in Japanese art and poetry, which delights in such combinations, though not more so, perhaps, than we, who systematically put bees in clover and owls in ivy-mantled towers. In autumn, they say, the stag's cry becomes mournful, and the poet proceeds to gaze at the moon and compose a thirty-one syllabled verse, such as this:

"When dead leaves fly,
The hart's sad cry
Our hearts with sorrow fills."

The tea-house at Oji is a capital place to get a Japanese meal; the food is excellent and the service good, unless they are too very full and rushed with guests. Chestnuts, boiled with sweet potatoes, mashed and sweetened, are an appropriate dish for the maple season, and pink-tipped slices of raw tai–best of Japanese fishes–and golden persimmons to follow the meal. The house stands beside the river below the gorge, and the prettiest rooms look out on the water. Not only in the fall, but in spring, too, the maples are lovely, especially those small varieties which are so much used as shrubbery in America; the blending of pinks and pale greens has an unusual charm in a country where half the trees never drop their leaves at all, but go on pushing out new buds among the old. "Frogs' hands" the Japanese call these slender leaves, the delicate texture and strong veins making them think of what to us would be a very "moist, unpleasant" association, particularly so when they go onto call a girl's pretty little hand a maple leaf! I suppose they forget the frog, or else they don't mind him. These spring maples will not do to cut; but in the fall, among the trinkets and toys which they display near the gate, there will be choice branches to sell to the visitors, and the young men in particular are sure to purvey themselves each a bough to carry over his shoulder as he returns by train or kuruma, or very possibly afoot, the five miles back to Tokyo.

Maple-viewing is a very old custom, even older, perhaps, than the cherry-cult, which is attributed to a certain Emperor of the eighth century. The following legend has a flavor of still greater antiquity, though the names and the date ascribed are of the eleventh century:

One autumn day a knight of the Taira family went out with one serving-man to view the maples on a certain mountain. As he rode up the lonely path he was surprised to see a very beautiful lady and her attendants, who had hung up a silken curtain under an especially fine tree and were preparing a picnic meal. Not wishing to disturb them, the courteous knight got down from his horse and took off his shoes (sic, doubtless the sort worn for riding), intending to pass quietly by a little footpath among the rocks. But the lady saw him, and, calling out, bade him not incommode himself to leave the road, but rather to stop a little and share their feast. Sir Taira could not well refuse so pleasing an invitation; so he seated himself under the tree and received the cup of wine which she pressed into his hands. But no sooner did he drink than both he and his servant fell into a deep sleep. Then, as he slept, an old gray-headed man appeared to him in his dreams and bade him rise up, for he was in deadly peril. So, starting suddenly awake, Sir Taira heard thunder crashing about him and saw the beautiful lady changed into a horrible demon, who glared at him with burning eyes; and her attendants were fierce little devils, dancing and breathing out smoke and fire among the rocks. Such a terrible sight, says the legend, might well have frightened an ordinary man out of his senses, but the brave Sir Taira drew his sword, and, after a tremendous fight, he killed the demons, everyone!

Japanese stories are always intended to point a moral, so I suppose clemency is the virtue taught by the story of "The Emperor and the Broken Maple Trees." The hero of it is one of those pathetic figures, so numerous in Eastern history, a child-emperor raised to the throne, to be the tool of others, and forced to resign just as he reached manhood; and this Takakura's case was made still harder by the arrogant behavior of his prime minister, the Taira chief Kiyomori–the same who slew all the Minamoto, except the lad Yoritomo and his brothers.

The Emperor Takakura, then, had two little potted maple trees of which he was particularly fond; and that they might be well cared for he put them in charge of one of his gentlemen, named Nobunari. And Nobunari guarded them as if with his life, taking them home every night, and carrying them to the palace every day. But one cold evening, while he was obliged to be absent, some of his servants came in and sat down to drink; and getting rather fuddled, they broke off the little maple trees and used them to kindle the fire by which they were warming their wine. When the master came back and looked for the precious trees, his wrath and terror were unspeakable; however, the only thing to do was to confess all, so off to the palace he went, expecting nothing less than banishment. But when the young Emperor heard the tale, he comforted Nobunari, saying kindly, "Remember what Hakuraku, the Chinese poet, did when he went to view the maples of Senyuji; even as his poem says:

"I kindled a fire of the fallen leaves
    To warm my wine.
    I cleared the stone of its mossy coat,
    And on nature's tablet my verse I wrote."

"Let thy servants go; they have but emulated the poet."

15

KARUIZAWA AND THE WEST COAST

IN the old times there were two great highways between the Kwansei and the Kwanto-the Home Provinces about Kyoto and the Eight Provinces north, of the Hakone mountains; they were the Eastern Sea Road, Tokaido, which goes southward by Yokohama, and crosses the Hakone pass, and the Central Mountain Road, Nakasendo. They started together at Sanjo bridge, in Kyoto, and ended at Nihonbashi, in Yedo it was Yedo still in those days when the Daimyo and their trains used to march up from their provinces, following the coast or keeping inland by these mountain passes. There was a third road, the Hokurokudo, which went by way of Kaga and the other west coast provinces, but it was out of the way and comparatively little used. Not always peaceful retinues came over these roads; plenty of fighting there was, little feuds and great struggles involving the whole empire, such as the battle of Sekigahara on the lower Nakasendo-counted now part of the Tokaido railroad-where Ieyasu won his decisive victory, and began the two hundred and fifty years of the Tokugawa Shogunate. Indeed, in those days there was more effort to impede travel than to promote it; at the border line, where the roads crossed from one province to another, there were barriers kept by armed guards, who let no one by without credentials, and to go from one Daimyo's country to another, and perhaps hostile one, was no easy matter.

There is no actual record of the Nakasendo until the eighth century, but there is good reason to believe that some kind of a known track must have existed hereabouts very much sooner. Certainly the account of the adventures of Prince Yamato-take, when he came through this way after his conquering expedition, though full of preternatural marvels, at least points to definite travel over the mountains at an early period.

The whole central region is full of legends of this hero prince, Achilles-like in his bravery and beauty, and the sorrow woven in his short thread of fate. He was the son of the Emperor Keiko, the twelfth in line from Jimmu Tenno, the first Emperor, and his accepted date is the beginning of the second century. In those days the tribes living in the mountains and the neighboring islands were only half in subjection to the Yamato Son of Heaven, and there were frequent revolts, which the Emperor often went out to subdue in person; so that when the prince came of age there was no lack of foes for his steel.

According to legend, Yamato-take was just sixteen at the time of his first exploit. A tribe or clan in the island of Kiushiu, the Kumaso, rose against the Emperor's authority, and the prince took a band of knights to meet them. When they reached the place, Yamato-take got into the camp disguised as a girl–according to one account he borrowed the dress from his aunt, the high priestess of Ise–and danced and sang and coquetted so well that the delighted lords fell to disputing as to which should possess the charming damsel. The chief himself settled the matter by taking her by the hand and leading her into his own tent; but like the Norse giant, who wedded Thor instead of Freya, the Kumaso lord found himself seized by wiry young arms, and the prince's sword came out from under the spangled robe. Then the Yamato knights rushed in on the drunken revelers, and utterly destroyed them.

The South being thus quieted, Prince Yamato-take went forth to conquer the Emishi, who were troubling Ise and Owari. His father gave him a spear eight fathoms long, and sent two trusty lords as guards and councilors. When he drew near the shrine of his ancestor the Sun Goddess, at Ise, he left his sword under a tree and went up to worship; and his aunt, the high priestess, who seems to have been a very useful relative, gave him the sacred sword Cloud-Compeller, which was in her care at the shrine. This sword was the one which the Sun Goddess gave to her grandson Ninigi, grandfather of Jimmu Tenno, when she sent him down to earth to make order among the warring gods and demi-gods. Amaterasu had it from her rude brother Susa-no-o, who took it from the tail of the dragon with eight heads. This dreadful beast haunted the mountains, and took a meal as he felt disposed from among the fairest daughters of the earth-gods, who seem to have been quite helpless against him.

When Susa-no-o was banished from heaven for his bad behavior to his sister Amaterasu, the Sun Goddess, in his wanderings he came upon the parents of a beautiful maiden who were in great distress because of the dragon; so Susa-no-o told them to make a heavy fence, having eight gates, and at each gate to set a tub; and he brewed sake and filled the eight tubs, and lay down to watch. By and by the dragon came and smelled the sake, and first one head drank, and then another, and when they were all eight asleep Susa-no-o sprang up and cut the heads off one by one and hacked the dragon to pieces. But when he struck the tail his sword broke, and, looking closely, he saw something shining in the tail; he drew it out, and found it to be a sword of marvelous beauty; and he took it away and gave it to his sister as a peace offering. This, with the mirror and the jewel, were the "three treasures," which Amaterasu gave to her grandson, and they are the imperial insignia of Japan. The first Emperors kept them in the palace; but fearing lest harm should come to the precious things, the tenth Emperor, Sujin, had facsimiles made and kept them in the treasury; but the real ones he sent to a temple in Yamato, and afterwards to Ise. The mirror is still at the shrine, but the sword has been removed, and is in a temple at Atsuta, near Nagoya.

Armed with the Cloud-Compeller, Prince Yamato-take went northward, and was everywhere victorious. And once, as he crossed a desolate moor, the Emishi kindled a fire in the long grass, so that the flames threatened to destroy the prince and all his company;

but he cried to Amaterasu, and cut the grass about him with the magic sword, and the wind veered suddenly and blew the flames back against the enemy. So, in gratitude, Yamato-take changed the name of the sword to Grass-Mower.

Subduing all the country around Sagami bay, they crossed the Hakone mountains and came down to the Izu peninsula and the shores of Yedo bay; and here at Uraga the distance looked so small across to Awa that the prince made some careless jest, never guessing how the squalls rise and the tide races through the narrow channel. But Kompira, the sea-god, heard and was angry, and he raised a terrible storm against the ships, so that they were almost overwhelmed.

Now the Princess Ota Tachibana, his wife, went with Yamato-take on all his expeditions and when she saw that there was no more hope, she made prayer to the sea-god and cast herself into the waves, and they were still; and the prince and his fleet crossed in safety. The next day the princess' comb was washed ashore, and the prince built a little temple to her memory at the place where it was found, before going on to finish his task. Coasting northward, he set a mirror on the prow of his ship, and the sun dazzling on it struck the Emishi with terror, so that they came down to the shore and made submission.

Many other adventures Yamato-take had; but at last he came up from the coast and crossed over where the Nakasendo goes among the passes of the mountains, and so back to his own country again. And when he came to the top of the Usui pass and looked back over the great plain, and even to Yedo bay, he cried aloud, "Azuma, Azuma wa ya!"–My wife, alas, my wife! Therefore it is that in poetry the Tokyo plain is called Azuma till this day.

But it was terribly cold in the mountains, and the mountain spirits, angry at their coming, sent out blinding mists and poisonous volcanic gas, so that the knights fainted in the path; and these evil Kami appeared to them in the shape of a white deer, wishing to lead them astray. But Yamato-take threw wild garlic in its eyes and killed it, and he and his men ate the garlic and were saved from the choking vapors; and a white dog, which was a good Kami, led them over the passes into the safe plain. But Yamato-take presently fell ill, and though he drank of the "spring of recovery" and revived a little, his sickness returned, and he could only reach the pine tree where he left his own sword, and took it again, and sent his faithful general on to tell the Emperor of all his victories. Then he sought to reach Ise, hoping to recover at the holy shrine; but he died upon the way, lying under a tree in the green spring fields.

According to tradition, the Emperor Keiko made a visit to all the regions conquered by his son, and some caves near the Nakasendo are pointed out as the place where he lodged on the way. He laid down laws for the new country and appointed governors from the princes of the blood, who already numbered seventy-seven; but it was long before the mountain parts became really civilized. Indeed, to this day the great broken table–land which fills up the centre of the main island is far more sparsely populated, as well as less developed, than any other part of the empire, except in the north. Tradition lingers long here; stories of the Tengu, goblins or kobolds who haunt the lonely places; strange half-human creatures, having beaks and birds' feathers, or else extraordinarily long noses, which are the delight of Japanese artists. They were small, and very brave and active, but on the whole not unfriendly beings. It was one of these who, according to the legend, taught the exiled boy, Yoshitsune of Minamoto, to use the sword. The two met one day on a mountain, Kurama-yama, six miles north of Kyoto, near the monastery where Yoshitsune was being brought up in seclusion from warlike studies. Finding the lad quick and fearless, the Tengu made him his pupil, meeting him in the deep forest, and teaching him not only to fence, but to leap and bound and almost fly, as the dwarfs could. Ogres, too, lived in caves among the rocks–spidery, horrible ogres, which could sprout new limbs in place of old ones. A little to one side of the Nakasendo the villagers still show the place where one lived as late as the eleventh century, and stole a maiden every year at the annual festival. At last the elders decreed that every man who came to the feast should have a mark set on his forehead, and no one not marked should be allowed to go away; so they did it, and one stranger was found unmarked–an ugly fellow, very big and tall.

So they promptly cut off his head, and at once the body became so heavy that they could not possibly move it, and had to bury it where it lay, raising a great mound. The most amusing point in the story is that a visit to the grave is considered very good for headache.

The Nakasendo is often called the Kiso-kaido, because from Gifu onward it follows the valley of the picturesque Kisogawa, one of the "three great rivers" of Japan. The other two are the Tonegawa and the Shinanogawa, and all three rise within fifty miles of each other, in the central mass of mountains, the Tonegawa coming down across the plain of Tokyo, and emptying by one arm into the bay of Yedo, and by another into the Pacific, further north; and the Shinano flowing almost due north into the Sea of Japan. The Kisogawa rises on the eastern slopes of Ontake, an extinct volcano, only less high than Fuji San, and considered almost as sacred; from there it makes its way through the mountains, and at last out and across the plain into Owari bay, in all a distance of one hundred and sixty-three miles. It is a wild little river, always liable to rise in floods and ruin miles of the beautiful Owari plain. In feudal times the whole region along its upper course was covered with forests, which belonged to the Daimyo of Owari, and were most carefully preserved; but now that the land has passed into private ownership, the peasants cut as they please, with little thought of the future, and the only tract that is properly cared for is a forest belonging to the government.

The Torii Toge (pass) is so named from the torii, which stands at its highest point, put there in honor of the god of Ontake. Here is the water-shed between the two river systems, the Kisogawa flowing down to the east and south, and the Shinano and its many tributaries rising among the slopes on the other side.

There is one other important pass on the road besides the Usui Toge, namely, the Wada pass, and it is the longest and highest–over five thousand feet. The Nakasendo is kept in good order most of the year, and a jinrikisha trip over it can be made in five days from Gifu to Karuizawa without any serious difficulty. It would seem more natural to take the road the other way–down instead of up–but it is much easier to get good jinrikisha men at Gifu; at the other end one could only take one's chance of catching men who had just brought up a party, and might or might not be fresh enough to run well the other way. The ascent is so great that at least two men apiece are necessary, and even so it is needful to walk up some of the hills, or else hire extra men. The views all the way are charming, and the peasants are simple and unspoiled by modern civilization. The inns are very fair, and some European food can be had at most of them.

The Daimyo of the west coast provinces used to come up from their side to meet the Nakasendo at the top of the Usui pass, and in those days there was quite a town at the summit, and several highly aristocratic inns for the accommodation of their lordships and their lordships' men. But in 1868 the Shogunate was done away, and with it compulsory residence in Yedo; and their lordships departed to their provinces and came no more journeying to Karuizawa. They arrived with such volcanic suddenness, these changes from old to new Japan, and they were so sweeping, so utterly disorganizing to half the conditions of life! Surely the national centre of gravity must be marvelously hung to have kept the whole structure from tipping over in hopeless ruin.

So it was that when the railroad came through in the early nineties, via Takasaki, over the pass and down to Naoetsu and Niigata, on the Japan Sea, it found only a miserable tumble-down village, instead of a fine post-town. However, even before the railroad got all the way, certain foreigners had discovered the place and its possibilities, and were taking possession.

"And thick and fast they came at last, and more, and more, and more."

The Canadian missionaries began it; H. B. M's legation followed and built itself a house, the mountain retreat of which Mrs. Hugh Fraser writes so delightfully; "foreign residents" came likewise, and took to themselves lands in the name of their cooks and houseboys–this was in the days of Extra-Territoriality and passports; tiny

Japanese houses were rented and built for renting; and the prongs of alien rocking-chairs played havoc with the fragile shoji.

When the Presbyterian Convention settled here, and an annual General Conference of Missionaries, Karuizawa's future was made. The butcher and the baker and the laundryman have brought their English signs to hang in the village street, the foreign hotel is distinctly good, and Kameya–Kameya, the enterprising, the invaluable–opens a branch grocery for the summer.

It takes a large piece of the day to come up from Tokyo, changing cars at Takasaki and climbing through twenty-seven reeking tunnels, and along the edges of ravines, and among rocks and precipices, all tumbled, jagged and stood on end. From this tormented wilderness the train sweeps out at last into a grassy moor, edged with hills, starred with lilies and orchids and all the mountain field-flowers of Japan, and drops you at a station perhaps half a mile from the summer town, where the strong, keen air sets the blood hurrying.

Now, it is not well to suggest to Karuizawa people that there may be more beautiful spots in the empire; still, Mr. Chamberlain is more truthful than polite when he calls it "a dowdy village," and adds remarks about the back woods. There really are no "attractions," except the many walks, which are pretty, if not deeply interesting; and there are several excursions, which make pleasant diversions in a Karuizawa summer, besides the one great trip to Mount Asama. But about the air there are no two opinions; whatever is the reason, it is drier, cooler, more bracing than even at Ikao–than anywhere in Japan, short of the Hokkaido and its cool northern summers. The village lies seven hundred and eighty feet below the summit of the pass, which leaves it still thirty-two hundred and seventy feet above the sea, lying against low hills, which thrust out their spurs into the plain. It is not really a plain, though, but a wide, high valley–almost a plateau–and the very dividing ridge between the two sides of the island. The sea-winds seem to drop most of their moisture before they get so high, and, though the mists roll up over the hills behind, making Scotch people talk about the Highlands, there is less rainfall than anywhere else, except in the northern island. The soil is light, even for dry-soiled Japan; for Asama rises across the valley five miles away, and Asama burst out into a great eruption a century or two ago and spread a layer of ashes four feet deep over miles of rice-fields and unsuspecting villages; and the streams were dried up, and the fields became a barren moor, overgrown with knot-grass.

Since then Asama only puffs and mutters, or sends out an occasional little sprinkle of ashes, and the climbers–they come by scores all summer–can scramble up the last steep cone to the very edge of the crater. There are no awful fires to behold, only ashes and blocks of lava, and sudden clefts split down to unknown depths, and at all times an abundance of blinding, choking, sulphurous smoke.

There are two or three ways of going up Asama, all taking a good long day for the trip; but though the path is steep in places, it is a good cinder-track most of the way, and there are no special difficulties. The total height is eighty-two hundred and eighty feet, making it about five thousand feet above Karuizawa.

The prettiest way is by Oiwake and a fine little waterfall, but the easiest and most usual is by the bump on the side of the mountain called Ko-Asama. You ride across the moor and up the slope to Ko-Asama, and climb from there in about three hours to the crater.

From the path, as well as the top, the view is superb, if you are lucky enough to get it; there are all the ranges, north, south, east and west, the sea far away to the east, and to the south even the cone of Fuji San. There are those who think it well worth while to come to Karuizawa just to climb Asama and see that view.

Of course, the railroad did not come up this way for the sake of scenery, but because it was the least difficult crossing over the mountains to the west coast; but, nevertheless, it is perhaps the most picturesque line in all Japan, even the Tokaido not excepted. At first, after crossing the Usui Toge to Karuizawa, the road sweeps across the nearly level moor to the shoulder of Asama; then it follows a tributary of the Shinanogawa among deep ravines, scooped by torrents out of the reddish, gravelly soil; far below there are glimpses of the sunny rice-fields, and behind, the sides of Asama no longer slope smoothly down, but are scarred with clefts and ridges of dark lava. Of the places on the way, Komoro, Takata, Uyeda and Matsumoto were all castle-towns in the feudal days, and at Komoro and Nagano there are two very famous monasteries. That at Nagano is one of the oldest in Japan, having been founded in 670; of course, there are no buildings standing that are anything like so old–the wooden architecture of Japan is always short-lived but it contains a very sacred image of Amida, with two companions, said to have been carved by Shaka (Gautama Buddha) himself, and brought to Japan in the very earliest period of Buddhism there. Matsumoto is not on the railroad itself, but is reached by kuruma, over a fine pass, some thirty miles in all from Uyeda. Walkers go to Matsumoto, making it a centre for expeditions among the mountains; but there is little or no European accommodation to be had at the inns. The one remaining watch-tower of Uyeda castle stands up sharply from the river as you leave the town.

Nagano is the present capital of the prefecture of Nagano, created after the Restoration from the province of Etchigo; it is unlike many others of these new divisions, in that it has followed the lines of the old Daimiate, instead of taking fragments of several.

The Daimyo of this region were all closely attached to the Tokugawa, and suffered in consequence on the downfall of the Shogunate. But between the monastery and the pilgrims, and the new government buildings and the numerous officials in residence, Nagano has a very flourishing air, and does a great deal of business with the country around. The mountains almost lock it in, and the railroad passes, as it were, through a gate in the hills to reach the valley of the Sekigawa and follow it down to Naoetsu.

Here there is a fairly good port, where the steamers call which connect the west coast towns; but the place is absolutely uninteresting; and so, too, is Niigata, to which the railroad runs on, by way of eighty miles of coast. Niigata was one of the five ports which were opened to foreigners by treaty; but it has been of very little value to anybody, for it is not really a harbor at all, but only an open roadstead, exposed to the north and west winds. The Shinanogawa flows into the sea beside it, and, spreading out among the dunes, drops a mass of sand from the mountains, bringing down a fresh deposit with every storm; so that it is hopeless to cut through the bar across the harbor, which only allows small boats to enter. The tree-planted walks along the dunes and a certain stiff cleanliness about the little town, made Rein compare it with a Dutch village.

This entire coast is as different as possible from the picturesque cliffs and coves of the southeast; for miles it is a flat line of shale and red sand, on which the sea breaks heavily, so that for half the year boats cannot land, except in a very few places. The warm Black Current, too, only sends up this side a small branch, which slides off around western Kiushiu, and stands out from the shore line almost up to the west coast of Yedo. Add to this the sweep of the bitter northwest winds in winter, and the near mountain ranges which keep off the summer south winds, and Niigata has as unlucky a climate as could well be imagined–cold and snow–blocked all winter and intensely hot in summer. At present, its chief importance, as well as Naoetsu's, is due to the kerosene oil which is found in the mountains, and is more and more carefully worked every year. Modern machinery for the oil-wells has been put up in some places, but at many others the digging and pumping are all done by hand. Not only is it far easier to get common laborers than men with skill enough to run the complex imported machinery, but with interest high and labor still comparatively low, few Japanese are ready to make the outlay of capital necessary for an oil-plant of American pattern.

As a rule, this native oil is much less carefully refined and sells much more cheaply than the imported article, but holds its own for those who cannot afford better; the Russian oil is next best, and the American best of all, and also a little more costly than its Russian rival. There are oil-wells recently opened in the island of Yezo, too, and doubtless in time the Japanese product will supply the home market entirely.

In connection with the American oil, an odd side-industry has grown up in some places like Tokyo, where it is largely used. The oil comes in square, five-gallon tins, which, in America, would find their way in due time into the ash-barrel. But tin is scarce in Japan, and labor plenty; the frugal Japanese collects the cans carefully, rolls out the sides, re-burnishes and works them over into shiny pans and basins, and such like, which are eagerly bought by the poorer classes as a cheap, though flimsy substitute, for their native, well-wrought brass.

Along with the disagreeable climate, these western provinces have much mineral wealth, and also great stretches of well-watered lowland, producing a valuable rice crop; the fisheries are renowned, in spite of the stormy winter; while in the mountains the peasants raise silkworms, tea, paper trees, and a good deal of lacquer. From the fifteenth century on, the Daimyo of the west coast were among the most powerful in the empire; under the Tokugawa Shogunate there were seven provinces counted: namely, Kaga, famous for Kutani porcelain and fine bronzes; Noto, the peninsula of Percival Lowell's pilgrimage–a place of rice-fields and fish; Sado, a large island, which had valuable gold mines, now almost worked out–it was to Sado that Nichiren was banished for his over-zealous preaching; Dewa, most northern of the seven; and Koshi, or Etchi, which was divided into Lower, Middle and Farther Etchi, or Etchigo, Etchiu and Etchizen. Of all these, Mayeda, lord of Kaga, was the wealthiest peer in the realm, having an income of over a million koku of rice; only the Tokugawa of Owari and Wakayama approached him, with six hundred thousand and five hundred and fifty thousand koku respectively. The Matsudaira of Etchizen followed hard after these great lords; this was the family from which Tokugawa Ieyasu sprang, and thirty-two Daimyo bore the name in smaller provinces all over the country. The capital of Kaga–Kanazawa–is still one of the most important cities in Japan; it is the capital of the new prefecture, which takes in Noto as well as Kaga, and has a garrison of soldiers stationed in it. Quantities of Kutani ware go from the potteries all over the world–the fine, thin Kutani porcelain, decorated in red oxide of iron and gold, which has kept its old standards so much better than most Japanese china made for the foreign market. Griffis has made Etchizen famous among English-speaking people by his pleasant account of his service as professor in the castle-town of Fukui during the last days of the old regime; and by his sympathetic account of Lord Matsudaira's resignation of the Damiate when the changes came, and the ceremony of dismissing the retainers. We, who only know modern Japan, with its wider patriotism of the whole nation instead of the province, can but dimly guess what the breaking of those hereditary ties meant. "Even the sparrows in the bushes," said the old proverb, "chirp the word 'loyalty'–chiu, chiu!"

16

IKAO

"With time and patience the mulberry leaf becomes silk."
–Japanese Proverb.

KARUIZAWA, as a summer resort, would never attract the Japanese, for it has not a single boiling spring. That is their first demand–hot water–whether for a sanitarium or a pleasure resort to stay in; and almost everywhere in the empire nature has provided it for their enjoyment. From Yezo to Kiushiu there are hundreds of springs sending up water at a temperature of eighty to a hundred degrees Fahrenheit, which the people of this land consider very delight- ful for bathing in; these springs are, most of them, very slightly impregnated with sulphur, and have also a small amount of iron, not enough to make them very different from ordinary hot water. The more sulphurous ones often come out of the ground hot to the boiling point; and the number of places called Yumoto, hot water source, is only equaled by the Springvilles of America.

Among them all, Ikao has long been a favorite. The place is pretty enough to be worthy of its musical reason for existence being the water breaking in half a dozen places from the hillside, scalding hot, slightly gaseous, and heavily charged with salts of iron. It is crys- tal clear as it reaches the air, but the moment the gas escapes it drops a rusty deposit on the stones and the river-bed and all it touches; the bathing tanks are turbid with a yellow cloud, and pieces of cloth, set to steep in the stream, take a bright rusty orange color; so dyed they are worn round the body and thought to be highly strengthening, the iron being supposed to be somehow absorbed. Bathers come from far and near to be cured of rheumatism and skin diseases, both a great deal too common in Japan; and pilgrims come, too, for the Kwannon temple below, at Mizusawa, is one of the "Thirty-three Holy Places." And well people come, both Europeans and Japanese, for the beauty of the place and to escape from heat and mosquitoes. There is a good foreign hotel, and a number of cottages to let, besides Japanese hotels and boardinghouses of every grade, for the pilgrims and bathers.

Now, why is it that Japanese bathing arrangements excite foreigners more than anything else in the national life? It is unique, certainly, this passion for hot water among high and low; some find it a virtue, and commend a race which owns no great unwashed; others point to the gregarious tub and declare succinctly, "The Japanese are not an immoral people; they simply have no morals." And the successive system distresses them, too; that which makes guests at an inn "first come first served" at the same tubful, and dips a household with feudal decorum, from the Danna San to the kitchen maid. "Disgusting custom!" Verily disgusting, indeed, if one "used Pears' soap," in European fashion, in the tub itself-which is something a Japanese never dreams of. What he does is to scrub thoroughly on the slatted floor of the bathroom, where basin and pails are provided for that purpose, and where he will dash himself plentifully with fresh cold water on getting out of the tub. Only when thus perfectly clean, and rinsed from every particle of soap, he enters the big wooden tub, and sits soaking blissfully up to his neck in water heated to steaming by a charcoal stove partitioned off at one end-just such an arrangement as the immortal Orthodocia dealt with. Mr. Kipling's experiences were less thrilling than hers; he was not parboiled, but he complains pathetically of sliding paper screens as scant protection for an Englishman "clad in his virtue and his spectacles." There is no denying that it is very trying and improper-especially for an Englishman. Hear what Dr. Rein says-Rein the statistical, the coldly accurate. In the days when both sexes bathed together, he declares, "they indulged in nothing unseemly, even according to our ideas." Contact with Europeans put an end to this paradisaical simplicity, which he holds "by no means a sign of moral corruption, or even of want of decency." "Bashfulness is undoubtedly a product of social life and civilization, as was pointed out long ago by Rousseau. *It is no criterion of morality*, appears in different forms, and varies with the education of mankind *and the climate in which they have to live.*" "Italics mine," as Mr. Ruskin says. Well, be content; the roadside tub is banished nowadays from all but the remotest villages, and certain conventional separations and restrictions are enforced by a paternal government, feverishly anxious to offend no proprieties of the Western world; and therewith the people continue–just as calmly and truly modest as they ever were. Except near the Treaty Ports; there the worst influences of all civilizations have done what they always do. But, once again, let us not judge Japan by the open ports, till we are ready to have others judge America by Chinatown.

Of course, all this tubbing is in hot baths; nobody in Japan uses cold water for pleasure, except for the final splash after a good boiling. And, by the way, it must be remembered that very hot water acts quite differently from warm or even moderately hot; where warm water relaxes, the stinging heat braces and stimulates the skin, else the Japanese race had long ago perished by reason of the national habit of running out, all glowing, into a wintry air of perhaps forty degrees Fahrenheit–very likely barefoot, except for straw sandals. Mr. Chamberlain insists that even Englishmen find the hot baths somehow suited to the climate, and it is a fact that those who have lived longest in Japan, and most happily and healthily, are just the ones who have adopted this with other Japanese customs.

But cold bathing is occasionally practiced, after all, not as pleasure, but for purification–religious, of course–or as a penance, and sometimes a very severe one. For instance, in the story of the Cat of Nabeshima, related by Mitford in his "Tales of Old Japan," a priest, looking out one night, sees a young Samurai bathing in the icy tank in the garden; when he has finished and taken his garments again, he bows before the shrine and makes prayer for the recovery of his lord. With the help of the priest, the young man afterwards succeeds in baffling the wicked enchantress cat, and finding herself discovered, she changes from a lovely lady into her true shape, and bounds over the roofs and disappears, whereupon Lord Nabeshima recovers from his sickness. Washing the hands at the well in the temple court is a usual practice before approaching to worship. The primitive Shinto nature-worship is especially fun of rites and formulas of purification from ceremonial uncleanness. It is carried even to a special cult; up in the mountains, in the most solitary places, live hermits who are seeking after perfect purity; eating only herbs, drinking only water, and bathing–it makes one shiver to think of!– bathing night and day, winter and summer, in the mountain streams and icy waterfalls. Sometimes they stand for hours under the dash of the fall, or up to their necks in a pool; on the coast, such rites are sometimes performed in the sea. If the Gyoja–the mountain hermits–die under such trials, there is reward for faithfulness in an after life; if they survive and continue, wonderful powers come to them–power to perform marvelous feats, to see and hear things hidden from grosser eyes. Such are the exercises and manifestations of the exorcists on Mount Ontake, near the Torii pass, which Percival Lowell has studied and written about so fully.

The Buddhist hermits generally lead a less severe life, devoting themselves instead to reciting the proper prayers to Kwannon or Amida. There is a pious legend of one of these, who lived in the mountains near Lake Biwa, praying and giving counsel to the villagers who came to him in his retreat. They brought him food and cared for his few wants, as pious folk will in the East; but one winter there came a terrible snowstorm, which blocked the path, so that for days they could not climb the mountain. The holy man was all but starved, and had given himself up for lost, when he found at his door a stray deer, which had come to his hut seeking shelter and had fallen there frozen. Here was food; but even though he did not have to take its life, the priest hesitated to break the rule and eat flesh, which was forbidden even to the laity. Yet he bethought him of his people; for if he died, who would say prayers for them and give them spiritual aid? So, at last, with many misgivings, he cut off a piece of the flesh and cooked it and ate a little, leaving the rest in the pot. When the storm was over, the villagers hurried to see what had become of their priest, and, to their great joy, found him safe and lustily chanting the daily office. He told his tale, and looking in the pot they found-not a piece of meat, but a bit of gilded wood. Here was a miracle; and, going to the nearest Kwannon temple, they found a piece had been cut from the side of the image. When the bit of wood was laid on the place, it exactly fitted, and at once grew fast without leaving any mark. So then they knew for a surety that the Merciful Kwannon had given of herself to save the life of her servant.

Such deeds as the Gyoja practice daily, penitents undertake for a certain time, as an expiation, or to fulfill some particular vow; pilgrims, too, bathe long and often at this or that sacred lake or stream; or, unwillingly enough, some poor demented creature is held shivering and struggling under a waterfall, that he or she may be set free from "Fox possession." Various kinds of dementia or epilepsy are accounted for in both Japan and China by a fox being supposed to have entered the victim's body, and it is thought that, if the residence is made very uncomfortable, the undesired tenant will leave. So the possessed one is subjected to all kinds of exorcisms and penances, this ordeal of waterfalls being thought especially effi-cacious-and it might really be, perhaps, if the case is a hysterical one. It is something of this sort that the skeptical villager tries, in Mitford's amusing story of the man who makes a bet that he will cross a certain lonely moor by night, without being deceived by the foxes who haunt it; and so, meeting a girl on the way, who seems to be the daughter of his friend, he decides at once that she is a fox in disguise, goes to the house and tells her parents, and undertakes to make the creature show its true form, which he does so vigorously that the girl dies in his hands. The infuriated parents only consent to spare his life if he will at once become a priest; so his head is shaved on the spot, and, as the last lock falls, there is a shout of mocking laughter, house and parents vanish, and the unbeliever finds himself alone on the moor, with his head shaved as bald as an egg.

Sometimes the fox disguises himself as a human being and lives with his victim, instead of entering his body. An Emperor once shot at a fox, which lay under a chrysanthemum bush in his garden; it was wounded and ran away, and afterwards one of the ladies of the court was found to have a wound in her forehead, just where the Emperor's arrow struck the fox. Thus detected, the evil thing was promptly disposed of.

Naturally the wise modern doctors do not countenance this sort of water-cure for epilepsy, and modern law has not a little to say on the subject; but the new rules do not greatly trouble the remote mountain villages, and the new science affects them still less. However, the modern schools have come now, and, with the young generation, Brer Fox's days are surely numbered.

Ikao's little town seems pinned, like a swallow's nest, against the green mountain; its main street climbs so steeply that it has to make steps to get up, and the houses straggle after like a flock of goats. Little side streets wander out right and left, in an irresponsible sort of fashion, all given over in some way or other to the housing and amusing of visitors.

As for the bath-houses, they advertise themselves by perpetual clouds of steam, like so many huge wash-boilers. The story goes that doctors are wont to lodge certain indolent patients well down the slope, and send them up the long steps for a morning and evening drink–a kind of unofficial "Terrein Kur," for people who will not exercise unless they are made to.

There is a great deal of exercise involved in merely getting to Ikao at all. The railroad sends out a branch from Omiya on the main line to Takasaki and Maebashi, and thence you proceed by kuruma, or by an execrable tram; or, if the road is in condition, by kuruma, via Mizusawa and the Kwannon temple aforesaid. Either way is warranted to provide a liberal jolting; but I hear the road has been improved, exceedingly pretty, through more steep, up and up into and at least the ride is green valleys, more and the towering hills.

The Kwannon temple at Mizusawa is one of a second set of "Thirty-three Holy Places," provided for the needs of the more out-

Street of Ikao

of-the-way provinces. The original ones are all in the region round
Nara and Kyoto, and the knowledge of them was first revealed to an
abbot of the devout eighth century. The abbot, who seems to have
been a most saintly man, fell suddenly ill and apparently died; but
his body did not become cold, and his disciples therefore waited to
bury him, hoping he might return to life. And, indeed, after three
days, he suddenly woke, as if from sleep, and told them he had been
to the under world. Two attendants led him before the judge of the
dead, Emma-O, who received him most graciously, and explained
that he had been sent for to deliver a message to men. This was
that the Merciful Kwannon, full of pity, had taken thirty-three spots
under her special care, so that, if any man made pilgrimage to one
of these, no matter what his sins, he should be saved; for such a
pilgrim would radiate light from his feet, and would have strength
to crush to fragments all the one hundred and thirty-six hells which

were waiting for him. This remedy Kwannon had provided; but, for lack of knowing it, men went on "falling into hell as plentifully as the raindrops fall in a summer shower." Emma-O then told the abbot where these places were, and bade him return and tell the good news; but the careful saint asked for a sign, lest men should not believe. "Thereupon Emma-O gave him his own jeweled seal, and he was led back by the same two attendants into the sinful world." (Chamberlain.)

The good abbot and his disciples at once made the first pilgrimage, taking all the holy places in the order laid down; but perhaps mankind were still too skeptical, for these particular pilgrimages did not become popular for a couple of centuries. Then the Emperor Kwazan, who was one of the rois faineants under the tutelage of the Fujiwara prime ministers, lost his young wife; and being but a boy, and deeply in love, he fell into despair and left the throne to become a monk, spending his life in pilgrimage to the Thirty-three Holy Places of Kwannon. From this time they were known and honored. The temple at Miidera on Lake Biwa is one of the series, and another is Kiyomidzudera, in Kyoto itself. The new series was added later, when the more northern provinces became populous, and naturally is less celebrated, but the temples are believed to have no less efficacy than the original ones.

All about Ikao the views are wonderful, even for Japan, taking in wide valleys and distant peaks, and near crumpled hills with deep gorges between, furrowing down the slopes of Haruna, each gorge adding its torrent to the Azumagawa and Tonegawa, which meet below and, passing south between Haruna and Akagi San, merge their valleys in the Tokyo plain. And beyond Akagi, peak behind peak, is the Nikko range, Shirane and Nantai San, and a sickle-like curve of mountains sweeping round to the north and west. Part of the town lies along one of these deep ravines, down which the stream rushes from Yumoto–that is to say, hot water source–where are seats for the water drinkers, and shade, and glimpses of the valley and the far hills.

The walks naturally are all up hill and down, and the excursions are either tramps or chair rides, or both impartially combined.

Kompira San is a very little ascent and a very fine view. Mount Soma and the "Haruna Fuji" are both pretty stiff climbing, but on Soma you get more than two thousand feet above Ikao-nearly five thousand feet from sea level-see Asama to the west, and the real Fuji far to the south, and overlook provinces and rivers and towns and more mountains than one can count.

Then there is Haruna Lake. Mount Haruna, of course, was once a volcano-every great mountain in Japan either is or has been or means to be-and what was once the crater is now a lake, with a good tea-house on its banks, where you may admire the prospect and dine on the salmon and other fish with which it has been recently stocked. Indeed, to admire seems quite necessary. Haruna lake has a guardian dragon, a "laidly worme," of a most jealous disposition; and he has a rival in the lake over on Akagi San, with whom he will brook no invidious comparisons. So if any mortal standing by Haruna lake should be so rash as to speak in praise of Akagi Water, saying that it is larger or more beautiful, let not that one think to reach home unscathed; either he will lose his way on the moors, or a terrible storm will overtake him.

The Haruna god seems to have a special influence in bringing down storms. When the early rains are delayed much after the middle of June, the farmers are in great trouble over the young rice; and if the drought lasts long, they gather from neighboring villages and pray for rain. Then a number of bands, made up from the several villages, set off for Mount Haruna to fetch some of the water of the lake. The water must be carried very swiftly, else the sky-water will come down to join the lake water in the wrong place; so the several groups station themselves at different points to receive and carry it on. The first band goes all the way to the top, and gathers the water in large bamboo stalks, which are closed up at the end to make light, strong vessels; running all the way, they reach the foot of the mountains and hand over the tubes to the next band, and so the water is carried forty or fifty miles in a day. They carry it to a proper temple and make prayer there, and afterwards one of the bamboo holders goes to each village, and the peasants carry them through the fields night and day, singing and shouting and beating drums. The whole affair is apt to end with a grand drinking and merry-making at the expense of the villages.

Tenjin pass goes westward from Haruna over the edge of the crater a little way above the lake, and wanders up the Azuma valley into a mountain trap, from which it struggles out somewhere in Echigo province; it is one of the old highways, but has never compared in importance with the Usui Toge, which lies to the south of Haruna. Following the path down the other side of the ridge from the crater, you reach an old, old Shinto temple in a grove of cryptomeria trees, set among vast rocks that are torn, flung, piled one on the other, as if all the mountain goblins had been at play, or as if the Earth God and the Fire God to whom the temple is dedicated had chosen the glen for a last desperate battle; while the carved dragons on the porch might have kept watch between, twisting and curling in evil delight of the fray. Though Shinto in origin, the place used to belong to the wild Yamabushi, or mountain priests, who were Buddhist in profession, but for two or three centuries it has been in quieter hands. The priests' families live in the village below, for this temple has always kept a traditional right of marriage for its servants.

This central mountain region is a great silk-growing district; the three provinces of Nagano, Gumma and Fukushima raise two-fifths of all the cocoons produced in the empire. In many villages the large, well-built houses show how profitable the industry has been to these high places, some of which could hardly raise a koku of rice on the hilly fields. Indeed, the peasants of the highlands learn to look upon rice as a luxury, to be reserved for the sick and weakly, and depend for food on their barley and millet; but where the white mulberry appears, there the people are flourishing and well to do. Part at least of this prosperity is due to the Shogun Tokugawa Yoshimune, who, early in the eighteenth century, extended and improved seri-culture in the midland provinces.

Through this part of the country almost every house in the little villages has a separate room, or sometimes a whole second story built for the worms, which will not flourish unless they have a clean, airy place, sufficiently warm, but sheltered from the direct rays of the sun. The room is filled with slatted shelves or racks, piled from floor to ceiling, and on the shelves stand shallow trays of mulberry leaves, where the host of pale green or whitey-brown creatures squirm and eat, eat, eat all day and all night. If you put your ear down you can hear them eating, with a faint, crisp rustle which is most uncanny. At first, when they are very small–from the hatching till the second or third casting of the skin–the leaves must be cut up for them; and at times some one has to watch all night. Well conducted human babies are really twice as hardy as these pampered specialists. The beds must be cleaned daily, except when the worms are casting their skins, which they do four times, at intervals of six and eight days. To get them transferred, the usual way is to spread a hemp net over the tray, and cover it with fresh leaves; the worms crawl onto it, and are then lifted to a fresh tray. Most of the time they are fed four times a day; between the last change of skin and the moment of beginning to spin they eat three-fourths of all the food they take in their entire existence.

When they show by their appearance and movements that the time for spinning has arrived, the caretakers lay twigs of rape or small faggots of brush across the trays, and the caterpillars climb up and hang themselves comfortably. When the cocoons are finished– which takes several days–the best of them are picked out for breeding, and the rest killed, either by exposure to hot sun, or in an oven or by steam. The eggs are very thin and easily broken, and to keep them from injury a stiff card is provided for the moth, on which they stick and can be safely handled. The best kinds are raised in the mountains, and most of the egg cards come from a few special districts. They must be carefully kept in a dry, cool place, and protected from mice.

Early in May, as soon as the young leaves begin to put out, the egg cards are brought from the storehouse and set in a warm room, or in a shady place out of doors, and the "haru-ko"–spring children–coaxed to come out and begin their career. In the lower parts of the silk districts the mulberry trees are carefully planted in rows three feet apart, and kept trimmed back to low bushes; at a little distance they look rather like one, of the low vineyards of Italy. Higher on the hills they are allowed to grow taller, perhaps four to six feet, and are still well cared for in a good deep soil, and carefully headed up; on the slopes of some valleys they are permitted to grow into trees, and in such places the leaves are less fine and thickly set, and the trees are said to last only forty out of a possible sixty years.

Besides the ordinary silkworm moth, of which there are many varieties more or less alike, there is another of a different species which is used to some extent; this is called the yama-mae, literally wild (or mountain) cocoon. The moth and worm are larger and the silk coarser. These feed on the chestnut oak, and are raised out of doors, on plantations of low trees set out for the purpose; scarecrows and boys with clappers and various other devices are used to protect the worms from birds and other enemies. But they are restless feeders, and difficult to keep together, instead of liking to herd, as the true silkworms do; and the silk is more difficult to reel off the cocoon. Though a good deal of it is raised in certain places, this yama-mae silk is seldom made up alone, but is used for weaving into certain kinds of loose crape manufactured for special purposes.

Women do most of the work of caring for the silkworms; little girls who seem hardly more than babies know how to pick the wriggling things up without hurting them, and tell by the size, color and transparency how old they are and how soon they will begin to spin, and many other mysteries hidden from the unskilled. But it is Oba San (grandmother) who understands all and directs all–bow-backed, cheery-faced Oba San, with her bright eyes and skin like wrinkled leather, who remembers days long before the Black Ships came to Japan, and has grandchildren working in the new water-power filature under the hill. She and Oji San cannot do with these newfangled ways, so when the cocoons are spun she and he will get out the old hand-reels and sit on the cottage floor winding off the skeins with marvelous deftness. Indeed, in many cottages the old hand-looms are still in use, and the old weaves are kept up–those distinctive local weaves by which you could tell the fabric of one province from another. Often still the tree is grown, the worms raised, the thread spun and woven and dyed at the same little mountain cottage.

The first filature in the country was one started at Tomioka near Takasaki in 1869, by a Frenchman, who was engaged by the government for the purpose. Now this filature is one of the largest in the empire, and there are many more, besides the large spinning and weaving factories that have sprung up in Osaka, always commercial and industrial, and in Tokyo and Kyoto, and the very many small establishments scattered through the silk-growing provinces.

The Hon. Robert P. Porter, United States Tariff Commissioner, puts the situation in a nutshell: "The Japanese simply throws away the old device when he can get the new; like all good workmen, however, he does not stand idly by waiting for better implements; he pounds away at his rice, and runs off beautiful silken threads from the ancient spinning-wheel, wholly oblivious of the hum and rattle of modern machinery in the surrounding factories. He cannot afford to stop, but he is none the less awaiting his turn to secure the newer machines." Spinning machinery to the value of over two hundred thousand pounds was imported from England in 1898-not all, of course, intended for silk; the weaving of cotton increases yearly, and of linen likewise. It is a curious fact that nearly all of the best Japanese embroidery is done by men; but of nine hundred and fifty thousand persons engaged in weaving in 1894, nearly nine hundred thousand were women and girls.

Rein explains in detail the various kinds of thread spun, which, of course, are essentially the same as in other countries–the floss silk worked up from waste, and from the outer portion of the cocoons, and the reeled silk which is wound off from the cocoons and spun into threads for the loom. From three to fifteen threads of reeled silk, representing as many cocoons, are spun into these threads for warp and woof, according to the weight of fabric desired. The secret of making chirimen or crape is that the woof threads are very tightly twisted, half to the right and half to the left; the two kinds are woven in alternately, and when the web is dipped this reverse twisting makes the crinkle. The twisting is done on a special wheel, the large hand wheel one sees in so many cottages, o-guruma, the great wheel, they call it. The dipping is really a boiling which goes on for several hours, in water mixed with ashes made from straw, and often slightly colored with a little indigo. Then the fabric is washed out, stretched, and rolled on a wooden cylinder to dry. The crinkling shrinks it to about three-fourths of its original width, but in length it alters much less. Silk waste, ma-watta, looks very like what we call cotton wadding, and they use it to line the nicer dresses for winter; it is delightfully warm, and light as down almost. The bottom of a lady's dress is padded out into a stylish roll, and both men's and women's winter garments are often lined with ma-watta. The bits of flock working through to the outside are cherished, because they show the nice quality of the lining–a cotton wadding does not come through.

The government makes wisely paternal efforts to improve the methods of raising the silkworms, the quality and quantity of the silk, the reeling and manufacture. Soon after the country was opened to foreign trade, the silkworm disease in France and Italy gave a great impetus to the export of Japanese egg cards, and they are also shipped over the empire from the best breeding places in large numbers. At certain seasons of the year the railroads all but refuse to handle ordinary freight, they are so taken up with moving eggs and young worms. A strange contrast all this to the anxious days at the time of the opening of the country, when Japanese statesmen tried to prevent the export of silk, fearing lest the supply should be too small, and prices should rise and drive it out of the home markets.

A dozen years ago there was danger that Japanese silk might fall behind in quality, if not in quantity, but now it has advanced in both, and more than holds its own in the markets of the world. Official returns show that in 1895 one hundred and thirty thousand yen worth of silk goods was exported; in 1899 the value rose to twelve million yen. France gets most of it, America next; so, too, of raw silk, which reaches still higher values. Often the thread is spun and woven in Japan, dyed in France, sold in America, and perhaps carried across the continent and worn on the Pacific slope. So the skeins that run through the withered old hands may have far to go.

Weaving must certainly have been known to the early inhabitants of Japan, for the Kojiki relates that Amaterasu, the Sun Goddess, was weaving with her maidens, when her rough brother broke in upon her, with his unseemly pranks; but the material used in prehistoric times may have been hemp, or possibly bark fibre, such as the Yezo Ainu use to the present day. Hemp was certainly used at a very early period in Japan, and was almost the only wear of the common people till the seventeenth century, when the Tokugawa encouraged cotton, and it came into general use as the ordinary dress of the middle and lower classes. According to one legend, an Indian queen shut her step-daughter up in a hollow mulberry trunk and threw her into the sea, and she was carried ashore on the coast of Japan; the people cared for her kindly, and when she died she gratefully turned into a silkworm.

Sujin, the tenth Emperor, commanded his subjects to bring tribute of the products of the bow and arrow–evidently skins, horns and tusks of animals, slain in hunting–and also of women's handiwork, which must have been materials woven or embroidered. Probably silk formed a large part of this tribute, as it was already in use for royal gifts; thus it is recorded that Sujin's son, the grandfather of Prince Yamatotake, received a prince from a neighboring country, and on his departure made him and his suite presents of scarlet silk. Also, when the Empress Jingo conquered Korea, she required, besides hostages of the King's relatives, that "a tribute of eighty shiploads of gold, silver and silk should be paid annually." Better still, weavers and embroiderers were imported and made to settle in Japan, and from these Korean artisans came two great families, the Hada and the Aya, who were scattered all over the country to give instruction in silk-culture. Finally, in the fifth century, along with the introduction of Buddhism and Chinese writing, an envoy sent to China brought back skilled workmen from there, and a department of tailoring was founded to oversee the costumes of the court. In this period, so much silk was presented to the Emperor that a special storehouse had to be built to receive it.

Brocade was always the special wear of the court. There is an endless variety of these beautiful old fabrics, some of which are kept up or imitated now; but the modern pieces are too apt to be colored with the imported aniline dyes, and have neither the brilliancy nor the harmonious quality of the old indigo and warm safflower reds. The gold used in the old brocades was sometimes a genuine gold thread, but more often the well-known paper-gold–a silk thread wound with paper to which gold-foil has been attached. These fabrics were all, of course, woven on hand-looms, much like those used in Europe before Jacquard looms were invented; the threads which wrought the damask effect were handled by bobbins, which a boy, sitting above the loom, threw back and forth. When the court adopted foreign dress, in 1886, the brocade-weavers lost their best patrons and the world a great deal of beauty; yet, however one may regret the change to our inartistic European clothes, it is impossible not to see how needful it was. The motive was not only to prevent the other nations from laughing and looking down on the long-sleeved Orientals; with the costly and elaborate court costumes went a load of ancient ceremonial that would have utterly swamped everybody, if the modern conditions of court life were added to it. Possibly, if Japan had not been so pushed into the rush of things, the change might have been brought about gradually, without sacrificing everything of the old life; but, as the case stood, the only way was to get rid of it all at once.

The "Brocade Banner" played, with the mirror, sword and jewel, the part of imperial representative.

When the Emperor sent Prince Arisugawa, with General Saigo, to take possession of rebellious Yedo, in 1868, he gave him the banner in token of his imperial command; and there can be little doubt of its moral influence with the uncertain. When the imperial forces entered Yedo, all the loyalist Samurai fastened each a bit of brocade on the sleeve of his dress, whereupon the Tokugawa clansmen dubbed them "Kingire" (brocade rags). For weeks there were constant brawls on the street, between the clansmen and these Kingire, ending in the battle of Uyeno Park and the retreat of the Tokugawa adherents to Utsunomiya. Now the sun-flag leads the army, with its ball of the red, rising sun on the white ground, and the banner of the Red Cross Society goes ever beside it; but the old-time brocade remains a symbol of nobility, whether material or spiritual. As the pretty saying goes: "Coat of rags, but heart of brocade"–tsuzure wo kite mo kokoro wa nishiki.

17

NIKKO-THE SHRINES OF THE SHOGUNS

"Dans tonte la description que je vais essayer maintenant, je voudrais pou voir rappeler it chaque ligne Ie bruit de ces eaux que l'on divine si froides, et la voute de ces feuill ages d'un vert noiratre etendue au-dessus des choses, et cette penombre toujours, et cette sonorite profond de dessous bois."

-Loti, "Japoneries d' Automme."

ABOUT ninety miles north and east of Tokyo the central mountain chain lifts into a range of graceful peaks, wooded almost to the summit, Nantaizan, the highest, reaching over eight thousand feet; the region is full of streams and waterfalls, and a beautiful lake, called Chuzenji, lies four thousand feet up in the heart of the range. So wild is it still in parts, that monkeys swing and chatter in the trees near the Chuzenji road, and back a little on the heights there are only wood-cutters or charcoal-burners' huts. "Could a Greek come back here, he would find his "soul-informed rocks," and all that he thought divine or superstitious, even to the very "impressions of Aphrodite." . . . I feel as if I were nearer than I can be through books to the old world we try to rebuild by collation of facts and documents." So wrote La Farge, whose "Letters of an Artist" show a grasp and insight into the deep things of Japanese thought, at times surpassing even Hearn's. In truth, this universal primitive sense of holy places, always strong, is still vividly alive in Japan; Mount Fuji, Nara, the Ise peninsula, Enoshima, and Miyajima and Kinkwazan–these are only a few of the hundreds counted special abodes of the Kami, all the way up to the solitary Sail Rock, on the wild coast of the Hokkaido, to which fishermen lower their sails. Pilgrimages to these shrines are the delight of the common people, particularly of those elderly couples who have become "inkyo"–retired in favor of the younger generation; you meet them everywhere, generally in parties of a dozen or more, under the leadership of the most experienced, and a capital time they seem to have of it.

The name Nikko belongs not to a single place, but to a whole mountain region, which has been haunted of divinity from the earliest times; before history began there was a purely Shinto shrine here, most probably several, dedicated to the spirits of the mountains, both bad and good. The most troublesome of all was a vicious old rain-dragon, who lived far up the side of Nantaizan, and from his cave sent out terrible storms which devastated the neighboring country. He seems to have continued his yearly disturbance without let or hindrance, till the coming of that arch-exorcist, Kobo Daishi, the great Buddhist saint of the ninth century. He at last subdued the dragon, and changed the name of the place from Niko, Stormy Mountains, to Nikko, Mountain of the Sun's Brightness. Nevertheless, even his spells would seem to have wrought no permanent cure; since, for centuries after, a certain family of Shinto priests went twice yearly, at the period of the dragon's accustomed outbreaks, and performed at the cave certain mysterious rites, the secret of which was communicated to their ancestor by the saint himself.

But Nikko shares the honor of Kobo Daishi's ministrations with half the early Buddhist temples in Japan; instead of him, it has a patron saint all its own, one Shodo Shonin, whose whole life was devoted to discovering and worshiping at Nikko and Nantaizan. Shodo's time was half a century earlier than Kobo's, and his life as written by one of his followers is scarcely less full of marvels than the Nara saint's. His parents, desiring a son, prayed at a cave sacred to the Thousand-handed Kwannon, which is far in the mountains as you go up to Ikao from the plain; and when the child was born thunder rolled and flowers and sweet perfumes fell from the sky. When the boy was grown, he stole away to that same cave, and lived there in solitude for three years, fasting and seeing visions. Then, in a dream, he saw a shining mountain, and on it lay a great sword; and awaking, though it was midwinter, he felt an irresistible impulse to seek the place. So, toiling through the snow, after many trials he reached a hill whence he could see the mountain of his dream. Here he lived another three years, practicing the austerities of mountain hermits, and a miraculous being came and fed him.

This trial over, Shodo came back to the neighborhood of his home, and went to a monastery of the Healing Buddha, where Chinese monks-this was in the days of Buddhist missionaries from the west-received him as a novice. But a sheltered monastic life was not for him. After five years of probation, he shouldered his bundle of images and holy books, and went back to his mountains in the north. As he went towards them, he saw in the distance four clouds of different colors rising straight up in the air; and following the sign, he almost reached the place, only to find a roaring torrent across the way-the foamy, glacier-green Daiyagawa, plunging down its gorge among masses of tumbled rock. Then Shodo Shonin stopped beside the stream and prayed; and suddenly some one cried to him from the other bank, and looking over he saw a terrible being, larger than human, wearing strange garments of blue and black, and for a necklace a string of skulls. "Trust thyself to me," he cried to the hermit; "I will bear thee over, even as I bore the pilgrim Chang over the River of Flowing Sand." Then Shodo saw that in his hand were two snakes, the one blue and the other green; and the King of the Deep Sand held out the snakes, and they reached over and changed into a long bridge floating from bank to bank, as it were a rainbow upon a cloud. And Shodo Shonin took up his pack and crossed over the bridge, and when he turned, both the bridge and the terrible king had vanished. So he built a hut and lived there, fasting and praying.

Now, after a time, an old man came to him in a dream and told him that the hill beyond was the abode of four gods, who kept the four peaks. Then Shodo climbed the hill, and at the top he found his four rainbow clouds rising into the air, as he had seen them before; so he knew that the vision was true, and he built a shrine and founded the monastery of the Four Dragons. By this time disciples gathered about him; and with them he tried to climb the last peak, his shining mountain, Nantaizan, which is over eight thousand feet high and not a little steep. Preparing themselves by religious exercises, they climbed till they reached lake Chuzenji, but snow and thunder drove them back; and they returned to the monastery to fight the demons with spiritual weapons. And so at last, after fourteen years, Shodo and his companions attained the summit of the mountain, the place of his dreams. Here they built a little shrine, and at Chuzenji a Buddhist temple and a life-sized image of the Thousand-handed Kwannon, Shodo's protector.

Buddhist Temple, Nikko

Likewise they built at Chuzenji a Shinto temple to the Three Guardians of Nantaizan, the god Onamuji and his wife and son, who were Gongen (avatars or manifestations) of the Buddha, and who appeared to Shodo on the mountain and promised to watch over Japan.

The people believe that the defeat of the Mongol invasion and many other deliverances are due to their care. Also, beside the Daiyagawa, Shodo and his followers built a monastery and a temple to the King of the Deep Sand; and this was the beginning of the great Nikko monastery.

The sanctuary remained an important one, but its great glory began in 1617, when Tokugawa Ieyasu was buried here, and the present temples erected in his honor. At that time the abbot of Nikko was one Tenkei, a man of great ability, who had been tutor to Ieyasu's son, the Shogun Hidetada; and he may very probably have influenced Ieyasu in his choice of a resting place. Yet it is likely that he had in mind most of all the prestige and advancement of the Kwanto, the provinces about Yedo, which it was ever his policy to connect firmly to his house.

For the Tokugawa power was altogether of Ieyasu's making. Beginning as the ruler of a little province, Mikawa, which lies to the south of Owari bay, surrounded by enemies, and forced like all the rest to protect himself or go to the wall, in that ungoverned period of the sixteenth century, he had forced his way up less by ability as a general than by genius for organization. So low were his fortunes at one time, that after a defeat at the hands of his neighbor, Takeda, he retired to a village house and prepared to end his life. But, as he was about to strike, the dagger turned in his hand, and thinking something must be wrong with the blade, he stopped to try it on an iron mortar. The steel point entered the iron, and Ieyasu, astonished, was about to strike himself again, when his followers broke in and forced him to escape to his own province. Joining with Oda Nobunaga, he afterwards defeated Takeda, and received part of his territory. He concluded that the spirit of the dagger had made it turn aside, and from that time weapons made by the Yoshimitsu family, who had fashioned this, were considered especially lucky for the Tokugawa; while the famous Muramasa blades were believed to have a particular grudge against anyone of the name.

Like other great men, Ieyasu had his fancies, and one was to take a bath just before going into battle. One of the curious instances of the belief in luck is the "evil averting pillar" at one of the gates at Nikko, the beautiful Yomei-mon; the delicate arabesque carving on it is done upside down, that the flaw in the perfect jewel may turn aside any misfortune from the Tokugawa house.

Conqueror though he was, Ieyasu averted war whenever he could. When the Regent Hideyoshi died, Ieyasu kept on good terms with his son as long as possible, choosing to go to Kyoto when summoned to do so, though he knew it was at the risk of his life. "The country needs peace," he told the councilors who tried to dissuade him. "Better I should die than bring on another civil war." To his followers he was always fair-minded and ready to listen, even to a rebuke. Once a Samurai came to him and presented a paper containing a lengthy protest; Ieyasu heard him to the end, and thanked and dismissed him kindly, though the objections were worthless and unsuitable.

To reproach one's chief, he declared, needs far more of courage than to fight in the front rank of battle. "There a man can but die, honored arid mourned by his lord; but the outspoken servant, whose words offend the ear, risks the mockery of his comrades and the anger of his master, perhaps a prison and an inglorious death."

Ieyasu was already fifty-seven when the Taiko Hideyoshi died. Two years later, in 1600, the battle of Sekigahara gave him practical control of the empire, and in 1603 he was appointed Shogun. He only held the position three years, resigning it to his son Hidetada; but the retirement was only a nominal one, setting him free from tedious ceremony and leaving him to be from his retreat at Shizuoka the actual ruler and organizer. In 1615 he took part in the final overthrow of Hideyoshi's son at Osaka castle, and being wounded by a spear thrust, died in the following year at the age of seventy-five. His son at once set in hand the tomb and mortuary chapels at Nikko, and in less than a year the body was brought with great pomp from its temporary resting place at Shizuoka, and interred in its bronze tomb on the mountain. Thither pilgrims have thronged ever since for the honor of "Gongen Sama"-the beatified Shogun- and yet more perhaps for the splendor of the temples and the romantic beauty of the place.

Beauty of situation is, indeed, the keynote of Nikko. The charm is heightened by the gradual approach, and must have been even more so in the old days when Daimyo and common pilgrim alike followed the post road up from Yedo across the wide plain toward these peaks, seen first far off, cloud-crowned and opal-tinted, then lifting near and green; and from Utsunomiya-an important garrison town in Ieyasu's time and later-turning eastward, upward, into the very heart of the hills. In those days there were ninety miles of smooth road, shaded by magnificent cryptomeria trees; they are still standing for some twenty miles above Utsunomiya, but the rest nearly all perished in the troubled years that followed the opening of the country.

Nowadays everybody comes by train in five hours from Tokyo, and is set down at the end of Hachi-ishi village, to be pulled by jinrikisha a mile and a half more to the hotels and the temples. "Kanaya's" is on the near side of the Daiyagawa, the "Nikko" and others in Iri-machi village on the temple side. Where Shodo Shonin went over on the rainbow snakes stands the famous Sacred Bridge, once reserved for the Shogun-representative of the Emperor-now for the Emperor himself and the imperial family. It was here that General Grant won everlasting honor for himself and his people by declining an invitation to cross. The bridge is a remarkable structure quite apart from its odor of sanctity; the supports on either side are great stone uprights and cross-pieces, treated like wooden beams, on which rest heavy black rafters, and then the bridge itself, painted with dull vermilion lacquer like the temples. Dull, that is to say, in the sense of an unpolished or matt surface; the red is strong, without being vivid, being made of a mixture of red cinnabar (mercuric sulphide) with the brownish lacquer juice. The varnish helps much to preserve the wood, and the bridge has only needed repair four or five times in its three hundred years.

Just below the red bridge is another for common mortals, by which the road crosses and runs along the other side of the river and off into the mountains, and nearly opposite an avenue leads up through the forest into the sacred enclosure. Here nothing on wheels may come, nor any beast of burden; the path climbs between high banks faced with blocks of stone, spotted with gray-green moss and lichen, among giant cryptomerias, the branches far above crossing so thickly that scarcely a ray of sunlight strikes along the gray mast-like trunks; reaching by and by all open forecourt and a little garden, beyond which a tall pagoda shows red through the trees, and a great stone torii marks the entrance to the monastery and the shrines of Ieyasu.

The Mangwanji, or monastery enclosure proper, stands a little to the right, and in it is the so-called Hall of the Three Buddhas, named from the three gilded images in it–Amida, between the Thousand-handed Kwannon and the Horse-headed Kwannon, who has three faces, and a small head of a horse over the central one. In the open space before this San-Butsu Do there is a curious slender column of black bronze, supported by four rails, making a cross running out to bronze posts at the four corners of the high stone pedestal; the upper part of the shaft is made of seven lotus flowers, four erect and three inverted, from the petals of which hang little tinkling bells. The form is evidently of Hindu origin, and it is supposed to have the power of averting misfortune. Near the entrance there is a carved bronze lantern, a marvel of design in low relief. Many of these accessories were added at different times by vassals of the Tokugawa house, as, for instance, the pagoda, which was set up after Iemitsu's death by a Daimyo of the southwest. The little landscape garden is exceedingly quaint and pretty, especially when the iris is in bloom, in a series of beds irrigated by the stream which ripples down from a spring higher up the mountain. Everywhere, as Loti says, there is the sound of running water, of brooks and waterfalls, hurrying to join the deeper voiced Daiyagawa in the ravine.

A large granite torii, gift of a Daimyo of Kiushiu, stands before the wide flagged walk leading to the mortuary chapels. Owing to their position on the steep hillside, these buildings cannot follow

the conventional Buddhist grouping, which places bell, shrine, treasury, water-tank, and so on, in more or less regular positions about
an open court. Here instead is a series of terraces, faced with stone
and connected by massive stone steps, all shut in around and behind
by the dark, towering cryptomerias of the forest; on each gray terrace stands a cluster of buildings, glowing with color, quivering with
the play of light and shadow on a maze of graceful ornament, like
some jeweled altar in the gloom of a vast cathedral. The wide, heavy
roofs, curving upward at the corners, rest on a wilderness of rafters
and cornices, ending in dragons and strange beasts; every column is
wrought over in low relief, every space carved with frieze and panel-
birds, flowers, monkeys-handled with a freedom and naturalness,
a boldness of color, that almost take one's breath. Each terrace is
enclosed and entered by a roofed gate: first, the Niomon, Gate of the
Two Kings, or guardian gods-the images have been removed to the
gate of Iemitsu's temple and replaced by the lion-like Chinese monsters called Inu; then Yomei-mon, most beautiful of all, with carved
white columns and birds and peony-arabesques, and Karamon, the
Chinese gate, which leads to the main shrine, through an enclosing
wall of carved and painted trellis which surrounds the entire court;
and not least famous, the little door leading to the hillside and the
tomb, over which Left-handed Jingoro, the master carver, placed a
sleeping cat, as they say, to keep away mice from the temple. They
say the present one is not the original pussy; she used to go off
mousing at nights, and finally stayed away altogether. And Jingoro
had to make a less restless guardian in her place.

A heavy fence, painted red like the bridge, encloses the first
court, which has two platforms, divided by steps; in the middle of
the first platform is a great bronze torii, bearing the Tokugawa crest
in gold on uprights and tie-beam-three holyhock leaves, enclosed in
a circle. The form of the leaves is so like the well-known "leaf and
dart" motive, that it must surely have come from the other end of
Asia-brought, like so much else, with the "Graeco-Buddhistic" art
of the Chinese missionaries. These Nikko torii are all of the modified, or Ryobu Shinto form, their bases resting in sockets, instead
of directly on the ground, and the ends of the cross-beams curving

upward. Near the bronze torii stands a tall pine, which is said to be the very tree which Ieyasu carried about with him in his litter; after his death they set it in the ground near his temple, and it grew up to its full height in the forest.

On this platform are the three treasuries, where they keep many relics of Ieyasu, and the stable of the sacred white horse, who seems to be sacred chiefly because he is an albino; he has an extraordinarily vicious temper, even for a Japanese horse. His business is to draw the sacred car at festivals. Across the front of the stable is a charming carved frieze of monkeys playing; one covers his eyes with his hands, another his ears, a third his mouth, in token that we should see nothing, hear nothing, say nothing evil.

The second terrace is faced like the first with a mossy stone wall, on which rests a stone balustrade cut out of great blocks; at the back of the terrace another flight of stone steps leads up to the Yomeimon, an exquisite little building, which somehow puts one in mind of the tiny gem of a church beside the Arno, in Pisa, Santa Maria della Spina. There is the same perfection of proportion, the same sense of quaint elegance and marvelous refinement of detail; though here the comparison must stop. Nothing, of course, could be more unlike Gothic forms–unlike any forms known to the West– than the curved overshadowing roof, with its white tiles and gilded ridgepole, its carved and gilded cornices, and the grinning Chinese dragons in the gables, Of the pawing unicorns which form the capitals of the columns. A little balcony, with carved and colored panels in the railing, runs round the second story, well under the eaves of the great roof, and supported on a mass of carved beams and brackets which rest in turn on the white and gold architrave and columns; the inner walls and the sides of the niches are likewise white and gold, wrought all over with peony-arabesques in low relief, like the laciest of diaper patterns; it makes an admirable background for the life-sized seated figures in either niche. To the right and left of the gate a high-roofed wall rests on the stone facing of the next terrace; this wall, too, is divided by red lacquered posts and rails into panels of birds and flowers, peacocks, pheasants, pine trees, and oak and plum; and below these again are narrower bands, in which ducks and other water-fowl splash in curling conventional waves.

Many votive lanterns and candelabra stand about the courts— there are one hundred and eighteen lanterns all told–the gifts of Daimyo and of subject states, of which last Japan considered Holland to be one. The most beautiful is the bronze Korean lantern, called also the revolving lantern, because it turns on a pivot; it probably did not come from Korea, but from Europe by the hands of the Dutch. A great bell, gift of the King of Lu Chu, hangs in a fine bell tower, which is balanced by the drum tower on the other side.

At the edge of this second platform is the temple of Ieyasu's patron saint Yakushi, one of the Five Buddhas of Wisdom–the Buddha at whose monastery Shodo Shonin studied; it still retains the Buddhist furnishings, removed from most temples since the Restoration reinstated Shinto; and the interior is rich with color and gold, in a soft half light that filters through dangling bamboo curtains, subduing strange forms of dragons and Buddhas, half revealing the shrines and lanterns and tall vases and embroidered altar cloths; over all there is a delicate smell of incense, not heavy with centuries of dirt, but mingled with the sweet pine-scented air blowing gently through the transparent hangings and carved screens. Presently a priest strikes one of the melodious gongs, stroke by stroke, with long pauses between; a band of pilgrims kneel on the pavement without, while another priest recites the noon-day office in a droning singsong, rising and falling in a mournful chant. Strangely like the Romish ritual, yet strangely different, too; most of all different, perhaps, in the sense of out-of doors, of belonging to the forest.

For, after all, the greatest marvel of Nikko is the way in which all this wealth of detail, this profusion of ornament, is kept in place and subordinated to a central thought; no part is an end in itself, not the individual temples even; they are cellae, shrines of the sacred grove, one with it as by a sort of instinct. The want of height, of mass, is supplied completely by the trees; even the color-scheme has a strange unity, as if it were the forest-motive accented, set in a higher key. Those raw emeralds, toned in the shadow of the roofs, are repeated where the sun glints across a blue-green branch of cryptomeria; the fretted white columns are lighter but not less tender than the straight gray trunks; and where the bark breaks away in places you see almost a repetition of the vermilion lacquer in its strong dusky red. And the lavish use of vermilion becomes clear, too; after all, it is but little in proportion to the mass of surrounding grays and greens; just enough, no more.

The next terrace is a small one, and contains only the building for the sacred car and other paraphernalia of the festivals, and the stage for the sacred Kagura dance. A Shinto priestess of the imperial house is always in charge here. A little open building close by is used for burning the fragrant cedar wood during the rites.

At the back of this enclosure the Kara-mon, with its inlaid pictures of dragons and plum trees, leads to the last terrace of all,

Sacred Stable

which is almost filled by the Honden or oratory; this is really not one building, but a series of halls or chambers opening one behind the other. The great folding doors of the entrance are gorgeous with carved and gilded peonies, but beyond it the empty matted hall in its cool quiet seems most restful after so much splendor. The ante-chambers at either end are again magnificent with polychrome carving and pictures of lions on a gold background; while the coffered ceilings glow with Buddhist angels and chrysanthemums and the Tokugawa crest, and again and again repeated is the mystic Howo bird, which seems created out of memories of pheasants and peacocks, and the southern bird of paradise, which could never have come so far north as Japan.

Only the mirror and gohei remain in the oratory; the Buddhist trappings have all been swept away, leaving an empty hall. A lower chamber beyond leads to the gilded doors of the inner chapel, beyond which strangers may not go. But the ashes of the Shogun are not here. Off to the right more flights of stone steps lead far up the hill to a little platform having a stone balustrade and a heavy bronze door, within which stands a bronze cylinder under a square bronze roof, turning up at the corners; a stork candelabrum, an incense burner, and a great bronze vase holding a brass lotus are the only accessories. All is plain even to bareness up there alone among the trees; "the acme of costly simplicity," said LaFarge, and De la Mazeliere, "autant le temple est riche, autant le tom be est simple; en bas la gloire du heros-dieu, en haut les restes de l'homme." It is a concrete expression of the Buddhist doctrine, All earthly things must pass.

Ieyasu was perhaps too great to have a great son; it was the grandson, Iemitsu, son of Hidetada, who carried out his political plans and completed his work of centralization. Iemitsu's group of temples lies to the left, reached by another fine avenue of cryptomerias; something in their situation, closed as they are in the hollow of the hill, lends them a remoteness and secluded charm that rivals the wide terraces of Ieyasu.

Built less than fifty years after his, they are almost identical in style; on the whole rather less magnificent, but not less beautiful. The tomb is on the hill behind them, a structure of plain gold bronze like Ieyasu's, but the shiny brass characters on the bronze gate detract somewhat from the dignity of the effect. Taken together, the two groups of temples stand for what is undoubtedly the high-water mark of art in Japan.

Iemitsu was chosen for the Shogunate during his grandfather's lifetime. Hidetada had two sons, of whom the younger was gentler and more popular, at least with a certain clique, and while they were still boys intrigues were afoot to get the younger named heir. Tradition has it that these schemes were frustrated by the energy and courage of Iemitsu's governess, the Lady Kasuga, wife of a Daimyo who had forfeited his estates. When she knew of the plots against her charge, she set off alone for Shizuoka, gained admittance to the ex-Shogun in his retreat, and besought him to make the choice between the lads.

Ieyasu had them both brought before him, and subjected them to close tests of character, and as Lady Kasuga had brought up her boy in the stern simplicity of warlike times, he proved himself altogether worthy, and Ieyasu proclaimed him Shogun after Hidetada. When the lady was asked to name her reward, she desired that her husband might be restored to his title and estates; but the husband declared such a request was improper and dishonoring to him, and divorced her. Then the ex-Shogun offered to make Lady Kasuga Daimyo in her own right, but she refused to be honored above her husband; and in the end Lord Kasuga was reinstated on his own merits, and forgave and restored his wife—all of which appears in a modern drama quoted by Osman Edwards.

Iemitsu's problems were very different from his grandfather's; the one was the last of the great sixteenth century adventurers, the other inherited absolute power and that tradition of conservatism which was to harden later into an almost Chinese rigidity.

Ieyasu's high places had been fortified camps; Iemitsu's was a brilliant court, and he was a patron of literature and all the arts. In truth, during Iemitsu's youth there was danger of a relapse into over-luxuriousness, which was checked in time by the faithful councilors bequeathed by Ieyasu, the old Daimyo Abe and Okubo. Their remonstrance with the young man forms the subject–or, rather, one of the subjects–of a lengthy and involved drama, in the course of which Okubo rides to the Shogun's castle in a tub, as a demonstration against the soft living of the younger knights. In an amusing dialogue he explains to a friend how the Shogun has lately told him that since he is now seventy-eight years of age, he may ride to the castle in a norimon like the other ministers. "But, unfortunately, I have nothing to ride except my favorite wild horses; still, I thought it would be very impolite to my lord to disobey his kind advice, and after much consideration and anxiety I found this tub and put the poles on as you see. Isn't it a splendid idea?" Fine, says the friend; but–well–really, a vassal of the Shogun must be able to get a proper norimon, instead of that queer thing; if he happens to be hard up, any of his friends–and so on and so on. Best of thanks, says Okubo; but after all it is no queerer than a sliding door, on which he has been more than once carried from battle; and what with arming his men and looking after poor friends and unlucky Ronin, if he once began buying useless things like litters, he would soon be calling on all his friends for help. So off he goes, and dances a spear dance before the Shogun–an improvization in the style of the No dance–ending with the solemn last charge of Ieyasu:

" 'Though we conclude the war and restore peace to the nation, it is not an easy task to keep it tranquil. Though we secure control over the country, if we do not know how to govern it, it will fall into disorder. After my death, if my grandson go astray, there is no one but you to remonstrate with him.' Thus did Gongen Sama lay a charge upon me. Subjects always pattern after their lord, and now all the Daimyo and officers have become luxurious, and the government is becoming disorderly and corrupt. O, my dear lord, to me the sorrows of the people are like the tormenting fires of hell!" (Translated by K. Kimura)

The young Shogun acknowledges his fault, and vows to put away his follies; Okubo dances a final No, celebrating the glory of Minamoto no Yoritomo, Iemitsu's ancestor, and the curtain falls on the prosperity of the Tokugawa line.

18

NIKKO AND LAKE CHUZENJI

THE chapels of the Shoguns are of such surpassing interest that one almost forgets the other shrines of Nikko; yet, if it were anywhere else, the Shinto temple of the "Three Guardian Deities" of Nantaizan would be thought quite worth looking at. It stands between the two great groups, and, like them, is bowered in green depths of forest. A little lower than the main building stands a kind of double house, connected by a covered gallery, and all painted with the Buddhistic red, which, it is true, the modified Ryobu Shinto allowed, instead of the purer uncolored wood. This temple, however, is not Shinto at all, but Buddhist, and dedicated to Amida and Fugen, and Kishi Bojin, the protector of children. Kishi Bojin was once a wicked ogress, who devoured children, but she was converted and became a Buddhist nun; so, now beatified, she atones for her evil deeds by taking special care for the little ones–a task which she shares with the benign Jizo. Mothers bring pathetic tokens to her shrine–the little frocks and dolls and toys of their lost children. The Honden, or oratory, behind the Shinto temple, contains a number of interesting relics, among them specimens of the curious curved pendants called maga-tama "curved jewels"–which used to be run on a string and worn as necklaces or girdles. The shape is most nearly like a comma, the hole for the cord passing through the thick part. These maga-tama were probably worn as part of a dress of ceremony as late as the seventh century. In the double temple are still more relics, notably Yoritomo's bones, which ought by rights to be at his own temple in Kamakura, where he is supposed to be buried. However, such multiplications are not unknown in other lands. Behind these temples are the tombs of Tenkei, the abbot of Ieyasu's time, and a number of less distinguished prelates.

Above the red bridge the right bank comes down in a steep rocky cliff, round which the river hurries with a great deal of noise and foam; a little farther up, the sides of the ravine slope more gently, and here a small footpath crosses over to the right side by a bridge of logs and brush, and leads along the river to the "Hundred Gods." They are ranged in an irregular row along the bank, a gravely quaint assembly of stone images of Amida, all seated in the conventional attitude of contemplation, feet crossed under the robe, and thumbs together in the lap. Some are upright, some toppling, all weather-worn and green with moss and splashed with gray and black lichens. The largest sits at the far end of the row, looking down the path, an oddly impressive figure against the trees; there is something in the pose of these stone Buddhas as immovable as the rocks themselves–not only motionless, but as if they had never wished to move. The tradition is that no one can ever count the hundred up exactly; however often one goes over them, the tally never comes out the same. One figure was washed away in a freshet some years ago and landed some distance down stream, where the villagers joyfully received and cared for it.

Back across the foamy green river is a charming little garden, the Dainichi Do, where you may sit on the edge of the little tea-house and sip pale tea and nibble delicate tasteless cakes, looking out to the valley and the mountains, and hearing now and then over the rush of the river a far-off temple bell, full and deep and sweet, with a brooding sound like the call of doves in the wood. It is a beautiful view at all times, but most of all when the maples turn and the color flames up to the very peaks, and loses itself on Nantaizan in purple and amethyst. The jinrikisha men carry the kurumas up through the garden, and so out on to a pretty hillside road leading back through the upper village to the hotels again.

Nikko is particularly rich in gardens. Besides the Dainichi Do and the monastery enclosure, there is the public park, and pretty specimens of landscape art around Kanaya's and the other hotels; and about a mile from Irimachi, the village across the stream, is the cool, shady deer park-a government preserve, which anyone may enter for the asking, if he presents a visiting card. The grounds and building belonging to the monastery, which used to be reserved for guests of rank, is now the summer palace of the little imperial princesses, who come up from Tokyo, with their ladies, almost every year.

There is nothing even remotely like a town at Nikko; everywhere the forest is all about you, as in some wild part of the Adirondacks. The village of unpainted little houses stretches out, as Japanese villages do, for a mile along the old highway, and another small group of cottages lies across the river among the hills. As in all places where Japanese pilgrims come, the inhabitants frankly live by supplying their wants, and especially their desire for small purchases to take home as gifts; the larger part of these being woodwork, black "Sendai-wood" trays, with pictures of the red bridge or the temples cut in intaglio, and curious cups and bowls and tobacco trays, carved out of fantastic knots and roots. This is done in and around Nikko itself, and there is a great deal of lacquer besides, brought for sale from Wakayama, in the neighboring province. Much fur comes to Nikko from the mountains-skins of fox and badger and hare, and sometimes a monkey skin or a black bear. The women make delightful soft slippers, without any heels-most comforting of a cold morning. Deerskin rugs are to be had, too; and a good deal of the fur makes its way to Tokyo, when the tourist and pilgrim season is over.

Many Japanese folk-stories concern themselves with the badger, who plays some of the parts which belong to the wolf in other countries, and some which seem more appropriate for the fox or jackal. One very curious notion is that he loves to distend his hairy stomach and drum on it with his fists, producing sounds which not only delight himself, but bewilder any mortal who may be unlucky enough to hear him. Sometimes, in return for a kindness, the beast will show himself grateful and render much service; but more often he takes on human form, to entice people to their death. Mitford gives, as an example, the story of a young noble, who was out walking at night in a lonely place, and found a very beautiful young girl lying by the roadside; his squire was exceedingly smitten with her loveliness; but, after talking a few minutes, the young man drew his sword and cut off her head. The horrified attendant reported the deed to his lord, the young man's father, who declared he must kill such a son on the spot; but the youth quietly explained that he had merely disposed of an evil spirit, and requested them to go look on the bank by the moat and see what was there. Sure enough, on the spot where be cut down the girl, lay a huge old badger, with his head cut off. The young man explained that he looked closely at the creature and saw that, though it was raining heavily and she professed to have been lying on the bank for hours in great pain, her clothing was not even moist; the evil spirit had forgotten this little detail, which could not escape a Sherlock Holmes trained in Chinese philosophy.

Just over the bridge a horse tramway passes along the river, and every hour or two a line of small, flat cars comes by, drawn by shaggy ponies in great straw shoes; each horse has a man at his head, to lead him by a straw halter, for Japanese horses are seldom driven. This tram goes up over the mountains toward Ashio, where the great copper mines are, the largest in Japan. The way over is across the Hoso-o pass, two thousand feet higher than Nikko, and at the highest part the cars transfer their load to a steel cable wound on drums three miles apart, which carries the charcoal and coke to another tramway on the other side of the pass and brings back bars of ore in return. The mines have been furnished with the most modern machinery, and, as a first result, the increased activity sent out a mass of poisonous waste into the stream which drained the slope, and ruined the crops watered by it in the valley below. The farmers were almost up in arms over it, and a great deal of agitation has ended by forcing the owners to put in a filtration plant, which takes the injurious part from the water used in working.

Japanese law regards the surface of the land as alone belonging to the proprietor; the right to mine is a government monopoly, and is let out to those who work the ore at a certain percentage; the surface of the land used must also pay the regular land tax, or a set fraction thereof. The mines of Yezo and the west coast of the main island are but little developed as yet, compared to what they might be if there were more capital available in the land.

Nikko has long been a favorite haunt of the Anglo-Saxon contingent, being cooler and rather less rainy than the coast; and they have found many excursions in the neighborhood, both short and long. Distant views are not to be had from Nikko proper; the valley is too shut in for that; but a sharp climb to the top of Toyama gives a wide outlook among the nearer peaks, Nantaizan and Shirane San and the rest, and to the east the notched peak of Mount Tsukuba rising to the north of the plain of Tokyo. Most of the paths are too hilly for jinrikishas, but the ride back towards Utsunomiya, through the old cryptomeria avenue, is fairly level, and the road is good, except during the summer rains. The trees stand so close together that their trunks almost touch, and the shade is dense and cool on the hottest days.

The rain dragon cannot have entirely deserted his caves on Nantaizan, for the whole Nikko region gets a full share of both the June and September downpours; however, a dozen streams and waterfalls are all the more beautiful for that. There are charming excursions to the mist-falling cascade, and the pitch-dark cascade, and the back-view cascade, where you can walk behind the sheet, and several lesser falls, besides the two on the way to lake Chuzenji. The foreign residents have adopted the pleasant Japanese custom of going off on impromptu picnics, and live out of doors almost as much as the Germans do in summer. At first the reception apartments of temples were let to the strangers who wanted to stay at Nikko, as well as the better houses of the village, but this accommodation has been long outgrown; many cottages have been built for and by the foreigners, and not only these, but the hotels, are usually full from July to September. The American Church Mission has lately built a pretty little church for English services, and there is a large colony of missionaries at Nikko, though Karuizawa probably takes the greater number.

Every year more people go all the way to lake Chuzenji, notwithstanding the difficulty of housekeeping so far from railroad and supplies. The lake is four thousand feet above the sea, and in spite of much rain, the air is cool and bracing all summer. It is, on the whole, the most beautiful body of water in all Japan, Biwa and Haruna, and even Hakone, not excepted; but the Japanese have much fewer associations with it of a literary and artistic kind; so they do not rave over it so much. Chuzenji lies in a circle of wooded hills, almost at the foot of Nantaizan, and it is just big enough for beauty and not too large to enjoy all at once; it is three miles across and some eight or nine miles long, and at the upper end exceedingly deep. Foreigners have taken very kindly to it, and living there becomes less impossible every year; indeed it bids fair to become the most aristocratic of the summer resorts, though all this may change now that the revised treaties allow everybody to rent cottages and live where they will, without taking out leases through the Japanese go-between.

The road to Chuzenji is not too easy to travel at any time, and after the rains it is often too much washed to be possible for jinrikishas, especially in the part along the gorge of the Daiyagawa. The distance is eight miles, and the rise two thousand feet, the steepest part being near the top. When the jinrikishas cannot run, the alternative modes of conveyance are horseback, kago and chair, of which the last is least trying to American feelings, for the kago or litter is only fit for people who can fold themselves up conveniently, like a jack-knife, and the horses are raw-boned, half broken beasts of execrable gait, and temper none too good. As for the so-called English saddles which are to be hired, they are desirable only by comparison with the native mountain pack-saddle, on which the rider sits doubled up, or with his legs sticking out on either side over the horse's neck. But the road is exceedingly pretty, taking in a picturesque village and specimens of mountain farming, and beautiful views along the river and up the steep hillsides. Part of the way the path clings to the side of the cliff, and here it is that the rains give so much trouble.

The Daiyagawa

Nantaizan is so sacred that the old rule still obtains, and no woman is permitted to pass through the gates and make the ascent. Only very good walkers are likely to be much grieved, for it is said to be a hard climb, much of it over slippery log steps, though the view at the top must repay a good deal of effort. Another and still stiffer climb is up Shirane San, which is six hundred feet higher than Nantaizan–eight thousand eight hundred feet in all, according to Chamberlain. Shirane San is an active volcano, but has not been in eruption since 1889.

A wide moor lies between the mountains, covered in summer with iris and lilies, and in the autumn beautiful with a kind of tall reddish grass. On the Shirane side lies a second lake, Yumoto, one of the innumerable sources of hot water. Yumoto village lies on the moor side, beside the cluster of springs, which are so strongly charged that they make the lake water quite sulphurous. The bath-ing arrangements are much more primitive than at Ikao–in fact, they are very primitive indeed, because, as a rule, only pilgrims go there to bathe as a part of their round of exercises.

Those who come on pilgrimage to Nikko visit first the tombs of the Shoguns, and then make their way up to Chuzenji, where the tem-ple of the Thousand-handed Kwannon, founded by Shodo Shonin, is still an important shrine; from there they ascend Nantaizan, and enjoy a soak at Yumoto before returning again to Chuzenji. For the few days in July and August when the mountain is officially "open"–and then only is anyone allowed to ascend–the village is packed to overflowing; as many as ten thousand pilgrims sometimes stay there for the night. The time of opening varies, following the old lunar calendar. Some stout-hearted pilgrims take in four other mountains in the round, giving several days to the whole expedition and sleeping at Nikko or Chuzenji. In maple time they come down bearing crimson branches from the sides of Shirane San, where the finest grow. All about Chuzenji the forests are full of oak and birch and other familiar deciduous trees, besides Wistaria vines and a glorious display of wild azalea in the early summer, the pink and white and red azaleas of our greenhouses, reaching here a height of ten or fifteen feet among the undergrowth on the edge of the woods. In many places the trees are draped with a long trailing moss called monkey grass, and the monkeys are there, too, swinging and chattering, and not at all afraid of the few human beings who come their way. Master Jingoro could have had little difficulty in finding models for his carvings. He is a rather large beast, the Japanese ape or saru, short-haired and pink-faced, and plausible looking; he does not hang by his tail, because nature has deprived him of that con-venience. In folk tales he is mischievous and ill-mannered, like all his race, but at the same time rather easily gulled–especially those of their tribe who, according to the old belief, inhabit the bottom of the sea. Here is one of the stories the grandmother tells the young ones around the warm kotatsu of a winter evening:

Once on a time there were a great many monkeys who lived in the sea, but now there are only a few, because they were foolish and would not stay there. In those days people used to brew sake on the seashore, and the monkeys came up and watched them, but at first they did not come near, for they said, "If we look we shall smell, and if we smell we shall taste, and if we taste we shall drink, and if we drink we shall dance, and if we dance we shall fall down, and the men will kill us." So they were very careful for a long time. But at last they said, "We might just look a little, but we must not smell, for if we smell we shall taste"–and so on and so on. And, when they smelled, they thought it would not do any harm just to taste a little; "but we must not drink, for if we drink we shall dance, and if we dance we shall fall down, and the men will kill us." So they tasted a little, and the sake was so good that they thought they would really have to drink some, but they would be very, very careful not to dance. So they drank and drank, and presently they began to dance and dance, and they all danced till they fell down, and the men killed them every one! I suppose in Japan,

> "This is the sorrowful story,
> Told when the twilight fails,
> And the monkeys walk together,
> Holding each other's tails."

Only, as I said before, the Japanese monkeys, poor things, have no tails to hold by.

19
BENDAI AND MATSUSHIMA

"My master bids me govern the far lands of his kingdom, the deserts of Koshi, the hills white with the wintry snow.

"I have no consolation save the flowers, the lilies and the tender carnations, springing beside my door.

"I watch the flowers blooming, and I think of my bride; white as the lilies, tender as the carnations is she.

"But for thinking of her, my beloved, my bride,

"In this wilderness, even for a day, how should I endure!"

–Japanese poem, ninth century.

THE settlements in the Kwanto in the early middle ages have been sometimes compared to the Roman colonies on the Rhine and the Danube; the wild Ainu were all about the northern border, ever ready to press back on the softer region from which they were being thrust inch by inch. Those who kept the barriers on these northern marches had need to be strong men, who, while they drained and cleared the new land, were always ready to fight in its defence. Some of the outposts on the Oshiu Kaido–the old highway–have kept the name still, as the memory of Roman camps lingers at Worcester and Lancaster; there is Ichi-no-he, first gate, and San-no-he, Hachi-no-he, third and eighth gate, and so on. It was not until Yoshiiye's conquests, in the twelfth century, that the barbarians were driven finally beyond what is now Morioka, quite to the northern shores of the main island.

In the seventh century, the border lay about half way up from the Hakone mountains to the top of the island, just beyond what is now the bay of Sendai–a great curve sweeping round for twenty-five miles, sheltered on the north by a high promontory and the mountain island of Kinkwazan, which forms the outer end of the are, but open to the beat of the sea on the south and southeast. Islands innumerable are scattered over the bay, and among them here and there are sheltered little harbors for small boats, and one fairly good port, Oginohama, lying close under the outer arm. Around the bay lie many little towns, which carry their traditions back to the early centuries, but all are overshadowed by their younger neighbor, Sendai.

Like Yedo, Sendai owes its importance to a single family, almost to a single man, namely, Ieyasu's contemporary, Date Masamune. The Date family was ennobled in the twelfth century, but we hear little about them till the year 1500; then, in the general turmoil of that stirring period, the Date, like so many others, laid about them and took by fighting whatever their neighbors were not strong enough to hold. At the height of Hideyoshi's power, Date Masamune and the Hojo–who for generations had been Regents over the feeble Ashikaga Shoguns–were the only lords who did not acknowledge the Taiko's supremacy. Then Hideyoshi gathered his generals–Ieyasu was among them–and attacked the Hojo stronghold at Odawara, on the Tokaido; and after a time Date came to him there and made submission. It is said that Hideyoshi rebuked Date severely for not coming sooner, and, taking him to a high place, showed him all the great army encamped around Odawara; and Date owned himself convinced. To Ieyasu, and his house, he became one of the most trusted and faithful vassals, and after Ieyasu's death his influence probably counted for much in keeping the other nobles loyal to Ieyasu's son and grandson.

Sendai castle stands on a sharp hill, in a fine natural situation, and Masamune made it as strong as unsparing effort could; part still stands, part was destroyed in the war of the Restoration (1868), when the city held out for the Tokugawa, its ancient overlords.

What remains of the castle is used for quarters for the officers, Sendai being now one the most important garrison stations, and having extensive barracks. There is also a large convict prison in the city.

Under the new division of the country into ken (prefectures) Sendai became the capital of Miyagi ken; and it is now a very modern, progressive place, proud of its fine hospital and schools, and a college which hopes soon to become a university. It further possesses a so-called "foreign hotel," but unless this has recently mended its ways, it has all the shortcomings of such hybrids in Japan, which are dusty, cheerless rooms and poor food, and a clumsy, half-comprehending service. Unless beefsteak and bedsteads are absolutely essential to one's happiness, a good all-Japanese yadoya is far preferable to such as these.

The city lies in a fine open country, slightly rolling to the west and south, and spreading away in a smooth level stretch of rice fields to the bay, some five miles off. The little river Hirose flows around it, coming across from the mountains on the west, which send out long spurs toward the Sendai hills. On the north, a long narrow plain reaches up toward Nambu province, well watered by the Kitamigawa and its numerous branches, which flow together into the bay farther round. The plain is rich and well cultivated, and bears a large rice crop; according to Appert's chart of the Daimyo, the income of the Date of Sendai was over six hundred thousand koku annually.

The meibutsu or specialty of the region is a kind of fossil wood known as Sendai wood, very heavy and black, and a good deal like Irish bog oak, which comes from a hill not far from the city; they make carved trays and other fancy things of it to sell as mementoes, and a great deal of it is sold at Nikko. For, wherever you go in Japan it is proper to bring away little specimens of the local handicraft as gifts for friends at home; and something characteristic is always forthcoming, because in the days of sharply drawn feudal lines every province, every village almost, had its individual life and individual industries. Thus, north, away here around the old castle-town of Morioka, they make beautiful iron kettles; Nagoya produces blue porcelain and "eggshell" lacquer; down in Kochi they raise chickens with tail-feathers yards long, and so on, and so on, from Lu Chu to the Ainu country. Sendai wood, therefore, for Sendai, and extra-fine persimmons–not our little puckery American ones that must wait for frost, but sweet and large and yellow as oranges. In October the persimmon orchards flash gold like a pre-Raphaelite paradise, and later endless boxfuls, dried in sake, will go to Tokyo for gifts at the New Year. These Japanese persimmons are grown a great deal in California now, and all through the autumn they make a fine show in our large fruit shops. I don't think I ever saw anyone buy any!

Sendai, under the rule of the Date, counted as the best governed of all the provinces. Masamune built not only fortifications, but roads and bridges, and dug canals and planted forests, and conducted himself in an able and enterprising manner generally. But perhaps the most enterprising, and certainly the most original thing that he did, was to send an embassy to Europe to visit the Pope. Nearly thirty years before, in 1583, the princes of Bungo and Arima, in Kiushiu, had sent four young nobles as ambassadors to the courts of Europe, bearing a letter which declared they came "from the kings and Christians of Japan," and desired to render homage to His Holiness; also to see "the marvelous and invincible city of Venice, which had surpassed their imaginations." The messengers also visited Spain, and asked for an alliance with Philip II. They were absent seven years, and brought with them an Italian prelate, who was well received by Hideyoshi, then in the height of his power, and not yet hostile to the Christians.

Masamune's embassy left in 1614. Just why he sent it is a little puzzling. The Pope naturally understood it to be an act of submission and allegiance, and sent gifts and messages accordingly; but this view of the matter is difficult to reconcile with the rest of Date's character and actions. Certainly, if he ever had any genuine interest in Christianity for its own sake, by the time the ambassadors returned his ideas had completely changed; the edicts forbidding "the evil sect" were then being rigorously enforced, and Date was among the most zealous persecutors. It is far easier to believe that this wide-awake prince was moved, not by any devotion to religion, but by desire for material advantage–possibly even by ambition for foreign conquest, like Hideyoshi's in Korea, for he can have had no definite conception of the distance from Japan to Europe. Indeed, if the Europeans could come, why might not the Japanese go thither to conquer? The "Anglo-Saxons of the East," like ourselves, have always a healthy confidence in their own ability to do whatever anybody else can. It is more than probable that Masamune sent his messengers to spy out the land and report concerning its strength, having also in mind those advantages of foreign trade and improved weapons which had fallen to the Daimyo of the south. However, when the embassy returned, Date was busy restoring Buddhist temples and improving his province, and, when he heard their report, must have given up his schemes for profit from the outside world. Many of the gifts sent by the Pope are now preserved, with other Christian relics, in the museum at Uyeno, and the rest have been scattered in recent years. There are two rather handsome temples in Sendai, one of them standing in a picturesque situation among fine old cryptomeria trees; the carved monsters on the ends of the rafters are of the best period of art. On either side of the building are stone monuments, placed in memory of twenty of Date Masamune's closest retainers, who committed hara-kiri after his death, in order that their spirits might follow and continue to serve their master. Such faithfulness is not without parallel in Japanese history. I think it is in the dramatized version of the story of the "Forty seven Ronin" that one of his attendants tells Lord Asano, as he makes his farewell to his household, before going to his unjust death, that he will soon hear the clatter of his old nurse's geta coming behind him–karan, karon, karan, karon–along the Shadowy Way. Near the retainers' another monument has been erected, in memory of a thousand men who were killed in the war of the Restoration. The other temple, called Zuiho-den, from the name of the hill on which it stands, is in what was a part of the old castle grounds; and here Masamune was buried, and there is a fine statue of him placed upon his tomb. Outside the Zuiho-den, near the first torii leading to the avenue of cedars by which you approach it, a great irregular stone tablet commemorates the hundred and odd Sendai men who lost their lives in the Satsuma rebellion.

As a boy Date Masamune is said to have been of a timid and retiring disposition; but he must have either outgrown or overcome what in those days would have been an unpardonable defect. His life was spent in the saddle, and to the end he held himself ready for war at any moment, though the Tokugawa rule had already begun the two hundred years of the Great Peace. Masamune's father, Date Terumune, was a born fighter, always at war with his neighbors, always victorious, and always surrounded by traitors. Mazeliere relates that at one time Terumune's Karo (chief retainer) discovered a plot against his lord; he therefore had his own son married to the conspirator's daughter, in order to keep a watch upon their movements. But the young man yielded to the charms of his bride and was persuaded to join in the plot; then, repenting, he broke away and went to his father, told all, and took his own life–in old Japan the only honorable exit from such a situation.

But at last Terumune was trapped and caught. Masamune marched against the castle where his father was confined; the enemy sent out word that, at the first arrow shot, Date Terumune should be put to death. With that the fierce old lord cried out from a tower to his son, "Never trouble for my life; I want only vengeance." Masamune took the castle, found his father's corpse, and piled him a funeral mound of the heads of the slain.

Naturally, the later members of the house were of less remarkable mould than these two; but the family remained among the most powerful barons, being always closely attached to the Shogun, and faithful to him to the very end of the old order of things. One of the most popular historical dramas deals with the fortunes of the house–the play of the "Prince of Sendai"–the real events of which happened in the province about the middle of the eighteenth century. Briefly, this is the outline: Hyobu, a wicked kinsman of the Prince, formed a plot to get the Daimiate for himself; to this end he tempted Date to a life of dissipation, in order that he might be disgraced and deposed. The plot succeeded, in so far that Date's doings came to the Shogun's ears, and he was ordered to retire; but, instead of Hyobu, the Prince's little son was appointed Daimyo in his place. Then Hyobu tried to murder the boy, and, to protect him, the Prince's Karo sent his own daughter, with her son, as nurse or governess to the child.

The culminating scene of the drama is laid in a room of the castle, where the three are virtually prisoners; the children watch hungrily, while the nurse, who dares not trust anyone about her, prepares with her own hands their belated meal. Presently, to amuse them, Masaoka–that is the nurse's stage name–sends them to the balcony to see the sparrows, and, while they watch the mother bird feeding her gaping young, the half-starved princeling gravely reminds his comrade that it is all very well for the birds, who know no better, to push and twitter for their food, "but for a Samurai, when his stomach is empty, it is a disgrace to feel hunger."

At this moment a lady in waiting enters, bearing a box of cakes, which she says are for the little Prince, from his father. Masaoka, suspecting mischief, declares that the child is ill and cannot eat them today, but she will put them by for him; the messenger, on the contrary, insists that she must see him taste his father's present. While they are disputing, Masaoka's son suddenly snatches one of the cakes and crams it into his mouth, the mother making no movement to check him; indeed, he is but carrying out what she has carefully taught him to do for the protection of his young lord. But the frightened messenger, well knowing that the child will presently die of poison and so betray their plot, draws out her dagger and stabs him, exclaiming that he has dishonored his lord. I venture to think a European mother of the same period would have drawn in turn; not so the Samurai. Feigning to suspect nothing, she declares that the doom is just; that for such an evil deed her son deserves to die. With all ceremony, she dismisses the messenger over her trampled cakes, and only when alone with the body of the son whose life she has freely given for his Prince, the mother-heart at last has its way.

In all essentials, the tale is quite in accord with the facts, and it is a comfort to know that in the end the wicked kinsman was detected and brought to justice, and the little Prince was saved, though the faithful Karo, Masaoka's father, lost his life in the struggle.

A few miles south of Sendai, at the junction for the East Coast Railway, there is a curious old temple of Inari, the Shinto god of rice, whose servants are the foxes. According to its legend, the temple was founded by a certain nobleman named Ono Takamura, who came up from Kyoto about the year 900 to inspect the northern provinces. Being a pious person, he carried with him a pair of foxes from his home temple at Fushimi, near Kyoto. Temple foxes, by the way, are not wicked enchanters like the mountain fox, but bring good luck with them wherever they go. They have power over the hill foxes, and that is why a person suffering from fox possession is brought to the Inari temple, so that the white fox may cast out the evil one. After journeying long, and far, Ono Takamura came one day to a bridge over a little river, just before you reach what is now Iwanuma junction, and there he sat down to lunch and rest. While he sat there he opened the lid of the box where the foxes lived, because they were tame and gentle, but to his astonishment they both jumped out and ran away. One went this way and one went that, and as they ran they cried eight times: "One in the north and one in the south; one in the north and one in the south." This, it may be supposed, surprised their master still more, and he was much perplexed to understand the sign. At last he saw the foxes run into a little wood, so he decided that they wished to dwell there, and establish the worship of the god in these northern countries as well as in the south, and he obediently built them a small temple in the wood, so small, indeed, that very few people knew anything about it.

Then we skip five hundred years–into the time when this part of the country was beginning to grow powerful and important. A certain poet-priest of Kyoto learned of this wonderful manifestation, and set out on a pilgrimage to Ono Takamura's temple; but, when he reached the place he could find no one who had ever heard of such a thing. At last he stopped a boy riding on a bamboo stick for a horse, and asked him the way; the child pointed to the forest and vanished. The priest went where he pointed, and found the little temple still standing; so he was sure the boy who directed him was the god in disguise. Later the temple was taken over by the Buddhists, but Inari Sama still had his worship, even after a large Buddhist monastery was built there and named Takekoma-ji, Hobby-horse Abbey, in memory of the priest and the disguised god; and in the end the Shinto priests regained possession.

The temple stands in a wood surrounded by a high board fence, put up to keep out dogs and other animals; the foxes' caves are behind the temple buildings, and not even the priests may see inside the walls built around them. But sometimes the people of the neighborhood see the foxes at play in the fields at night. The young ones are rather light red; the grown ones have white tips to their tails, and the old grandfather faxes are quite white all over.

I quote from one of the Sendai missionaries, Mrs. Hoy, an account of the daily offerings:

"It is the custom of the priests to offer boiled rice, eggs, bean-curd fried in oil, and fish to the foxes once a day. A large table is placed in the temple yard, on which the offerings are arranged. The feast is spread before sunset, and then, just as the sun begins to set, the priests inform the foxes that their banquet is ready. This they do by beating drums very loudly and striking the hyoshige (two blocks of wood which are smitten together, making a very sharp sound). Then the foxes, one by one, come slowly out of their caves and carry the food away in their mouths. Any one who offers food may stay and see the foxes if he wishes." Mrs. Hay says that a friend of hers who stayed put a lighted candle on the table to see better, because the night was cloudy and dark, but an old fox snapped it up and ran off with it to his den.

They say that one of the Sendai princes once went hunting in the neighborhood of the temple and shot a wild goose, which fell on the ground, and a fox ran out and carried it off before his eyes. The prince sent to the Inari temple and reported the matter, requesting that the rude fox should be punished. What the priests did about it is not related, but the next morning a fox with a goose in his mouth was hanging on the temple gate.

At the time of the great yearly festival, which falls in the second month, the temple foxes invite their friends to attend; and they say that if you are bold enough to go out in the fields the night before you will see a great many lanterns moving along the little paths, all going toward the temple. The foxes who have to cross the river go to a certain ferry and change themselves into gentlemen wearing very fine clothes, and the ferryman on that night does not charge any fee, for he knows that he is carrying Inari Sama's servants.

According to Japanese poets and enthusiasts, there are three "chief places" counted the most beautiful of all in Japan. They are Nikko, Matsushima and Miyajima. Of the three, Nikko, of course, can be reached with no difficulty at all; Matsushima, or the "Pine Islands," fairly easily from Sendai, which is twelve hours from Tokyo and seven from Nikko on the main line north; and Miyajima, "Island of the Shrine," by rail and small steamboat from Kobe, quite away from the full-fledged European hotels. So far foreign tourists do not often visit either of the last two places, partly, of course, because they are off the track, and, besides, the stranger cannot be expected to thrill as the native-born does over the literary and historical associations of either place. Of them all, Matsushima has least to offer instead in the way of art interest, but as pure landscape it is most unusual, most picturesque, and, perhaps, too, most characteristic of Japan–certainly well worth a visit from anyone who cares for natural scenery.

Taken in connection with a trip to the Hokkaido, Matsushima comes in naturally enough, and makes a pleasant break in the long journey–twenty-six hours by rail–from Tokyo to Aomori, at the upper end of the main island. Coming this way the stopping place is Sendai, and the islands make a full day's excursion from there. Another way is to come up by sea from Yokohama on one of the large coasting steamers of the Nippon Yusen Kaisha line, which call at Oginohama on Sendai bay–the only place worthy of the name of harbor between Yokohama and Hakodate or Aomori. The run is about twenty-four hours from Yokohama; the steamers differ a great deal in size, and the smaller ones do not serve European food; but they are all clean and the service is uniformly good. Oginoharna is a pretty little place, lying in the hollow of a great hill, and the Japanese inns are fair. From there a little local steamer connects with the Nippon Yusen Kaisha, passing among the islands and landing you at Shiogama, the end of the branch railroad from Sendai. This branch line appears to exist chiefly to transport enthusiasts to and from Matsushima, though probably it gets some freight from the south by way of Oginohama; but the numerous handlings must make the advantage of this over the railroad exceedingly small. Passengers certainly depend as a general thing on the through trains to and from Tokyo, in spite of the unpleasant midnight hours at which they arrive and depart. Just why a city of Sendai's importance should be afflicted with such a timetable the benevolent paternal government probably knows, but it does not tell.

To reach Matsushima from Sendai you go by the branch road to Shiogama in about half an hour, and there hire a boat to sail or row across among the islands. Some vary the trip by taking a kuruma at Matsushima and riding back by the shore road. Shiogama itself is rather interesting; it was one of the oldest settlements on the bay-indeed, it claims to go back to the very Age of the Gods, and to be the place where the son of Isanagi, the creator of Japan, invented the art of making salt by boiling sea-water, and it is from this circumstance, they say, that the town gets its name, Shiogama, which means salt pans. If any should doubt this piece of history, they will show you the very pans the god used for his boiling–four of them–standing on a stone pedestal. They are made of iron, very shallow, and measure about a yard across; the sides are exceedingly thick. They are very much eaten with rust, and, whether we accept the inventive deity for a solar myth or a real culture hero, anybody can see that they are immensely old.

Tradition further relates that these pans came originally from the wonderful palace under the sea, where the Jewel Princess lived who married the fisher-boy Urashima; and at first there were seven of them, but one night some robbers came and stole three, and made off in a boat. But the dogs began to bark and roused the god, and when he saw the robbers were out of reach, he raised a tremendous storm and sank boat and pans and all; for he said; "They came from the Jewel Palace, and back to the Jewel Palace they shall go."

However it may have been in prehistoric times, this part of the coast is not one of the principal salt producing regions now;

most of this is made in the south, and also in the neighborhood of Yokohama. Japan has no salt mines, and the only way of getting this necessity is from the sea; consequently the industry must be a very old one–far older, surely, than Japanese dominion in this part of the islands. In the official division of the country made for purposes of taxation, one class of land is specified as shio-hama ("salt strand")–flat stretches of sandy coast used for salt-drying and boiling. Rein says the process of making it is the same as in China; they take a flat, sandy strip lying above the tide line, and divide it into little fields, each worked by two men; after leveling a field carefully, they layover it a coat of well-worked clay, thick enough to act as a cement. On this goes a layer of sand, spread evenly, and when this is ready they turn in sea water by little ditches, let it stand till it evaporates, and then turn in more, repeating again and again till the sand is very full of salt, when it is gathered up and washed in a filter with more sea water, which carries off the salt and leaves the sand behind, ready to go back on the fields again. The water, which is now very briny, is boiled in shallow pans, made of woven bamboo, covered on both sides with a clay cement, or occasionally in iron pans somewhat like the old ones at Shiogama. The process of letting the water filter down through piles of brush, as in some parts of Germany and near New Bedford, Massachusetts, seems not to be in use anywhere in Japan. Japanese salt is damp, grayish, queer-looking stuff, containing a good deal of the original sand; but in old times there was nothing better to be had, whether for salting fish or seasoning soup.

From Shiogama to Matsushima takes from two hours to four or five, according to the wind. The boats are not unlike the craft on Lake Como or Lecco, except that the round, white canvas cover is wanting; instead they give you a yane-bune (roof-boat), which has a tiny cabin amidships, or put up a mat shelter to keep off the sun. There are tatami (thick mats) to sit on, and a red blanket atop for elegance, and perhaps a comfortable pot of red coals to warm your fingers over, if the sea-wind is chilly. If you are so exacting as to need any other seat, you will have to make a special contract–probably with mine host at the little inn beside the shore, where you wait while the boat is made ready. The men row standing, as the Italians do, pushing the long sweeps with an easy swing, till they can run outside the anchorage and catch a favorable wind. Then, like Ulysses and his crew, they will "hoist up the mast from the mast-crutch, and spread out the white sail"–only in all probability the sail will not be white, but pale-brown or straw-colored matting, rigged to the yard in strips hung lengthwise and laced together–not in horizontal strips, as the Chinese rig their mat sails.

And so away through a very fairyland of isles and islets, their gray tufa rock worn by the waves into all manner of fantastic shapes. There are eighty-eight, islands, they say, between Shiogama and Matsushima, and one hundred and eight between Matsushima and Kinkwazan. Probably the count is about as accurate as the numbering of the islands in Casco Bay. Matsushima is a little like the

Matsushima

Maine coast, a good deal like the Italian shore from Naples south; most of all, perhaps, like Bermuda and the cedar-covered islands of Hamilton harbor, for, the ragged coral rock takes on much of the same picturesque grace as this sea-washed volcanic tufa. Each smallest rock bears a pine–those gnarled, sweeping hama-matsu of the Japanese coast, whose long branches "seek down" to the water, the Japanese say, just as a child stretches out its hands to its mother. The shore, too, is pine-clad and broken, with deep, rocky inlets, and the bay, with its green flock of islands, reaches away in a wide curve to Oginohama, locked in its high, bare hills, and crowned by Kinkwazan, lifting far above the blue sea-line. Kinkwazan has been one of the very sacred places since the earliest times, and it is far enough a way from modern life to keep many of its old associations and customs, though the rule which forbade women so much as to gaze on it is of course done away with. The name means Golden-flower Mountain, but the reason for it nobody knows, unless, as Chamberlain suggests, it comes from the glitter of mica in the soil. The fame of Matsushima arose long ago, almost with the first coming of the Japanese to these parts. Their poets have raved of the Thousand Pines ever since the seventh century, and they have given to every smallest island an individual name, sometimes descriptive, sometimes fanciful, such as the Elephant, the Turtle, Buddha's Entrance into Nirvana.

While the wind holds, the men sit smoking and deftly steering the little boat as it winds in and out, mile after mile, slipping under low branches and rounding sharp corners, were you see the jagged bottom through the clear water; or creeping under sheltering cliffs, where the leaning pines are doubled on the still surface; and so at last into the little harbor of Matsushima, with its neat village and its colony of tea-houses and shops for the sale of sea curiosities. The meibutsu (specialty) of the place is the fine slate of Ishinomaki, which is made into very smooth and beautiful ink-stones. Anyone who has tried to rub down a cake of India-ink on an ordinary glazed porcelain saucer knows what a hopeless task it is to try to get anything off on the slippery surface; the peoples who have written exclusively with this medium could never have done it if they had not had something different to work with. The slate is first cut out in a deep hollow at one end, running steeply into a shallower hollow at the other, and then polished smooth, and finally varnished over with India-ink and a wash of vegetable oil. It is perfectly smooth, and yet there is just enough tooth to work the ink to the thick, velvety black liquid good brush writers love. Besides slate, a green serpentine or a colored marble is often used, and the border of the hollow is frequently enlarged to give room for very beautiful carving in intaglio or low relief, sometimes pine or plum branches, sometimes figures, or Benten's tortoises climbing up the rocks.

The little Kwangetsuro and the Matsushima hotel are as clean and neat as the Sendai house is slatternly, and it is pure delight, after the long sail, to sit on the springy mats and consume the freshest of fish, with shoji pushed open to the salt air and all the beautiful bay spread out before you, showing here and there a sail among the dark islands. There are pretty little walks along the shore, and out by a bridge to Oshima, the Big Island—a more than usually fantastic thing of rock and pine. At Matsushima one begins to understand where the Japanese took some of their models for landscape gardening; odd and twisted as some of their creations are, they yet fall behind what nature has fashioned here by force of winds and waves. And therewith one perceives afresh how true to the actual appearances of things are many of the Japanese painters' most startling conventions.

During the comparative leisure of the latter part of his life, Date Masamune spent much effort and a large amount of money in the restoration and beautifying of the temple at Matsushima, gathering for the purpose the best painters and artists of the time, which was that of the shrines at Nikko. The gold backgrounds are tarnished now; but even so, the effect of the decorations in the reception rooms and other apartments is unusually rich and fine. The temple stands a little back from the sea, in a grove of pines; as you enter the enclosure, near a little cave, you are confronted by two tall figures of Kwannon, carved in black slate—probably from the quarries of Ishinomaki. The Ihai, or ancestral tablets of the Date family, are here, and many interesting relics of them: likewise a second portrait-statue of Date Masamune himself, carved in wood, which stands in a chapel behind the main altar. The effigy is life-sized, in armor, seated on a camp-stool, such as knights used to carry for their lords; a one-eyed, stern old warrior, grasping sword and war-fan, and wearing on his helmet the crescent, in token of increasing power. The feet are apart, the mailed hands on the knees, and the head lifted with a suppressed energy that is very telling.

Assuredly he was a man to admire; a man of iron will, of flawless honor, of wise, far-seeing statesmanship. Tokugawa Ieyasu was his friend, as well as master. Hidetada, Ieyasu's son, was a man of far less vigor of character; dying a few years after his father, he felt that the great Shogun's work was incomplete, the Tokugawa power hardly secure enough to be held by his own young son, Iemitsu; and he bade his followers yield the Shogunate rather than plunge the country again into a civil war. Some of the princes hesitated; Date Masamune alone spoke openly, bidding them remember the favors they had enjoyed from Ieyasu, and adding, "Before you touch his grandson, you will pass over my dead body." Iemitsu became Shogun, and proved the ablest of his line.

A year later Date came to Yedo to render formal homage to the new ruler; but he arrived too broken down with age and sickness to leave his yashiki, and shortly after he died there, "in my bed, and not in the saddle, as I had hoped," he said regretfully to the young Shogun, who came to visit him. "The empire is at peace, but who knows how long peace will endure? Order and quiet enervate men, and when the moment of action arrives, there are no longer any soldiers. See to it that men do not degenerate. You alone can do this, and I shall command my son to aid you. Do not forget my last counsel." (De la Mazeliere, "Histoire du Japon.")

Such was Date Masamune, Prince of Sendai, the last of the great men of the sixteenth century. Of such a man we may well believe the Matsushima statue to be a true portrait.

20

THE OSHIU KAIDO

THE old post-road north, Oshiu Kaido, is still kept in very good condition, although the railroad follows it quite closely most of the way and takes most of the long-distance traffic. Leaving Tokyo and crossing the great plain, it climbs a little to reach Utsunomiya, where the branch road turns off to Nikko; then it keeps nearly due north, following the trend of the island, passing through the inland provinces about half-way between the central mountains and the sea, except at Sendai, where it swings out a little towards the bay. All the earlier part lies in a rich and well-cultivated country, and in some places the beautiful old pines and cryptomerias are still standing, which made it a stately avenue for the princes to ride through. Beyond Sendai, both road and railroad follow the Kitamigawa, climb the hills in which it rises, and so make their way by Morioka and the great moors to Aomori, on the northern strait.

Utsunomiya was a castle-town of some importance, belonging to one of the Fudai nobles; that is to say, those who had given their allegiance to the Tokugawa before the final battle of Sekigahara; and, as the capital of a prefecture, it has kept its former prosperity, and is favored with one of the ten-minute stops of the through trains. As the carriages slow into the long, covered station, you feel as if pandemonium had been let loose. The guards hurry down the platform, opening doors with a click and a slam; the stone pavements ring with the sharp scrape and ping-pong of countless excited geta, and above the shouts of the guard, the din of voices sound the staccato cries of the lunch and tea-pot men–"O bento!" "O chaya!" "O bento!" responding to each other like an antiphonal chant. A Japanese Baedeker must surely star these Utsunomiya o bento–"honorable lunch" boxes; even for a foreigner, after one has grown a little used to Japanese food and a little hardened to the shock of cold-rice sandwiches, the neat whitewood case and its daintily-arranged contents become very appetizing. Washed down with small cupfuls of freshly-made tea, from the o chaya's teapot, a Japanese, or a well-taught foreigner, will make an excellent meal. These station-lunches vary in freshness and quality, just as railroad restaurants do all over the world; and Utsunomiya's are among the best. The men come from the hotels, which make a point of sending them down to meet the trains; and it must be a very good business. Wheaten biscuits, fresh and hot, are sold at some of these larger stations, not far from Tokyo; they are, of course, an innovation, perhaps an imitation of the English penny bun. Sometimes a national touch is added–a stuffing of sweet black-bean paste!–a most startling compound to meet unawares in the heart of an innocent-looking bun! The result is a cross between a sugar-biscuit and a Japanese manju, which is a round, flattened cake of rice dough, filled with this same form of pease-porridge cold; and if your manju happens to be toasted over a hibachi of charcoal, on a crisp autumn evening, you have no idea till you try how good it can be.

Utsunomiya has sorrowful memories of the war of the Restoration; a terrible fight took place near there, and the clansmen were obliged to retire to Aidzu, the last province that held out, which lies over the mountains almost directly to the north. The Aidzu clan was really, as the angry Imperialists said, "the root of the rebellion." For generations they had been charged with the care of the city of Kyoto, and they had watched over the doings of the palace party with the eyes of a hawk; to have been deprived of this office was grievance enough for their pride. They had the reputation of being harder, less polished, but more soldierly than the other Samurai, unless, perhaps, Satsuma, who plumed themselves on their Spartan qualities. Whatever the rest did, Aidzu was ready to hold out for the Tokugawa to the last drop of blood, even though they fought against the "Brocade Banner;" for if the young Emperor was, as they believed, coerced or led astray by evil counselors, they considered themselves justified in setting him aside for another of the house-namely, the boyish prince-abbot, whom they had carried off from Uyeno.

Wakamatsu, the castle-town of Aidzu, lies in a beautiful plain twenty to thirty miles long and half as broad, famed throughout the country for its loveliness and fertility. To the north lies Bandaisan, a volcano some eight thousand feet high, which blew its crest off suddenly in 1888, pouring a mass of mud and rock down the valley on its northern side; more than four hundred people were killed, and four villages were overwhelmed, while seven were partly destroyed. The avalanche blocked the course of the river Nagase, and its waters spread out and formed a lake eight miles long and two wide; a village by it was left partly in and partly out of the water. The damage was greatest on the north side, where the huge mass was flung out almost horizontally, though hot stones and ashes fell all about the foot of the mountain. The western and southern sides of the Aidzu plain are surrounded by lesser mountains, from which a number of streams flow down across the open and fall into lake Iwashiro on the east, watering miles of rich rice-fields; and on the hills are plantations of lacquer trees and mulberry. The city, Wakayama, is still in a flourishing state, but the noble castle on the hill near it was torn down, even to the gateways, and hardly anything remains but a few of the old trees.

Wakamatsu castle was not taken by assault; when provisions failed the lord of Aidzu surrendered. Had it been otherwise, probably few, whether men or women, would have been taken alive. Old men and children fought ill that war; the women ardently desired the privilege, but it was denied them, on the ground that it would be a lasting disgrace to the clan to have it said that they lacked men, and therefore were obliged to employ women on the battlefield. I have before me an account of the siege, written in English by Mrs. Iwamoto, of Tokyo, from her own childish recollections and those of three friends, who were children in the castle during that terrible time. It begins with the first summons, when at eight o'clock one summer morning the clanging bells in the watch tower warned the retainers to hurry with their families to the shelter of the castle. There had been hot fighting in Echigo and at Shirakawa pass, and the imperial army had pushed its way up faster than anyone had dreamed; those who made most haste only gained the castle gate in a shower of flying bullets. So close was the firing that some gave up the attempt to reach the castle at all, and "whole families killed themselves rather than fall into the hands of the enemy," the men alone remaining alive in order to fight to the last.

Among those who went up to the castle was the mother of a Samurai, named Chikara, who had been killed in the fight at the pass a short time before. "The lord of the clan had condescended to visit the house after the head was brought in from the battlefield, and, taking the young child on his lap, commanded them to bring him up to be like his loyal and gallant father." Chikara's mother therefore told her daughter-in-law to take the child and hide him, while she herself went up to the castle, believing, as all did; that it could not hold out long. "In fact, nobody thought of living in those days, their only concern was how and when they might die most honorably." But the young widow refused to survive her husband and mother; nor would she yield until the mother-in-law exercised her right to disown her daughter-in-law, and sternly bade her go, or she should no longer belong to the family. Then the widow took the boy and fled, happily without injury.

Entering the castle in breathless haste, the women of the clan were ordered to attend on their lady, and going to her apartments they found her quietly arranging every detail with coolness and dignity, showing neither haste nor flurry. "During a whole month's siege, while the roar of the battle was heard without; Lady Teru did not once omit her usual toilette, nor did she ever show the least trepidation. Her quiet manner strengthened the hearts of all who came before her."

The siege lasted just a month, and all had time to settle into a routine of service, caring for the wounded, preparing food, even making bullets. There were several ladies who made up their minds to take their own lives, "but having seen many who were alarmed into death when there was no necessity for it" (which in Japan is almost as shameful as to refuse at the right time), "they resolved to wait till the great crisis should come, and then dispatch themselves with coolness and composure." They knew already just how to do it–to bind the knees together in the usual sitting posture, then take a sip of water and apply the sword.

The children had their plays, the little girls filling the small sand bags with which Japanese children play jack-stones, and the boys fishing with bent pins in the castle pond, or even flying kites, which the enemy took for some ruse meant to deceive them. On the night of the September full moon the ladies held a "poem party," as was proper to the season, an occasion for moon-gazing and composing uta, thirty-one syllabled poems, didactic, or fanciful. "But after the middle of September," continues Mrs. Iwamoto, "hoski (rice boiled and dried and stored for use on extreme occasions) was brought out from under the watch tower and began to be used. Then we knew that the worst had come. . . . Then came a command from our lord. It was to sew a flag with 'kosan,' (surrender) written on it. The women objected, and said they could not sew the flag of surrender. But there was no help for it, and they were obliged to obey the command." The next day the whole body of inmates filed out of the castle gate–"a sorry, crestfallen picture."

I have quoted at perhaps undue length, because in many ways the account is so very characteristic of old Japan, and because the same spirit exists today, however turned aside into other channels and modified by new conceptions of what is or is not right and suitable to do. For this was the atmosphere in which the men and women grew up who are the present generation in Japan; the siege of Aidzu castle was in 1868, something less than five years after the close of our own civil war. In the wider outlook, many things once great seem little; but, happily, the Samurai spirit has not altogether disappeared.

Aidzu was punished, but briefly. In the wise amnesty that followed the surrender all was soon forgiven, though for a time the sufferings of the Aidzu Samurai were pitiful beyond the troubles of the other clans. But the province has recovered, and carries on all its old industries as vigorously as ever.

The Aidzu specialty is lacquer–both the juice and the finished ware. What we know as shellac or lacquer varnish is quite a different substance from the Japanese ro or urushi, which is the juice of a kind of sumach, rhus vernicifera, akin to our poison ivy and the sumachs that flame across our swamps in autumn. It grows much larger than our sumacs, though, the trees reaching twenty-five to thirty feet in height, and as much as two feet in thickness; the timber is highly valued for its close grain and golden-yellow color toward the heart, and the seeds produce excellent vegetable wax, much used in making candles.

The tree flourishes best away from the sea, and in the more northern provinces, though Yoshino in Yamato produces the finest quality grown; but this is easily understood, because the Yoshino district is wild and mountainous, the peaks running up to five thousand and six thousand feet, and the loose, rather gravelly soil is exactly what the lacquer thrives best in. Naturally, the usual practice is to utilize land which cannot be cultivated in any other way, such as the steep sides of valleys, where even wheat will not grow.

The juice is gathered at any time after the sap begins to flow, in April, till it stops, in October or November, but the best and most comes out in the hottest months. The man who takes it goes from tree to tree, making a horizontal cut with a knife, and then, returning in a short time, scoops out the juice, which has filled the cut, but does not overflow it. To do this he uses a curved spatula, well oiled, scraping off the juice against the side of his pail or joint of bamboo. Trees begin to bear fruit and give sap at about seven or eight years, but their best yield is from fifteen to thirty. The branches and twigs cut off for trimming are steeped in water, and give an inferior grade of juice, which is mixed with drying oil and used for an under varnish. The season's yield averages about a pound of good sap to every fifty trees. For shipping they pack it down in tight kegs, well wrapped in oiled paper, which takes the place of tarpaulin for many such purposes in Japan.

As it comes from the tree the sap is thick and sticky, and of a grayish color. Before being used it must be strained through a cloth to get out the dust, bits of bark, etc., and then well stirred in shallow tubs and set in the sun for several hours, to dry out the superfluous water. In places where the manufacture of lacquer wares is considerable special dealers do this part, and retail to the real lacquer-workers.

There is a vast difference in the way pieces are prepared for lacquering, and in the kind of wood used to make them. The finest decoration is only put on articles made of the lightest and finest grain, and all the joints are cut down with a sharp knife, making a triangular hollow, which must be filled with cotton cloth, carefully pasted down, and varnished over with an under coat or two, before anything else is done. Then the worker lays a coat of juice, mixed with his ground color, usually either black or cinnabar red; the black (roiro) is a fine iron compound, the same that the women used to use for blackening their teeth. The coloring matter does not combine with the urushic acid, which is the principal ingredient of the juice, but is suspended as a body color in it.

Each layer of the varnish must be thoroughly dried and polished before another can be placed; and since a fine piece may have as many as twenty to thirty coats, it may be many months in the making. The drying takes from one or two to several days, and the curious part of it is that it must be done in a moist atmosphere and at a moderate heat. If the stuff is heated very hot, or if it is put in a dry place, it simply will not harden at all. Experiments have proved the reason to be that what happens is not mere drying, but a kind of fermentation. The juice contains between two and three percent of nitrogenous matter, and when it is exposed to the air, this acts on the urushic acid so that it oxidizes, and becomes not only perfectly hard, but entirely insoluble in alcohol, benzine, and several other substances which dissolved it easily before. Of course, the old lacquer-workers bothered themselves about reasons just as little as our grandmothers did when they "set a fresh risin'," but they learned to place the pieces in a special drying box and keep it warm and moist; and they knew that the best time in the year for working was in the wet summer months, when the temperature keeps between seventy-five and ninety degrees most of the time. For this reason, too, the moist air of Tokyo and Kyoto is well fitted for lacquer working, and a large proportion of the finer wares are made in the two capitals. Some of the earlier coats are polished with a powder of calcined deer's horn, which gives a smooth matt surface; the later rubbings are made with soft charcoal and the same powder used very fine and applied with a cotton cloth; and lastly the workman uses his finger and a little oil, till he attains the most brilliant gloss. The texture of a fine piece of lacquer is delightful to the touch, and is one test of its quality, and another is the lightness of the wood. I have handled a box several inches square which did not weigh more than a sheet or two of writing paper. Another test is that the grain of the wood does not show through the varnish.

Yoshida and other Japanese writers claim that the lacquer tree is indigenous to Japan, but Rein thinks there is no positive proof, and that the probability is that both the tree and its use were imported from China, with other arts. This seems the less likely, as there was an imperial Bureau of lacquer in the fourth century, before the great wave of Chinese influence. In the sixth century lacquer is named among the articles which may be offered in payment of taxes. The Nara period was one of development in this, as well as the other arts; and another time of rapid advance was under the luxurious Ashikaga Shoguns, in the fourteenth century.

But it was in the last quarter of the seventeenth century that this most Japanese of the arts of Japan, as Gonse called it, reached its highest expression, under the artist Korin, whose name is almost identified with lacquer. This period–the time of the fifth Tokugawa Shogun, a younger son of Iemitsu–is known in Japanese as the Gen-roku. It was a time of the greatest activity in literature and all the arts, a time of temple and palace building, and of increasing demand for the accessories of luxurious living. This Shogun Tsunayoshi was a great patron of classical studies, so much so that he not only founded professorships and encouraged the clan schools of the provinces, but himself delivered courses of lectures to audiences of feudal nobles, Samurai, and priests, both Buddhist and Shinto.

One may imagine the hearers were attentive when the professor was the actual ruler of the country. This period was also the time when trade intercourse with the Dutch was at its height, and when much of European thought and science was filtering into Japan, in spite of the exclusion laws. There is evidence, too, of renewed Chinese influence in Genroku art, as well as in the ornamentation of the Nikko temples, which immediately preceded. The Shiba temples belong to this time, and there is an exceedingly fine specimen of lacquer work in the shrines of the main temple.

But if the phaenixes and peonies and grinning lion monsters of the Buddhist temples seem to smack of Chinese taste, Korin is altogether of Japan; and the gold lacquer for which he chiefly designed is the happiest of mediums for his style–flexible and delicate, yet compelling a broad and simple treatment. The use of gold oil lacquer, as well as inlays of metal and mother-of-pearl, was at least as early as the Heian period–the ninth century–when the court removed from Nara to Kyoto. The decoration is laid on a surface already grounded and polished; the design is first drawn on paper, and the outline retraced on the under side with lacquer, which has been boiled to destroy its hardening power, so that it can be cleaned off when done with. The paper is then laid on the article to be decorated and rubbed gently, when the mark of the lacquer remains on the surface. This outline is then filled with fresh lacquer, on which fine gold dust is applied while it is still wet; after which the piece is put away to dry, and again the decoration is painted over with a coat of transparent lacquer. When this last has hardened, the design is rubbed down with hard charcoal, and finally polished with deer's-horn powder and a little oil. If the piece is large–say a writing-desk or small cabinet–only a little of the design can be laid at a time, so that with the successive dryings and polishings the old leisurely days were none too many for the lacquer-worker.

One of the wonders of Korin is the fertility of his imagination and the quantity of his designs; they created a school of lacquer which has been little altered since his time. He was also a landscape painter of considerable note, but the fame of his lacquer has quite cast his other works into the shade. His subjects were ideal landscapes, birds and flowers, such as a group of crows sitting on a branch, a graceful iris flower, or a flight of storks across the moon. Korin studied first the Kano school of painting, then the more delicate Tosa style, and finally worked for a time with a famous artist in metal; and his own style undoubtedly profited by all three. His subjects are treated with ideal grace, yet with the most perfect fidelity to nature–to those aspects of nature which can be expressed by the broad, flowing lines of the Japanese brush on a flat surface. Surely that is the essential quality of Japanese art–that it never attempts more than it can readily accomplish.

Naturally the more artistic works are not produced in these northern provinces; their wares are generally simple trays and bowls and boxes, the common articles of Japanese daily life. Bowls–the small covered bowls of plain brown or black lacquer in which the Japanese serve their soup–are rather a specialty of Fukushima, an important town about fifty miles south of Sendai. The city lies in a beautiful little plain encircled by hills, which is said to have once been the bed of a lake, but if so it has long since disappeared, and there are only a few historical allusions to support the idea. It is known that in the twelfth century Yoshitsune fled across this region to a neighboring castle, escaping from Yoritomo's unjust anger; but Yoritomo's spies pursued him even here, and he fled yet farther north toward the wild Ainu country, and put himself under the protection of a kinsman who was governor of the province. The kinsman was faithful, but when he died, the son was afraid or unwilling to oppose Yoritomo, and betrayed the trust. According to one version of the story, Yoshitsune and his companions died fighting against overwhelming odds, on the banks of a little river which flows into the Kitamigawa; and his head was cut off and sent to Yoritomo at Kamakura.

Like Sendai and so many others, Fukushima was an old castle-town and is now the capital of its prefecture; it is a great market for raw silk and silkworm eggs, as well as for the woven silks made in this and the neighboring provinces. A branch railroad soon to be opened will go westward, and will bring in easy reach another large silk-growing region, the town and prefecture of Yonezawa.

They say the silk trade of Yonezawa is largely in the hands of the old Samurai families, who were very numerous and very thrifty and well to do, so that they suffered less than most Samurai by the changes of the Restoration. The reason for this satisfactory state of affairs goes back to Ieyasu and the battle of Sekigahara, and concerns the rise and fall of the great Uyesugi family, whose vassal, Ota Dokwan, founded the first Yedo castle.

This great clan belonged to the feudal nobility of Yoritomo's time, and several of the chiefs held the office of Kwambaku or governor of Kamakura under the Ashikaga Shoguns of the fourteenth century; they were among the number of lesser lords who rose suddenly to great power, through the Ashikaga policy of making large grants of land to their followers, without any definite system of control over the lords so enriched. In this way the Uyesugi obtained Echigo, on the west coast, and held it far several generations, in spite of fierce wars. Their special enemy was Takeda Shingen, whose castle was at Kofu, in the mountains behind Fuji San. A typical specimen of the age was Takeda; brilliant, reckless, fighting for pure love of danger, so, able that the last battle between him and Uyesugi Kenshin became a model of tactics for after time. Takeda won this fight and greatly lessened the power of the Uyesugi, and shortly after shaved his head and became a Buddhist monk–renouncing all worldly matters except war; this, though, was nothing out of the way for a monk of his land and age.

By this time Hideyoshi came upon the scene. The Uyesugi were not prompt enough in making submission to him, and as a punishment were deprived of Echigo; but Aidzu, which they received instead, was not a bad substitute. But a generation later they sided against Ieyasu; and this time, when the retribution came, they were transferred to a little mountainous territory to the north of Aidzu, with no, coast, and not even a large lake or river. Yonezawa yielded a bare one hundred and fifty thousand koku on which to support the retainers who had been maintained out of a revenue of one million in Echigo. The clan ran heavily into debt, and the people were taxed beyond endurance.

To this unhappy province came a boy ruler, a lad of seven-teen, adopted from a neighboring family, because the old lord of Yonezawa had no heir. It is recorded that the boy reached his terri-tory on a chilly autumn day, and as he rode among the wretched vil-lages and scanty harvests, the attendants saw him carefully blowing up a charcoal fire in a small hibachi which had been placed in his litter. One of them offered to bring his lord a fresh fire, but Yozan declined, saying, "I am learning a great lesson; afterwards I will tell you." At the inn where they halted for the night, Yozan called his train together and said, "Today despair took hold of me, as I saw with my own eyes my people's miseries. Then I noticed the little fire before me, which was on the point of going out; and I took it up, and by blowing carefully and patiently I succeeded in reviving it. May I not be able in the same way to revive the land and the people that are under my care?"

The first necessity was to lighten taxation. Yozan cut down his own expenses to one-fifth, and the retainers' allowances to one-half; whatever revenue could thus be saved went toward paying the clan's debt. But it was no less important to bring back thrift and decency among the people, demoralized as they were by want and wretchedness. "As well expect an eggplant from a cucumber vine as look for wealth from a misgoverned people," says the Japanese proverb. Yozan sought out men of the highest character and ability, and made them governors and sub-officers; then he appointed a number of itinerant teachers, who were to instruct the peasants in morals and ceremonies–"of filial piety, of pity towards widows and orphans, of matters of marriages, of decency in clothing, of food and ways of eating, of funeral services, of house repairs, and so on." And thirdly, he sent out the strictest of police, bidding them "show Emma's justice and righteous wrath, but fail not to store Jizo's mercy in your bosom."

It was the time of the Great Peace, and Yozan set his idle Samurai to tilling the ground and bringing wasteland under cultivation. Every Samurai family was required to plant fifteen lacquer trees, and every temple twenty. Whoever set out more was rewarded; who-ever did not replace one that died, was fined. The result was over a million trees in a few years, to the very great profit of the district; and as many paper trees were also planted in waste places. To be able to plant mulberry, Yozan cut fifty gold pieces out of the allowance of two hundred and nine, which he had reserved for his own household, and used them as far as they would go, and, after fifty years, the few thousands of trees which he had been able to plant had grown up and were replanted from cuttings, till there was no more space left for them in the land.

But this was all hill-cultivation. There was land fit for rice, if only it could be sufficiently irrigated; so this poorest of the Daimyo undertook two of the greatest engineering works in old Japan; the one brought water for twenty-eight miles, through viaducts and on long and high embankments, and the other changed the course of a large stream, carrying it through a tunnel in a mass of granite rock– a work of twenty years, accomplished by a self-taught engineer, an awkward, silent man, whom everybody thought a dolt, till the chief discovered him to be a mathematical genius. When we consider the rude instruments of the time, such work is not small. Thus supplied with abundance of water, Yonezawa became one of the most fertile of the provinces.

Even this was not all. From their earliest beginnings, the Uyesugi had been distinguished for their love of letters and patronage of scholars; one of the family had revived a college of the Ashikaga time, and many had promoted the study of classical Japanese. As soon as his material reforms were well under way, Lord Yozan followed the family tradition, by re-establishing the Clan School, as the Samurai colleges were called, and endowing a number of scholarships, so as to bring it within the reach of even the poorest of his retainers, With this he also started a medical school, favoring the new Dutch system, which a few Japanese had learned at Nagasaki.

Yozan lived to be seventy, keeping his frugal habits to the end, wearing only cotton and eating the simplest of food. He saw his house free from difficulties, his people well nourished, and "the clan that had not been able to raise five pieces of gold by their united effort, could now raise ten thousand at a moment's notice."

258 JAPAN AND HER PEOPLE

No wonder that the people wept for him, or that the little province has been prosperous ever since.

The region through which the railroad passes is very different; indeed, soon after leaving Sendai, the whole aspect of the country seems changed. Instead of villages, making an almost continuous line along the highway, and fields cultivated to the last inch, from sea to mountain's edge, as in the south, you pass for hours through districts sparsely populated, and scanty acres, leveled with toil, between ravines and steep hills; or, again, miles of grassy moor, stretching away and away, without a sign of life. The wildest, most beautiful and most desolate portion is on the upper waters of the Kitamigawa, and on the pass which crosses between Fukuoka and Morioka, where the railroad follows up one little branch to its source, then crosses over the divide and winds down the narrow valley of another stream. Morioka is a fine old town, the capital of a prefecture now, and formerly the castle of the Daimyo of Nambu. It lies in the centre of a beautiful cultivated plain, dominated on the northwest by a fine volcanic cone, rising six thousand eight hundred feet, in those sweeping lines which Japanese mountains take so often.

It was the coast of this province which received the full force of one of the greatest tidal waves of modern times, in June of 1894. To understand the kind and extent of the damage, one should know the Japanese coast, with its little bays and chines, as they would call them in the Isle of Wight, shut in by high, steep cliffs, against which the little villages nestle, or creep down to the shore line. Against such a coast, from Kinkwazan to the Tsugaru strait, and even across to the Hokkaido, rose a sudden wall of water, variously estimated at from twenty to eighty feet in height, crushing the little houses together as if they had been eggshells, breaking trees short at the root and carrying the stone pillars of torii hundreds of feet. It was the day of the May festival, according to the old calendar, which is generally followed for such things in the country; and every house was keeping holiday. There was little warning; two or three slight shocks of earthquake, then a roar, said to have been like the firing of cannon; and then the wave. A few fled up the cliffs and escaped;

the most were caught and drowned, or killed by the falling houses. Some towns and villages were totally swept away; the estimate was between twenty-five and thirty thousand lives lost, eight thousand houses entirely destroyed and thirteen thousand damaged, besides immense destruction of nets and shipping. Large boats were carried far up the land and lodged in the rice-fields and orchards.

The news was telegraphed at once, and relief parties hurried to the district. In one village the telegraph operator saw his family killed before his eyes, but he gathered himself and his instruments out of the wreckage, and went to work without delay to summon help. The Red Cross Society is always ready for such work, floods and earthquakes, more or less severe, keeping them in far too good practice; and the governors and under-officers of the three prefectures came also, and after them the missionary bodies, which naturally were less prepared for such service, but did it gladly and well when they did arrive. It was not easy; the extent of coast affected was so great, and the distance from the railroad so considerable and over hilly, poor roads; but the system and care with which the government officials acted was beyond praise. The Emperor and Empress made personal gifts, besides the government grants for tools and fishing apparatus; and newspapers and large business houses, native and foreign, opened subscription lists, which were promptly and gladly responded to.

There were many strange escapes–one taken and another left. Two French priests were at an inn; the one fled in his stockings, the other stopped at the door to put on his shoes and was drowned. A baby was found in a tree, quite unhurt; another was floated out to sea. Now, the fishermen of the villages were far outside, engaged in their deep-sea fishing–it was eight o'clock in the evening when the wave came and their boats had been lifted on the long swell, without their noticing anything unusual. Thus they were rowing quietly home, when a boatload of them saw something floating in the water and went over to see what it was. The thing proved to be a tatami–one of the thick pieces of rush matting of a Japanese house– and on it lay a bundle wrapped in a quilt. They opened it, and found the sleeping baby, carried out from their own village.

Pack Horse

Up to this time these remote coast villages had been less touched by modern progress than any part of the empire; on account of the hills and ridges inland, they communicated with one another almost entirely by sea, and occasionally with the larger coast towns in the same manner; but with the rest of the world they had little to do. It is said that in some places the people hardly knew of the change of government, and when the papers entitling them to receive relief were given them, they thought the gift came from the Prince of Nambu, their former lord, and they lifted the papers reverently to their foreheads, expressing thanks to his lordship for his condescension.

Fukuoka is the only town of any importance between Morioka and Aomori, which is another eight hours by rail, making the full tale of twenty-six hours from Tokyo; and never a sleeping car to do it in, unless one has been put on lately. Above Sendai, though, the trains are seldom full, and that means plenty of room to lie down and be quite comfortable. As for food, one must either take it along, or cultivate a taste for Japanese o bento, which is the easier, since Morioka's lunch-boxes are uncommonly good.

Aomori lies at the head of a gourd-shaped bay, twenty miles long, which opens by a narrow mouth into Tsugaru Strait. It is the terminus of the mainline railroad, and the port for crossing to Hakodate, and it is also a garrison town; and that is about all there is of it. Once on a time the government had a stock farm near Aomori, but that has been moved away. A good many horses are still raised in the neighborhood, and there are orchards of apples, esteemed the best in Japan, and other fruits, likewise introduced from America. The whole region is open to the bleak Siberian winds, and the air is bright and keen, and often bitterly cold. The truth is, Aomori is a dreary little place, in spite of some good shops and a considerable trade; the streets look half-deserted, and far too wide for the low houses, which are not thatched or tiled, but loosely shingled and piled over with stones, to keep the shingles down, giving them an air of hopeless poverty and untidiness. The shop-fronts are darkened by a sort of arcade over the sidewalk, closed in winter by storm-shutters, to keep out the drifting snow, as they do also at Niigata and some other places on the west coast. Altogether, they have a look of forlorn compromise, these poor little towns that are trying to live Japanese fashion in the biting, un-Japanese north.

The inhabitants of Aomori seem to be either trim soldiers or unkempt fishermen, or peasants leading squealing, ill-tempered horses, which take every opportunity to engage in a free fight, regardless of the carts they are hitched to. An army of crows also quarters here, and their dances of a morning on the shingled roofs would rouse the Seven Sleepers. But very few travelers stay to hear them. The train from Tokyo gets in at four in the afternoon, and the Hakodate-Mororan boat leaves at ten or eleven in the evening; or, going south, you reach Aomori from Hakodate at daybreak, and take the train at ten in the morning. There is no pier; the steamers lie out in the bay, and you row to them by lantern-light in big sampans; the men push and swing back at the long oars, keeping time to a wailing chant that echoes weirdly across the dark water, and is taken up by boat after boat stealing out toward the high, black hull, with its winking lights. The steamers are clean and fairly large, and the sixty miles of bay and strait not often very rough so that, with a cabin–best engaged beforehand–there is no particular hardship in getting over to the Hokkaido; that is to say, the North, or, literally, Northern Road, as they call Yezo and the Kurile Islands together.

21

THE HOKKAIDO

TSUGARU STRAIT, which cuts Yezo from the main island, is a deep though narrow channel into which the waters of the Japan Sea sweep at the western end with dangerous currents. It is widest in the middle, and narrows sharply at the two ends, where the mountains rise like gateways on either side; indeed, the whole Yezo shore of the strait is almost a continuous wall of cliffs, with only one great break opposite the mouth of Aomori bay, as if the two openings were meant to pair with one another. Just here beside the break in the cliffs Hakodate Head thrusts out from the side of Hakodate Mountain, which lifts one thousand one hundred and fifty-seven feet clear from the water-line. "The Peak," as nearly everyone calls this mountain, is almost but not quite an island; a sandy strip a mile or so long connects it with the shore, which on the other side is quite low for some distance, and leaves room for several good farms. The slope of the promontory is wooded half way up, and covered with low undergrowth to the top; the base is circled on three sides by precipitous cliffs, while the third, lying between the sand strip and the bold point called the Head, curves around in a sheltered hollow to form one of the finest harbors in the world–deep and roomy, with anchorage for half a dozen fleets. The town curves after, following the line of the harbor, and spreads out along the neck of sand, and climbs yearly higher up the mountain by steep streets and terraces; a prosperous, growing, commercial city, getting small share of foreign trade, but very busy with the coast-wise service. It has a charming park on a rocky knoll overlooking the bay, and two fine reservoirs fed by a stream far back on the mountain, hundreds of feet above the town; the water is distributed by hydrants placed every few hundred yards along the street, where the housewives and maidservants come to draw, as elsewhere they come to the old wells, since few are wealthy enough to have water introduced into their houses. The waste water rushes down the paved gutters by the road, much as it does in the little mountain villages, and the police have some difficulty in persuading conservative grandmas that it is not equally pure and suitable to wash their fish and vegetables in, as the good dames used to do, no doubt, before they migrated from their hills in the south to this new region, for it must be remembered that in Hakodate few save the young can be native born.

Hakodate is sometimes compared with Gibraltar, but there is little real resemblance; what it is far more like is the bay of Naples and Vesuvius, if the crater of Vesuvius were carried up to its full height. But the coloring is utterly different; for the bare ash and lava, there is fresh green forest, and instead of warm Italian blue in sea and sky, the dreamy, opalescent light of Japan.

The harbor is thronged at all times with fishing craft and coasting steamers, and Maine schooners, and tramps from all over the world putting in here for food and water; in summer the motley crowd often includes the warships of half a dozen powers, sent up to keep watch–or, so they say–over the sealing and whaling of their nationals in the Smoky Seas. The cool summer air is pleasant for officers and men; the climate of Hakodate is exceedingly like that of Newport, R. I., except that the Japanese port gets less fog. The British fleet often winters at Hong Kong, comes to Yokohama in the early summer, and goes on to Hakodate for the hottest months. They say that when the ships come beer shops spring up as if by magic; indeed, the foreign sailors are a serious drawback to residence in the place. When some of these are in port it is most unpleasant–not to say unsafe for ladies to go down near the harbor, or, indeed, toward dusk on the streets farther up, where the principal shops for European goods are. English officers say they dread to bring their men to Hakodate; crews that have done well almost everywhere else seem nearly sure to get into difficulties in the grog-shops there as soon as they have a chance to go ashore. For one thing they say these Hakodate sailors' taverns keep American drinks of a peculiar vileness and potency; and partly, too, the men have a sense of being almost up to the end of the world.

When the fleets are not in port there are few foreigners about; only the Consular people, and a small body of hard-working missionaries of many denominations. The English make Hakodate a base for their labors among the Ainu, and do much also by seamen's missions and the like for the shifting sailor population; both the Greek Church and the Roman have long had stations here, and up on the hill there is a large Methodist girls' school, which is perhaps the best institution of the kind in Japan.

From every street in Hakodate the views are exquisitely lovely, and they seem to grow even lovelier as you ascend the peak behind the town. It is a long climb, but nowhere steep; at first beyond the houses the path leads through a grass-grown cryptomeria forest, where lilies-of-the-valley bloom in spring, and in summer the clustering white wild roses stretch a bower over every sunny bank and lane; between the branches you look down on the gray shingled roofs of the town, looking flat as if some one had ironed them, and the flock of white sails in the harbor, and across to the blue wall of peaks closing the horizon, Komagatake's keen point centering all. To the left of the harbor on the low, green headland is the site of an old fort, dismantled now, which played a serious part in the war of the Restoration, when Count Kuroda and the rest stole away up here with the Tokugawa ships; the fort is a public park now, and the moats are used for skating–an amusement which the Japanese have learned from America, and enjoy thoroughly when they have a chance.

As might be expected, fishing remains the chief local industry of Hakodate; it is a pretty sight to see the fleet of little boats go out of an afternoon, rowing past the headland and round by the cliffs quite behind the mountain, till they lie off the neck on its outer side. At night, from the end of the town near the public garden, their tiny lights cluster like a galaxy of winking stars in the dark sea beyond the blacker rocks. The fish are plenty and of excellent quality, to judge by Hakodate markets; besides fine tai and other fish met with in the south, there are swordfish and salmon from the northern rivers, both fresh and dried, and oysters from Kushiro and Nemuro on the east coast of Hokkaido, and plenty of large scallops, with delicate white meat and shells four or five inches across. These pretty, light-brown, ridged shells make charming little individual baking dishes; I have seen them sold on the street in Tokyo, I suppose for that purpose, though I had not Japanese enough to ask. These hotate, as they call them, are very abundant in the Hokkaido waters, but do not seem to be found farther south. Seaweed, too, is a special "meibutsu" of Hakodate, and there are several edible varieties which are highly prized and frequently put up in neat little tins, for visitors to take to their friends at home. A great deal of fish goes to the south dried, canned, smoked and fresh, and much also

Hakodate

to China, along with boatloads of the large univalve awabi or sea-ear—beche de mer, as the French call it—from the southern waters; Japanese seaweed, too, is largely exported for the Chinese.

Formerly the rivers of Hokkaido must have been as full of salmon as the Columbia or the Alaskan waters, but till lately they have been recklessly wasted; still, they are very plenty even now, and there are laws to protect them in future. The Japanese cure salmon with a great deal of salt, but the Ainu method is merely to dry it in the sun—an arrangement which makes not only their huts but themselves unpleasantly perceptible a long way to leeward.

The Ainu, who supply the folk-lore for the Hokkaido, have a legend to account for the plentifulness of fish and flesh in Ainu land. Once, they say, long, long ago, there was a dire famine, so that the Ainu were ready to die of hunger. But they gathered together the crumbs that were left, a little millet and a little rice malt, and with it they made a cup of wine, and poured it into six lacquer cups; and the sweet smell of the sake arose from the cups, filling all the house.

Then the gods were called together, the gods of all places, from this side and from that; also the goddesses of the mountains and the goddesses of the valleys, the goddesses of the rivers and the goddesses of the mouths of rivers. And they were all pleased with that delicious wine, and the goddesses of the mountains and the valleys, of the rivers and the mouths of rivers, danced and sang before the assembled gods; and the gods laughed and were glad. Then as they danced the goddesses plucked out two hairs of a deer and blew them over the tops of the mountains, and on the tops of the mountains two herds of deer came running, one of bucks and the other of does; and they plucked out two scales from a fish and blew them over the rivers, and in the rivers shoals of fish came swimming, insomuch that there was not room, and they scraped upon the stones.

So the men set their boats upon the rivers and took fish; and the young men went forth and slew deer upon the hills, and they ate and did not die. Therefore, from that day, in the land of the Ainu, there is fish and flesh without stint.

Hakodate people go for picnics and other such amusement to the hot springs at Yunokawa, on the coast farther to the east, a mile or so beyond the neck of sand; and to Yunozawa, which is two or three miles inland from the last; also, a longer excursion, best made on horseback or by carriage, to a chain of lakes which lie at the foot of Komagatake. The ascent of this volcano can be made in a long day from Hakodate, but nearly everyone stays over a night at Junsaimura, on the first lake. Beyond here horses can be used for nearly three-quarters of the way; the rest is a stiff climb over sand and crumbling ashes to the edge of the crater. On the side of the cone is a great mass of rock towering far above the rest, and it is this which makes the spear-like point of Komagatake as it is seen from Hakodate and along the coast. The crater is still but thinly crusted and treacherous, with boiling springs and sulphurous smoke breaking out here and there, altogether a risky place. The great volcano of the north no one seems to venture on; it is Mount Ezan, the most eastern point of the southern peninsula, and the first mountain sighted in coming up from Yokohama by steamer–which is really the easiest, if not the most interesting way.

This sea route takes only two days, with the call at Oginohama besides, where you can usually go ashore for a few hours while they load and unload; and a very pleasant run it is too, if you are so made as to be able to enjoy a voyage in a clean little steamer, rocking nicely on a long ground swell. They lie twenty-four hours at Hakodate to leave and take on freight, and then run on through Tsugaru Strait and up the west coast of Yezo to Otaru; while the Aomori boats touch at Hakodate for a few hours only, and then turn out around Cape Ezan and head across Volcano bay to Mororan. For the present, one or the other line has to carry all there is to go, for it will be a year or two longer before Hakodate is connected by rail with the rest of the world. A line from Mororan, on Volcano bay, to Sapporo and Otaru was built long ago, in the early days of Yezo colonization, and held the world's record as the cheapest line ever built anywhere; but its route was a fairly easy one, offering nothing much worse to contend with than swamp and forest and a few rivers, whereas the part of the island south of Volcano bay is only a peninsula, so crowded with rocks and mountains that it is much easier to take a boat and go round than attempt to climb over. However, in these days there must be railroads, and so, although the neck of the peninsula is the very most spinous of all, a line is on the way, opening up new tracts of country as it goes, after the manner of colonial railroads. One special reason for pushing this one is that oil has been found in these mountains; the extent of land already opened for wells in Hokkaido exceeds the whole amount in the rest of Japan, which last is mostly located in the mountains, near Niigata, on the west coast of the main island.

Yezo must have been separated from the rest of the group since very early geological time, for its flora and fauna are quite distinct from even the northern end of the main island. There are no monkeys–which of itself would not be unnatural, Yezo is so much colder–and the bear is a huge grizzly, while the proper Japanese bear is small and black; there are grouse instead of pheasants in the north, and a number of singing birds not found in the other islands. Elms and other northern trees grow in great abundance all through the Sapporo plain, and elsewhere in the interior, and the wild forests along the Mororan-Sapporo railroad might be anywhere in central Pennsylvania.

According to the Ainu, the creator god Aioina did not himself make Yezo, but entrusted the task to a god and goddess, giving him the south and east, and charging her with the western part. So they both went to work at once, trying to see who could finish the job best and most quickly. But while they were working, another goddess came along, and woman-like the first stopped to have a bit of gossip with her friend. So they talked and they talked, for quite a long time; and meanwhile the god was working away fast and steadily. Then all of a sudden the goddess looked up and saw that he had almost finished, and she was frightened and ashamed, and hurried very fast, piling up the rocks and mountains any way at all, so that she might get done in time. And the consequence is that the west coast of Yezo is so wild and rocky that no one can do anything with it to this day. Moreover, anyone may see the axe the god used in making his part, for he stuck it up on the shore when he got done–a large dark rock, standing on the coast near Mororan.

The shape of Yezo is rather like a Japanese kite, its head pointing to the northeast, and the part below Volcano bay serving for a short, bent tail. Not only this southern peninsula, but the main part of the island, is more than half mountainous, and far the larger portion of it is still covered with forests, through which the roads are few and, as a rule, anything but good. The government has made considerable surveys, however, and the character and resources of the region are fairly well mapped down. Coal and coal oil and sulphur are the chief mineral products, a very large part of the sulphur produced in Japan–and it is a great deal coming from, Yezo and the Kuriles. The Russians destroyed most of the fur-bearing animals on the Kurile group, before they consented to give up their unproved claim on the islands in return for the far more valuable cession of southern Saghalien. The sulphur on Kunashiri and Iterup is the one useful product to be had there now.

The single plain of Yezo is a wide level, seventy miles long and some twenty to thirty across, running from Volcano bay nearly north to the Sea of Japan. It must have been at one time a part of the bay, and probably not so very long ago either, as geology counts time, since the Sapporo botanists say that certain purely beach plants still linger on its border hills. The Ainu called this region Satsuporo (the dry plain), in distinction to the vast stretches of peat bog and morass near the lower part of the Ishikari and other rivers; and the Japanese Colonial Department kept the name, when they chose the upper end of the plain and placed there the new capital, Sapporo. The other towns of the Hokkaido, like Topsy, "just growed," and they are all on the sea–Hakodate, Otaru, twenty miles north of Sapporo, and Kushiro and Nemuro, on the dreary east coast, ice bound all winter and fog hung the rest of the year. With some government help in the way of harbor improvement, these self-made towns have thriven finely; it was only official, made-to-order Sapporo that had rather a hard time to get started; as for Otaru, shipments of coal and herring-oil and fish guano have made

it boom at times like any American town in the wild West, specula-
tion in building lots and all.

It is really almost more American than Japanese, this lively,
new Hokkaido, which, only thirty years ago, was altogether vir-
gin forest, given over to bears and Ainu. There was a Daimyo, it
is true, and had been since the sixteenth century, whose revenues
came from fishing dues, and whose castle and single town of any
size was Matsumae-now renamed Fukuyama-at the west end of
Tsugaru strait. Hakodate was only a little bigger and better than
the other wretched fishing hamlets fringing the coast, which were
hardly inhabited, except in summer, when fishermen came up from
the main island for the season. On the main island people would
believe anything about Yezo; they were quite sure that in winter
fire froze and turned into coral; and certainly nobody would go
there who could help it. But when the West was discovered and
American vessels began to sail the north Pacific, Hakodate was the
safest and most convenient place for the sealers and whalers, and
consequently it was one of the first ports asked for, opened, and
provided with consuls of the various nationalities.

Still, this coming of a few foreigners did not affect Japanese
interests much. The real opening of the Hokkaido was begun in
1868, and it was the work of the unsubmissive Tokugawa clansmen.
When Yedo was given up to the Imperialists, the ex-Shogun's ships
were to have been given up likewise, as part payment for sparing
the city; but, instead of fulfilling this part of the contract, the naval
commander and some of the followers of Tokugawa took it upon
themselves to slip off with the whole fleet, which consisted of some
five vessels. They sailed north and waited about Sendai, hoping to
be able to help the land force who were at Utsunomiya and Aidzu;
but, after the fall of Wakamatsu Castle, they were joined by the
chief rebel general, Otori, and went on to Yezo, taking possession
of Hakodate and Matsumae. The governor, seeing himself unable
to resist, departed to Aomori and sent a complaint to the imperial
government; and there was another brave but hopeless struggle to
be gone through before the leaders, Enomoto and Kuroda, found
themselves totally overmatched, and gave themselves up to save

their followers. And again, as after the fall of Wakamatsu Castle, the Emperor was "as a father" to his misguided children, whose sin, after all, was only loyalty misplaced.

It is worth while to look a little into the meaning of this raid on the north, for, in a way, it gave not only the first impetus, but set the keynote of Yezo colonization. This is what the leaders said for themselves, as Black translates their memorial to the Emperor. After speaking of the changes that had taken place, the Tokugawa revenues cut off and the retainers turned adrift, they plead: "Men who have the hearts of Samurai cannot turn into farmers or merchants, so that it appeared that there was nothing for us but to starve. But, considering the uncultivated condition of the island of Yezo, we thought it better to remove thither, that, even under the endurance of every hardship, we might level steep mountains, cultivate the desert, and employ hitherto useless people in a useful work." For this privilege, they say, they petitioned the government in vain, and "it seemed that the three hundred thousand clansmen must surely starve;" so, in despair, they had sailed on their own risk, using force only against Hakodate and Matsumae–both fortified places. "On application to the governor of Hakodate, he would not listen to us, but viewing us merely as a band of robbers, attacked us. Matsumae also murdered our messenger, and for these reasons we were obliged to set aside these men. The farmers and merchants are unmolested, going about their business without fear, and sympathizing with us, so that already we have been able to bring some land under cultivation."

"To employ useless people in a useful work"–there spoke the true Samurai spirit; the spirit of the man who must have service–and that a worthy service–or extinction. There is an amusingly familiar note in the guileless protest of these land-grabbers against being regarded as robbers; but there can be no question that they were absolutely sincere, as well as terribly in earnest, even though there was another motive underlying all, and quite frankly avowed. "We pray that this portion of the empire may be conferred upon our late lord, Tokugawa Kamenosuke; and in that case we shall repay your beneficence by our faithful guardianship of the Northern Gate."

That was their dream–a vision of repeating history, and winning for Tokugawa a new province, even as Yoritomo won the Kwanta from the wilderness seven centuries before; a province which their master should rule for the Emperor in all loyalty, that so the clan should be, as they say, once more the keepers of the Northern Gate. That was their hope; and some say that if they had chosen Mororan and fortified it, instead of Hakodate, they might have held it against all the forces of the empire.

They did not so choose, and in spite of the openly expressed sympathy of the foreign consuls, the "Three Days' Republic" failed. But there was no harsh treatment; rather the government sought to give them opportunity to repent. The newly-appointed head of the Tokugawa clan was ordered to go to the Hokkaido and restrain his clansmen; the Tokugawa asked that, as this new head was only a child, the ex-Shogun might be allowed to lead them. But this was refused, for fear that he might be forcibly taken over to the rebels, and so used to encourage others and prolong the struggle. After many delays, the chastising force reached Hakodate, landed on the steep cliffs behind the promontory, and marched over the mountain to a point from which they could command the entire fort, rendering resistance hopeless.

The leaders yielded, and were punished for a time, but presently Count Kuroda was back in the Hokkaido again–this time as an accredited government official, the head of the newly-organized Colonization Office. This office–literally, department for the development of the country–was intended to do precisely what the runaway generals had intended, minus the individual clan bias; and its hope was the same–namely, to provide for masterless Samurai. It was the day of great things, of wild endeavors to make Japan over in a night, and of foreign experts imported to do it at any price. So General Horace Capron was sent for, "to introduce the American system of agriculture into Japan"–which meant to be the actual head and organizer of a department with many branches, including stock raising and forestry, surveys of every sort, even engineering and road building; to establish agricultural schools and experiment farms, and to start new things generally. Of all the innovations, the

Hokkaido, being itself new and unprejudiced, naturally came in for the largest share; and moreover, being most like America in climate, took most kindly to American ways.

All this was begun in 1873. At first the results lagged far behind the lavish expenditure; indigent Samurai did not appear in flocks, perhaps because they were too busy getting educated in the new government schools to prepare for government offices, or studying abroad on government scholarships. Moreover, such expenditure could not possibly be kept up; the "American plan" was far too magnificent for Japan. Still, the thing was started, and the discovery of large fields of bituminous coal of an excellent quality, not more than twenty or thirty miles from Sapporo, made the future of the Hokkaido sure, if slow. In a few years public-spirited men who were fortunate enough to have a little means began to plant colonies of their dependents, many a gentleman going with his band, living with them as they lived, and working with them at clearing and draining the forest. It is not easy work; the land which is often best when put in order is swampy, as well as heavily wooded, and until it has been brought under cultivation for a year or two the settlers are sure to have malaria–genuine chills and fever–a thing hardly known to exist in Japan proper. The cold, too, is terrible to people from the south, for Yezo lies in the latitude of Maine, and except on the lower coast gets very little effect from the warm ocean currents; and the rough, poor little houses of the colonists are quite unfit to keep out such winters. Yet the settlers thrive. By 1895 they were coming at the rate of forty and fifty thousand a year. The government grants about twelve and a half acres as homestead to anyone who will take it up and develop it, putting a certain specified amount of improvement on it each year for a fixed term. There are already manufactures, particularly iron nails, bricks and linen, and the fisheries are being developed astonishingly. All around Otaru, and along the railroad from there to the point where it turns off inland to Sapporo, fish and fishing are very much in evidence, some being dried on frames, more, in the herring season, boiled down to make fish oil. On the beach, near every little village, you see large iron pots, sometimes propped on stones, sometimes set in a hole like a primitive oven.

Here they boil the fish and skim off the oil, drying the refuse and pressing it into cakes to be shipped for manure. These little villages on the Japan Sea are small and squalid, and the people have an air of untidiness and poverty; in fact, this fishing population is the poorest element in the Hokkaido.

There are not very many Ainu around Sapporo, except what some one called "tinned" ones, at Mr. Batchelor's excellent "Rest House," as he calls the little hospital he has built for them in his own garden. Occasionally a few of them wander into Sapporo to sell skins or carved trays and bark dippers, but as a general thing they stay apart in their own villages, which lie along the wilder streams and remote places on the coast. Professor Todd's astronomical party were quite among them in 1896, at Esashi on the north coast, and Mrs. Todd was able to make some interesting investigations. The most accessible villages are on the shore of Volcano bay, and their straw huts, thatched all over, are easily visible from the train at Horibetsu and Noboribetsu stations, and at one or two other places. But of these strange people more hereafter.

Perhaps it is because only the pluckiest and hardiest Japanese go to the north, and also the most lawless; perhaps the sharper climate braces both body and mind; whatever the reason, the people of the Hokkaido are both the best and the worst in Japan. The worst–let us hope–are survivals of the time when it was the custom to release prisoners at the end of their term–the long-sentence prisons, by the way, are all in the Hokkaido–and pay no further heed to them; the times when settlers feared two things, bears and "red men," as they call convicts, because of their brick-colored prison clothes. Now that is all past; the prisoners are returned to their own provinces and released there; and bears, too, are scarce, and seldom attack houses, as one great grizzly actually did in Sapporo in the early days, devouring a woman and a baby before he was hunted down and killed. He is stuffed in the Sapporo Museum now, along with other Hokkaido beasts and birds–which, as I have before said, are strikingly different from the rest of Japan among Ainu mats and carvings, and relics of the war of 1895, such as Chinese swords and spears and curious old firearms, brought home by the northern troops. Some of these

troops came from the Tonden or military colony which is being carried on as an experiment on a fine piece of land some miles from
Sapporo; and they made a good name for themselves both for bravery and physical condition.

For the best element in the Hokkaido, go not to lively, bustling
Otaru, with its ill-kept streets and hastily-built houses, its pushing
business men and rough dock hands, but to quiet Sapporo and
the Imperial College of Agriculture, now nearing its hope of being
promoted into a university. The place has a very attractive situation
in the midst of the open plain, with the stony Toyohira flowing by,
and mountains all about it, near or far. A few of the beautiful old
elms are still standing in the town, but most of them, unhappily,
were cut down through a mistaken order when it was first laid out.
Workmen had been sent ahead to begin clearing the land, and when
the higher officials arrived they found wholesale destruction of the
trees, which had covered all the site of the new city. Maple and
other quick-growing trees have been planted, and the place begins
to be well shaded in many parts, but it seems difficult to make the
elms grow again; probably they get too much sun in the open places.
As for the town itself, it looks far more like a bit of New England
than any part of Japan; the shingled houses, their roofs less projecting and steeper pitched to shed the snow, the wide streets and
the frequency of glazed windows, instead of shoji and amado, the
elms and maples and paling-fenced gardens, where the flowers grow
somewhat recklessly as compared to the neat south–all this goes to
make nearly every American exclaim as soon as he is set down in
Sapporo, "This is like home; it looks just like my own State!"

All around the city hay fields and grain fields stretch away across
the plain and to wooded Maruyama, five miles off, where snow lies
in the hollows till far into May. There is a great deal of flax too,
which goes to supply the large linen mill in the town, and acres
of beets for sugar; a little rice–not much; rice does not love the
far north–and out toward Maruyama a few plantations of mulberry trees. In the gardens, instead of flowering cherry or plum,
you will find American fruit trees–apple, pear, quince, and dark
red or ox-heart cherries, worthy of the best New York orchards; not

peaches–it is too cold for them where strawberries only ripen in time for college commencement parties, almost on the fourth of July. The original foreign professors were all New England men, and they have left their mark on the college and the town in many little habits and traditions. The very gardens bloom with sweet peas and nasturtiums and phlox, and have none of the formal stone set-ting of the real Japan–at least in most places. Some beautiful little specimens of conventional Japanese gardening there are, after all, even in unconventional, independent Sapporo.

The centre of the town is occupied by the large brick govern-ment building, known as the Do Cho, or district office; here the affairs of the entire Hokkaido are attended to, including the allot-ment of land to new settlers, who sometimes come and wait a good while in the town before they get just what they desire. The building stands in an open space and has a fine air of dignity and simplicity. The other important government building is one which was put up to accommodate the Emperor, when he made a visit here in the course of his long journey all through the empire; it is in charge of the imperial household department, and is used as a hotel in for-eign style. Only the four lower rooms are rented, unless by special permission from the officials. It is a big, barn-like sort of a place, with immensely high ceilings and huge windows. The lawn, though, is charming–a delightful stretch of grass, something rare enough to be prized in Japan, with a bit of a Japanese lake let and some trees and shrubbery in the midst. The Do Cho, too, has pretty grounds, and especially a fine lotus pond, where they grow flowers as large and fine as at Kamakura itself, in spite of a foot or two of ice on the pond all winter.

There is something pitiful, though, about a southern people who are trying to live in the north; as they trudge through February snows that hide the fence-posts, no one can help remembering that there is scent of plum-blossoms about his old home. One April, in Hakodate, some enterprising or over-homesick person got up a cherry-viewing, by taking a quantity of paper flowers, and arranging them in pots and on stands really very beautifully; and a number of people came and walked about and tried to admire and think they were enjoying themselves. Absurdly childish, of course; but there was something very pathetic about it, too. And you cannot help feeling the same homesick effort in the Sapporo crowds who go to the gardens there and look at fine lilies and roses and European annuals, very beautiful in themselves, but without a particle of association for a Japanese. The children growing up there will love the north, but the older ones must feel themselves exiles, however loyal to its interests. Just outside of Sapporo lies the experiment farm, connected with the college, where students taking the practical course study American cattle and American methods of farming generally. The stock farm proper, though, is not here, but away back in the country on other government land. In the prettiest meadow of all, among beautiful old elm trees, the new college buildings are going up; they have been long and sadly needed, and heartily deserved, for if ever an institution made the most of the scantiest resources, that one is the Sapporo No-Gakko. We who love the North like to think that this is the "Hokkaido Spirit"–the spirit of development, of service under whatever difficulties; to think that it is the old "Yamato Damashii," the spirit of Japan, translated into modern, yes, and Christian life–and a legacy, too, of Enomoto and Kuroda's brave failure.

Acknowledgments

We would to thank Rheba Massey for giving us the original text which inspired the republication of this book; and Lian Hearn for contributing the foreword to this new edition.

We would also like to thank Joseph Ryan, Brick McBurly, Randy Schadel; staff and members of the Samurai Archives Citadel for their support.